BOB DYLAN

Tempo
A Rowman & Littlefield Music Series
on Rock, Pop, and Culture

Series Editor: Scott Calhoun

Tempo: A Rowman & Littlefield Music Series on Rock, Pop, and Culture offers titles that explore rock and popular music through the lens of social and cultural history, revealing the dynamic relationship between musicians, music, and their milieu. Like other major art forms, rock and pop music comment on their cultural, political, and even economic situation, reflecting the technological advances, psychological concerns, religious feelings, and artistic trends of their times. Contributions to the **Tempo** series are the ideal introduction to major pop and rock artists and genres.

BOB DYLAN

American Troubadour

Donald Brown

ROWMAN & LITTLEFIELD
Lanham • Boulder • New York • Toronto • Plymouth, UK

Published by Rowman & Littlefield
4501 Forbes Boulevard, Suite 200, Lanham, Maryland 20706
www.rowman.com

10 Thornbury Road, Plymouth PL6 7PP, United Kingdom

British Library Cataloguing in Publication Information Available

Library of Congress Cataloging-in-Publication Data

Brown, Donald, 1959– author.
Bob Dylan : American troubadour / Donald Brown.
pages cm. — (Tempo : a Rowman & Littlefield music series on rock, pop, and culture)
Includes bibliographical references and index.
ISBN 978-0-8108-8420-5 (cloth : alk. paper) — ISBN 978-0-8108-8421-2 (electronic)
1. Dylan, Bob, 1941—Criticism and interpretation. 2. Dylan, Bob, 1941—Influence. I. Title.
ML420.D98B77 2014
782.42164092—dc23
[B]
2013044394

Printed in the United States of America

In memory of my mom, Elaine Taylor Brown,
and my dad, Fred Earl Brown

For Kajsa

CONTENTS

SERIES EDITOR'S FOREWORD

For a book series such as this, which examines popular and rock music within the cultural context of its time, one could not find a better case study than the American musician Bob Dylan. Born into the first generation of rock and rollers, he has marked time with his changing times since his first public performance in 1960. Every few years since then, there have been new songs, new albums, and new live performances, up through the publication of this volume, all of which have drawn their strength from the swirling forces of change Dylan has sought to bear witness to. His music often critiques forms of complacency and intolerance without mentioning a social ill or an institutional abuse by name. But because he first appeared in Greenwich Village at the start of the 1960s and melted right into the spirit of those times—a decade when protest was the conspicuous function of folk and rock music—many felt Dylan was their sympathizer. With each new offering, fans and critics alike have approached the singer-songwriter of Americana, that mixture of folk, roots, blues-rock, Western swing, and country, looking for a Jesus but sometimes meeting a Judas. Generally, though, Dylan has won everyone over for being both.

We would do well to remember that while Robert Allen Zimmerman was born in 1941, Bob Dylan didn't exist until 1960, and he didn't invent himself to be our friend. As a product of changing times, Dylan has embodied the constant of change and has offered us a commentary on the human experience by developing into one of the most enigmatic public performers in the history of American popular music. Once or twice a decade he has re-formed himself; or rather, he has revealed a new side of Bob Dylan the searching poet of the restless self. Keeping in mind that Bob Dylan is an invention crystallizes the fact (or is it a myth?) that Americans are as much inventions unfolding over time as they are a people connected to a place. In Dylan's search and out of his own unease has arisen a defiant spirit, fueling him to challenge cultural conventions and his fans' expectations of what Bob Dylan should do or who he should be. His particular defiance, as an expression of living the American Experience, can be heard in the dialect of snarl. As prolific as Walt Whitman, but with a lot less of that American bard's love for the self and optimism for mankind, Dylan sings the conflicted body electric. His has mastered this form of the American voice and his fluency has never been better expressed than in his now iconic question: "How does it feel / To be on your own / With no direction home / Like a complete unknown / Like a rolling stone?" In this question Dylan concedes the blessing and curse of America. Here, there is freedom to invent oneself and set out on your own; but here, you will live alone as you follow the long, frustrating path of turning dreams into lesser forms of reality. Dylan has clearly enjoyed the artist's freedom to create himself and explore his medium, but he declaims those who rest in America as though this is the promised land. Judging by the frequency with which Dylan himself adopts this perspective, one wonders if it's the voice he finds the most comfort in, too. Many listeners, however, like this side of Dylan and seem to revel in his Old Testament–prophet persona. Misery does love company.

But the trap of studying Bob Dylan as a cultural symbol, a seething-sage, or a cipher for the changing times he appears to be singing about is in listening to his work only for specific comment on the correspondingly specific modern dilemmas he seems to link himself to. As good a study as he is for hearing the decline of a cohesive cultural narrative of hope in post–World War II America, he is a better poet of the injustice felt in the human heart in any given time or place. Dylan lays the trap himself with a brilliance of familiar and obscure allusions, but if we are not ensnared in the literal lyric, then we find his art assays the timeless longings of the human heart: for an end to suffering; for justice against oppressors; for reward for perseverance; for love that remains.

As a troubadour, Bob Dylan arrives in mystery and includes the material of our lives and our times in his songs. Inasmuch as we think

Dylan speaks for us, we think so because we know our times as well as he does; he just helps us realize that we do. In as much as we feel he has an answer to our questions, we do so because he is amplifying what we already feel in our bones or hear "blowin' in the wind." It turns out that as an American troubadour, Dylan is us, only more so. But while he sings for us, he sings first for himself. He is on a fulltime, singular search for happiness while we typically search in snatches and bursts when we feel we can spare the time. He is as kind, as sincere, and as greedy as we are. He is as dissatisfied as we are with the incompleteness of things. But he spends more time dwelling on it, and then he plays us a song about it. He entertains us by performing the American consciousness, which we don't realize until the song is over and he is gone.

Scott Calhoun
Series Editor

TIMELINE

World Events and Cultural Items

December 7, 1941: Japan attacks U.S. Naval Base at Pearl Harbor, HI; U.S. declares war on Japan; December 11, Germany declares war on U.S.

1943: Woody Guthrie's autobiography, *Bound for Glory*

June 6, 1944: D-Day: Allied invasion of Normandy

April 1945: Deaths of Mussolini and Hitler; liberation by U.S. of Buchenwald concentration camp
May 8, 1945: V-E Day
August 6, 1945: U.S. drops atomic bomb on Hiroshima
August 9, 1945: U.S. drops atomic bomb on Nagasaki
August 14, 1945: Japan surrenders

Life and Career

May 24, 1941: Born as Robert Allen Zimmerman to parents Abram and Beatrice, in Duluth, MN

February 1946: Younger brother, David, born

World Events and Cultural Items	*Life and Career*
	1948: Family moves to Hibbing, MN
February 1950: Senator McCarthy's speech about "Communist spy ring" in the State Dept.	
June 1950: U.S. enters the Korean War	
January 1953: Death of Hank Williams	
June 1953: Korean war ends	
November 1953: Death of Dylan Thomas	
December 1953: First issue of *Playboy*	
1954: *On the Waterfront*: Best Actor award to Marlon Brando	
April–June 1954: Army-McCarthy hearings	
December 1954: McCarthy censured; segregation in public schools declared unconstitutional	
August 1955: Killing of Emmet Till	
September 1955: Death of James Dean; *Rebel Without a Cause*	
December 1, 1955: Rosa Parks arrested for civil disobedience; Little Richard's "Long Tall Sally" in pop Top 10; Bill Haley's "Rock Around the Clock" at number 1 for 8 weeks	

World Events and Cultural Items	Life and Career
September 1956: Elvis Presley on the *Ed Sullivan Show*	**Summer 1956:** Plays piano and sings on a 78 with high school friends **Fall 1956:** Attends Hibbing High School
September 1957: National Guard oversees desegregation in Little Rock, AR **October 4, 1957:** USSR launches *Sputnik*	**1957:** Plays piano and sings on two Little Richard songs in high school variety show
	1958: In high school band, The Golden Chords
February 3, 1959: Death of Buddy Holly; first U.S. casualties in Vietnam—military advisors killed in guerilla attack	**January 1959:** Appears at Hibbing High Jamboree as Elston Gunn & The Rock Boppers **January 31, 1959:** Attends Buddy Holly concert in Duluth **June 1959:** Graduates from high school **September 1959:** Student at University of Minnesota in Minneapolis; begins to frequent folk clubs in Dinkytown
February 1960: Black student sit-in at Woolworth in Greensboro, NC **November 1960:** Senator John Kennedy narrowly defeats Vice President Richard Nixon to become the youngest U.S. president and first Catholic president	**1960:** Reads *Bound for Glory*; first appears as Bob Dylan in folk clubs in Dinkytown **Summer 1960:** Travels to Denver for gigs
January 1961: President Eisenhower warns of the	**January 1961:** Arrives in New York City; visits Woody Guthrie;

World Events and Cultural Items	Life and Career
"military-industrial complex" in his farewell address **April 1961:** Fellini's *La Dolce Vita* opens in the U.S.; summer of "freedom riders" in the Civil Rights Movement in the South **August 1961:** The creation of the Berlin Wall	meets folksingers in Greenwich Village, begins relationship with Suze Rotolo, 17 **September 25–October 8, 1961:** Performs at Gerde's Folk City, reviewed by Robert Shelton; signs with John Hammond at Columbia Records **November 20–22, 1961:** Records 1st album
Spring 1962: Michael Harrington's *The Other America: Poverty in the United States* **Fall 1962:** Rachel Carson's *Silent Spring* **October 1962:** Kennedy addresses the nation about Soviet missiles in Cuba	**March 1962:** *Bob Dylan* **April 1962:** First performance of "Blowin' in the Wind," at Gerde's **April–December 1962:** 6 separate sessions for 2nd album **August 1962:** Signs with Albert Grossman **December 1962:** In London to appear in BBC play
April 1963: "Letter from Birmingham Jail" by Martin Luther King Jr. **June 1963:** Murder of Medgar Evers in Jackson, MS **August 1963:** Martin Luther King Jr.'s "I have a dream" speech at the March on Washington for Jobs and Freedom **November 22, 1963:** President Kennedy assassinated in Dallas, TX	**April 1963:** Town Hall Concert; final session for 2nd album **May 1963:** Walks off *Ed Sullivan Show* rather than substitute a song for "Talkin' John Birch Paranoid Blues"; *The Freewheelin' Bob Dylan* **June 1963:** Peter, Paul & Mary's "Blowin' in the Wind" **July 1963:** Takes part in voter registration rally in MS with Pete Seeger; appears at Newport Folk Festival and sings "With God on Our Side" with Joan Baez at the end of her set

World Events and Cultural Items	*Life and Career*
	August–October 1963: Five sessions for 3rd LP
	August 28, 1963: Performs with Baez and others at the March on Washington for Civil Rights
	December 1963: Receives the Tom Paine Award, makes controversial speech
January 1964: *Meet the Beatles!* released in the U.S.; Stanley Kubrick's *Dr. Strangelove, or How I Learned to Stop Worrying and Love the Bomb*; April, The Beatles have Top 5 songs in Top 10	**January 1964:** *The Times, They Are A-Changin'*
	February 1964: Cross-country road trip, visits Carl Sandburg; appears on *The Steve Allen Show*
July 1964: The Civil Rights Act of 1964 becomes law	**June 9, 1964:** Records 4th album
August 7, 1964: The Tonkin Resolution passed by Congress	**July 1964:** Newport Folk Festival, debuts "Mr. Tambourine Man"
August 1964: The Beatles film *A Hard Day's Night*	**August 1964:** *Another Side of Bob Dylan*
August 1965: Riots in the Watts section of Los Angeles	**January 13–15, 1965:** Records 5th album, using rock musicians
	March 1965: *Bringing It All Back Home*
	April 1965: Begins final acoustic tour, in England (with 4 LPs in Top 20), filmed by D. A. Pennebaker
	June–August 1965: Records 6th album
	July 20, 1965: "Like a Rolling Stone"

World Events and Cultural Items	*Life and Career*
	July 25, 1965: Newport Folk Festival with electric band (booing and outcry) **August 1965:** *Highway 61 Revisited* **November 22, 1965:** Marries Sara Lownds
May 1966: The Beach Boys' *Pet Sounds* **August 1966:** The Beatles' *Revolver*, and final U.S. concert, in San Francisco; Lenny Bruce dies	**January 6, 1966:** Son, Jesse Byron born **January–March 1966:** Sessions for 7th album **February 1966:** Begins tour of the U.S., half solo acoustic, half backed by The Hawks **April–May 1966:** Tour continues in Australia and Europe **May 16, 1966:** *Blonde on Blonde* **July 29, 1966:** In accident on his motorcycle; further touring canceled
January 1, 1967: "Human Be-In" at Golden Gate Park, San Francisco **April 1967:** Large marches against the war in Vietnam **June 1, 1967:** The Beatles' *Sgt. Pepper* **June–December 1967:** Height of "psychedelia" **June–August 1967:** Race riots throughout major cities in the U.S. **August 1967:** Jimi Hendrix Experience's *Are You Experienced* in U.S.	**Spring–Fall 1967:** Records with Rick Danko, Garth Hudson, Richard Manuel, Robbie Robertson in Woodstock, NY **March 1967:** *Greatest Hits* **May 1967:** *Don't Look Back*, film of the 1965 UK tour **July 1967:** Daughter Anna Lea born **October–November 1967:** Records 8th album, in Nashville **December 27, 1967:** *John Wesley Harding*

World Events and Cultural Items	*Life and Career*
October 3, 1967: Woody Guthrie dies	
October 1967: Huge anti-war march ends at the Pentagon	
November 1967: Debut of *Rolling Stone* magazine	
April 4, 1968: Martin Luther King Jr. assassinated, followed by riots in DC	**January 1968:** Performs 3 Guthrie songs, backed by The Band at Woody Guthrie Tribute Concert, NY
April 1968: President Johnson announces he will not run for reelection	**June 5, 1968:** Abram Zimmerman dies
May 1968: Student uprisings in Paris	**June 22, 1968:** Jann Wenner calls for the release of Dylan's "basement tapes" in *Rolling Stone*
June 1968: Robert Kennedy assassinated; Stonewall riots in New York begin movement for gay rights	**June 30, 1968:** Son, Samuel Abram born
July 1, 1968: The Band's *Music from Big Pink*	
August 1968: The Byrds' *Sweetheart of the Rodeo*; September, Jimi Hendrix's cover of "All Along the Watchtower"	
November–December 1968: Elvis's comeback album and Christmas special	
January 30, 1969: The Beatles rooftop appearance in London	**February 1969:** Records 9th album, in Nashville
June 1969: *From Elvis in Memphis*; formation of the Weathermen, revolutionary faction of SDS	**April 1969:** *Nashville Skyline*; begins recordings for 10th album, in Nashville
July 1969: Apollo 11 lands men on the moon	**May 1969:** Tapes *Johnny Cash Show*, airs June 7
	August 30, 1969: Performs at the

World Events and Cultural Items	Life and Career
August 15–17, 1969: Woodstock Festival, NY	Isle of Wight Festival, UK, with The Band
December 8, 1969: Rolling Stones show at Altamont Raceway	**December 9, 1969:** Son, Jakob Luke born
1970: Hal Lindsay's *The Late, Great Planet Earth* published	**March 1970:** Concludes recording 10th album, in NY
April 1970: Paul McCartney announces the breakup of The Beatles	**May 1970:** Recording sessions with George Harrison
May 1970: National Guard open fire on antiwar protesters at Kent State University, 4 deaths	**June 1–5, 1970:** Sessions for 11th album
September 18, 1970: Jimi Hendrix dies	**June 8, 1970:** *Self Portrait*
	June 9, 1970: Honorary degree from Princeton University
	July 1970: Partnership with Albert Grossman dissolves
	August 1970: Final sessions for 11th album
	October 1970: *New Morning*
January 1971: Congress repeals the Gulf of Tonkin Resolution; debut of *All in the Family*	**March 16–17, 1971:** Recordings with Leon Russell
March 1971: Weather Underground explodes a bomb in the U.S. Capitol building; East Pakistan declares its independence as Bangladesh	**August 1, 1971:** Performs at Concert for Bangladesh, accompanied by George Harrison, Ringo Starr, Leon Russell
April 1971: U.S. Supreme Court unanimously endorses busing for desegregation of schools	**November 1971:** "George Jackson"; *Greatest Hits, Vol. 2*
June 1971: *New York Times* begins publishing the Pentagon Papers	
August 1971: Nixon takes the U.S. off the Gold Standard	

World Events and Cultural Items	*Life and Career*
June 1972: The Watergate break-in	**March 1972:** *Concert for Bangladesh* film **November 1972:** Filming of *Pat Garrett & Billy the Kid* begins
January 1973: Ceasefire in Vietnam War **March 1973:** Last U.S. combat soldiers withdraw from Vietnam; Pink Floyd's *Dark Side of the Moon* **May–August 1973:** Televised "Watergate" hearings	**February 1973:** Film soundtrack completed **July 1973:** "Knockin' on Heaven's Door"; *Pat Garrett & Billy the Kid* **November 6–9, 1973:** Records *Planet Waves* with The Band
February 1974: Vote taken to investigate impeachment of the president **July 30, 1974:** Nixon relinquishes subpoenaed White House tapes **August 9, 1974:** Nixon resigns **September 1974:** President Ford gives full pardon to Nixon	**January–February 1974:** U.S. tour with The Band **January 17, 1974:** *Planet Waves* debuts at #1 **June 20, 1974:** *Before The Flood* with The Band **September 16–19, 1974:** Initial version of *Blood on the Tracks* **December 27–30, 1974:** Re-recordings for *Blood* in MN
April 1975: The fall of Saigon ends the Vietnam War **August 1975:** Bruce Springsteen's *Born to Run* released **September 1975:** Assassination attempts on President Ford **October 1975:** Springsteen on the cover of *Time* and *Newsweek* as "future of rock 'n' roll"	**January 15, 1975:** *Blood on the Tracks*, #1 **June 1975:** Attends Patti Smith show at The Other End in the Village, begins to frequent old haunts; writes most of the songs for next album with Jacques Levy; July, records *Desire* **June 26, 1975:** *The Basement Tapes*, with The Band **October 30, 1975:** Rolling Thunder Revue opens in Plymouth, MA, concludes

World Events and Cultural Items	Life and Career
	December 8, 1975: Madison Square Garden with "Night of the Hurricane," for Rubin Carter, portions of the show and staged scenes filmed for *Renaldo and Clara*
July 1976: Celebration of the U.S. Bicentennial; Democratic Presidential nominee Jimmy Carter quotes Dylan in his acceptance speech: "He not busy being born is busy dying."	**January 1976:** *Desire* released, #1 for 5 weeks **January 26, 1976:** Second part of Rolling Thunder commences with second benefit for Rubin Carter; show in Boulder, CO, taped for television, concludes in May **September 1976:** *Hard Rain*
April 1977: Studio 54 opens **May 1977:** *Star Wars* **September 1977:** Steely Dan's *Aja* **October 1977:** Sex Pistols' *Never Mind the Bollocks*	**June 1977:** Divorced by Sara Dylan
May 1978: First Unabomber attack **June 1978:** The Rolling Stones' *Some Girls* and tour; Bruce Springsteen's *Darkness on the Edge of Town* and tour **August 1978:** Pope John Paul I named **September 1978:** Pope John Paul I dies **October 1978:** First Polish pope: John Paul II named; Mudd Club opens; Sid Vicious of The Sex Pistols kills Nancy Spungen at the Chelsea Hotel, NY	**January 28, 1978:** Film: *Renaldo and Clara* **February–March 1978:** On tour in Australasia **April 1978:** *Street-Legal* recorded in L.A. **June–July 1978:** On tour in Europe **June 1–7, 1978:** At Los Angeles Amphitheatre **June 15, 1978:** *Street-Legal* **June 15–20, 1978:** At Earl's Court, London **September–December 1978:** On tour in the U.S.

World Events and Cultural Items	*Life and Career*
November 1978: Mass suicide at Jonestown	**November 1978:** Experiences a religious awakening while on tour in Arizona
December 1978: Two million demonstrate against Shah in Iran	
1979: *The Late, Great Planet Earth* (film) released	**1979:** Becomes a member of the Vineyard Christian Fellowship
January 1979: Shah flees Iran	**April 1979:** *Dylan at Budokan*
February 1979: Ayatollah Khomeini takes power in Iran	**April–May 1979:** Records *Slow Train Coming*, released, **August**
March 1979: Nuclear accident at Three Mile Island, PA	**October 1979:** Appears on *Saturday Night Live*; on tour in 1979 and into 1980, performs only Christian material and preaches about imminent Second Coming
May 1979: Margaret Thatcher becomes Prime Minister in UK	
July 1979: President Carter's "malaise" speech	
August 1979: *Apocalypse Now*	
October 1979: Pope John Paul II tours the U.S.	
November 1979: The hostage crisis begins in Iran	
December 1979: USSR invasion of Afghanistan, denounced by the U.S.	
August 1980: U.S. boycotts the Summer Olympics in Moscow in protest; Reagan denounces "Vietnam Syndrome"	**February 1980:** Best Male Rock Vocal Performance Grammy for "Gotta Serve Somebody"; *Saved* recorded, released **June**
December 1980: John Lennon murdered by psychotic fan	
January 20, 1981: The Iranian hostage crisis resolves on the day of Ronald Reagan's inauguration	**March–May 1981:** *Shot of Love* recorded, released **August**; beginning in shows in spring, Dylan reintroduces "secular" songs into his live set, including "Abraham, Martin, and John"
March 1981: Assassination attempt wounds President Reagan	

World Events and Cultural Items	*Life and Career*
June 1981: *New York Times* story on AIDS	
July 1981: Israel bombs Beirut	
August 1981: MTV debuts; first IBM PC model; Reagan fires striking air-traffic controllers, setting a precedent that undermines labor unions	
December 1981: U.S. divorce rate peaks near 50 percent	
June 1982: ERA fails to be ratified	**January 1982:** Howard Alk, Dylan's filmmaking collaborator, dies
November 1982: Michael Jackson's *Thriller* released	**March 1982:** Inducted into Songwriter's Hall of Fame
March 1983: Compact discs introduced in the U.S.; Reagan's "evil empire" speech and announcement of "Star Wars" initiative	**April–May 1983:** Records *Infidels*, released **November**
April 1983: Suicide attack kills 63 at U.S. embassy in Beirut	
October 1983: 241 marines killed in Beirut; U.S. invasion of Grenada	
January 1984: Apple Mac introduced	**March 22, 1984:** Appears on *Late Night with David Letterman*
May 1984: USSR boycotts Olympic Games in L.A.	**Summer 1984:** Tour of Europe with Santana
November 1984: Reagan/Bush win reelection with 59% of popular vote	**December 1984:** *Real Live*
January 1985: Reagan likens Nicaraguan Contras as the "moral	**January 1985:** Participates in "We Are the World" recording

World Events and Cultural Items	*Life and Career*
equivalent" of the U.S. Founding Fathers **March 1985:** "We Are the World" **October 1985:** Celebrity Rock Hudson dies of AIDS; Nintendo released **November 1985:** Microsoft Windows introduced	**June 1985:** *Empire Burlesque* **July 1985:** Appears at Live Aid with Keith Richards and Ron Wood of The Rolling Stones **September 1985:** Performs for Farm Aid concert backed by Tom Petty & The Heartbreakers **October 28, 1985:** Career-spanning compilation *Biograph* **November 1985:** *Lyrics 1962–1985*
January 1986: Space Shuttle *Challenger* disaster **March 1986:** Richard Manuel of The Band dies **November 1986:**Tower Commission investigates the Iran-Contra scandal of U.S. arms deals to Iran funding the Contras	**January 1986:** Televised appearance at Martin Luther King Jr. tribute **February 1986:** Opens tour with Tom Petty & The Heartbreakers in Japan **August 1986:** *Knocked Out Loaded*; in UK to film *Hearts of Fire*
June 1987: Reagan speech in Berlin: "Mr. Gorbachev, tear down this wall."	**July 1987:** Six concerts backed by The Grateful Dead **September 1987:** Opens European tour with Tom Petty & The Heartbreakers with first shows in Israel
February 1988: Rubin "Hurricane" Carter released from jail **December 1988:** Roy Orbison dies	**January 1988:** Inducted into the Rock and Roll Hall of Fame by Bruce Springsteen **May 1988:** Begins recording with George Harrison, Jeff Lynne, Roy Orbison, Tom Petty as the Traveling Wilburys; *Down in the Groove*

World Events and Cultural Items	*Life and Career*
	June 1988: First show with guitarist/band-leader G. E. Smith
	October 1988: Smith leaves the band after 71 shows
November 1989: The opening of the border between East and West Germany	**February 1989:** *Dylan & The Dead*
	September 1989: *Oh Mercy*
August 1990: Saddam Hussein's Iraq invades Kuwait; Operation Desert Storm, the U.S. leads UN coalition of forces against Iraq in the Gulf War	**January 1990:** 4 hour show at Toad's Place in New Haven, CT; made *Commandeur de l'Ordre des Arts et des Lettres* at Ministry of Culture, Paris
	March 1990: Dylan and Bruce Springsteen play onstage together for the first time, at a Tom Petty concert
	September 1990: *Under the Red Sky*
	October 1990: Performs "Masters of War" at West Point Military Academy
February 1991: Ceasefire in the Gulf War	**February 1991:** Lifetime Achievement Award at the Grammys, presented by Jack Nicholson, performs "Masters of War"
March 1991: Reunification of Germany takes effect	
December 1991: Dissolution of the USSR	**March 1991:** *Bootleg Series Vol. 1–3*
	October 1991: At Guitar Greats Festival in Seville, with Richard Thompson
May 1992: The Serbian siege of Sarajevo begins, the most devastating conflict in Europe	**October 1992:** "Bob-Fest," 30th Anniversary tribute concert at Madison Square Garden

World Events and Cultural Items	*Life and Career*
since World War II	**November 1992:** *Good as I Been to You*
January 1993: Inauguration of Wm. Clinton, first Democrat president in 12 years, and first president of the "Baby Boom" generation	**January 1993:** Performs "Chimes of Freedom" on the steps of Lincoln Memorial for Clinton Inauguration Concert; *World Gone Wrong*
February 1994: NATO intervention into Bosnian Civil War begins	**August 1994:** Performs at the 25th Anniversary Woodstock Concert
November 1994: "Republican Revolution": Democrats lose majority in both houses of Congress, in part due to reactions to Clinton's effort for health care reform	**October 1994:** Neil Young and Springsteen join Dylan onstage at The Roseland Ballroom, NY **November 1994:** Tapes shows for *MTV Unplugged*
August 1995: Jerry Garcia dies	**January 1995:** *Drawn Blank*, a collection of drawings **March 1995:** *Highway 61 Interactive CD-ROM* **April 1995:** *MTV Unplugged* **July 1995:** Opens for The Rolling Stones and joins them for an encore of "Like a Rolling Stone" **November 1995:** Appears at 80th Birthday Tribute for Frank Sinatra, performs "Restless Farewell" **December 1995:** Ongoing concert tour is joined by Patti Smith
February 1996: Official end to the siege of Sarajevo **May 1996:** *Bringing Down the*	**June 1996:** Prince's Trust Concert, with The Who and Eric Clapton, Hyde Park, London

World Events and Cultural Items	Life and Career
Horse, 2nd album by Jakob Dylan's band The Wallflowers released, sells 6 million copies	
	May 1997: Hospitalized with histoplasmosis, a fungal infection that affected his heart **August 1997:** bobdylan.com launched **September 1997:** Plays for Pope John Paul II at the Vatican; *Time Out of Mind*, first Top 10 album since *Slow Train Coming* **October 1997:** Receives the Dorothy and Lillian Gish Prize
January 1998: President Clinton denies relations with Monica Lewinsky	**May 6, 1998:** U.S. concerts with Joni Mitchell and Van Morrison **October 1998:** *Bootleg Series Vol. 4, Live 1966*
February 1999: President Clinton acquitted of impeachment charges	**June 1999:** Start of 32-week U.S. tour with Paul Simon
November 2000: Presidential contest between George W. Bush and Al Gore ends in contested voter counts in FL; Bush declared victor	**January 2000:** Beatty Zimmerman dies, aged 84 **March 2000:** "Things Have Changed" from *Wonder Boys* wins Oscar for Best Original Song
September 11, 2001: Agents of Al Qaeda destroy the World Trade Towers in NY and damage the Pentagon, using commercial airplanes; President Bush declares "war on terror" **October 2001:** U.S. invades Afghanistan	**September 11, 2001:** *"Love and Theft"*

World Events and Cultural Items	*Life and Career*
November 2001: George Harrison dies	
	February 2002: *"Love and Theft"* wins Grammy for Best Contemporary Folk Album **August 2002:** Performs at Newport Folk Festival in fake beard and blonde wig **November 2002:** *Bootleg Series Vol. 5: Live 1975*
March–May 2003: The U.S.–led invasion of Iraq to capture alleged "weapons of mass destruction" **September 2003:** Johnny Cash dies **November 2003:** President Bush signs $87 billion in supplemental spending for occupation of Iraq **December 2003:** Saddam Hussein is captured	**January 2003:** *Masked and Anonymous* opens
2004: Bush/Cheney reelected on "stay the course" platform of War in Iraq	**January 2004:** Tapes Victoria's Secret lingerie ad with song "Love Sick" **March 2004:** *Bootleg Series Vol. 6: Live 1964* **October 2004:** Autobiography *Chronicles, Vol. 1*; *Lyrics, 1962–2001* **December 2004:** Appears on *60 Minutes* and *The Simpsons*
August 2005: Hurricane Katrina strikes and devastates the Gulf Coast and New Orleans	**August 2005:** *Bootleg Series Vol. 7: No Direction Home* **September 2005:** Documentary *No Direction Home* airs; "Poems

World Events and Cultural Items	*Life and Career*
	Without Titles"—written by teenage Robert Zimmerman but signed "Dylan"—auctioned
May 2006: Peak of the "housing bubble" generally recognized **November 2006:** Mid-term elections turn control of Congress to Democrats; support of War in Iraq at all-time low **December 2006:** Saddam Hussein executed	**May 2006:** Inaugurates *Theme Time Radio Hour, With Your Host Bob Dylan* on XM Satellite Radio **September 2006:** *Modern Times*, first #1 album since *Desire*; Dylan becomes oldest person to debut at #1 in the U.S.
March 2007: Dramatic decline in housing prices	**February 2007:** *Modern Times* awarded Grammy for Best Contemporary Folk/Americana Album; "Someday Baby" wins Solo Rock Vocal Performance **November 2007:** First gallery exhibition of Dylan's artwork opens, Chemnitz, Germany
September 2008: Global economic crisis **October 2008:** Congress passes $700 billion "bailout" to stabilize Wall Street in the crisis **November 2008:** Barack Obama becomes the first man of African American descent to be elected president, defeating the McCain/Palin ticket	**April 2008:** Awarded special Pulitzer Prize for music
December 2009: Treasury Dept. announces unlimited financial support for Freddie Mac and Fannie Mae	**February 2009:** Appears on Pepsi commercial with rapper Will.i.am at Super Bowl XLIII, performing "Forever Young"

World Events and Cultural Items	*Life and Career*
	April 2009: *Together Through Life* debuts at #1 in the U.S. and in the UK (first since *New Morning*); Dylan oldest person to debut at #1 in UK
	July 2009: U.S. tour with Willie Nelson and John Mellencamp
	October 2009: *Christmas in the Heart*
March 2010: Patient Protection and Affordable Care Act signed into law by President Obama	**February 2010:** Performs "The Times, They Are A-Changin'" at the White House
April 2010: Devastating oil gusher in the Gulf of Mexico	**October 2010:** *Bootleg Series No. 9: The Witmark Demos: 1962–64*
December 2010: Start of "Arab Spring" protests	
May 2011: Osama Bin Laden killed by U.S. special warfare force	**April 2011:** Plays shows for the first time in the Far East, including Taiwan, China, and Vietnam
September 2011: Occupy Wall Street camp-out in Zucotti Park, NY, emulated by camps in major U.S. cities, protesting U.S. economic policies and income inequality	
October 2011: Global protests	
December 2011: U.S. declares official end to the Iraq War	
April 2012: Levon Helm of The Band dies	**January–March 2012:** Records *Tempest*, released September
June 2012: Supreme Court upholds constitutionality of the ACA	**May 2012:** Awarded Presidential Medal of Freedom by President Obama
November 2012: Obama/Biden re-elected	

World Events and Cultural Items	*Life and Career*
October 2013: U.S. government shuts down for 15 days	**May 2013:** Inducted into the American Academy of Arts and Letters **August 2013:** *Bootleg Series No. 10: Another Self Portrait (1969–71)*

ACKNOWLEDGMENTS

I want to thank those who have made listening to music a collective experience of tastes and songs and shows in common: my siblings Tom, Kathy Simpson, Jerry, Eric; friends, Tim Gilfillan, Paul Moliken, Lori Bachman, Pat Hinchey, Nancy Shevlin, Eddie Meisel, Mark Rohland, Harvey Weinreich, Mike Gallagher, Rick Moore, Joe and Gail Scuderi, Anna Livia Scuderi, Karen Smyser, Andrew Shields, Sumanth Gopinath, Rob Slifkin and Amanda Durant, Gabrielle Gopinath, Eric Brown, Jim Laakso, Ann Yi, Chang Suk Kim, Brian Francis Slattery, Jason Lee Oakes, Paul Grimstad. And for making this book a reality, I'd like to thank my editors at Rowman & Littlefield: Bennett Graff, architect of the Tempo Series, Scott Calhoun, its series editor, and Jehanne Schweitzer, this book's patient, helpful, and efficient production editor.

I'm thankful beyond words for the years, over thirty at this point, with my daughter Kajsa, who knew all the words to "Desolation Row" by the time she was ten, and for all the tapes and songs and shows we've shared. And there's no end of gratitude to my wife and companion Mary, for all the years and all she's done for me—"Something there is about you that strikes a match in me."

Finally, I'm grateful to Bob Dylan for his songs, his voice, his memorable words, and for being an inspiration, consolation, provocation, and vast source of entertainment and reflection in his fifty-plus years of recording and performing—for me and for so many others.

INTRODUCTION

When I was eleven, in the fall of 1970, my older brother Tom was seventeen and the arbiter of everything that was cool or worth knowing about in contemporary music. He had recently shared things like The Rolling Stones' *Through a Glass, Darkly*, Creedence Clearwater Revival's *Cosmo's Factory*, Crosby, Stills, Nash & Young's *Déjà Vu*, Black Sabbath's *Paranoid*, and the *Greatest Hits* of someone called Bob Dylan. On the back of Dylan's album were the covers of his seven prior albums. Unlike the posturing rock stars on most albums, Dylan appeared as a scrawny, odd-looking guy whose hair became more unmanageable as he got older.

The first side of the album contained the song Tom had been seeking, the one that said "everybody must get stoned," but wasn't called that. On other songs on that side, the voice sounded naked, uncomfortably so. I remember cringing through "It Ain't Me Babe." In our house, folk music was represented by The Brothers Four. Layered harmonies, catchy arrangements. I was about ready to pass on this one, until . . . the song that overthrew my pre-teen skepticism was the last track on side 1. "Like a Rolling Stone." Somehow I had never heard it before. I have a distinct memory—I can still picture where the plastic, fold-up phonograph player was located in the bedroom I shared with my brothers—of playing the song over and over again. Picking the needle up after each verse and putting it down again, until I was certain I knew every word. Such was my initiation to the unprecedented talent and fascination of Bob Dylan.

The purpose of this book is to give an account of Bob Dylan's career that may be helpful to anyone like I was in 1970, coming upon a body of work that is significant, changeable, disappointing, perplexing, inspiring, and still unprecedented and unmatched. Since 1970, much has happened in Dylan's body of work. If, as I didn't know then, two major phases of his career were already over, there were many others still to come. Now, in 2013, with Dylan's live shows getting much good press after the release of his latest album—*Tempest* (2012)—it's anyone's guess how many more shifts in perspective on this mercurial artist lie ahead. What is certain is that Dylan has made his mark, many times over, and that he continues to be lionized as one of the unavoidable creative forces of his generation in the popular arts—and mocked or criticized for not living up to "the false ideas, images and distorted facts" that often count as informed opinion about him.

Though Dylan has often belittled his own records because of the record-making process, preferring to play live to an audience, this book treats the albums as his primary artifacts. Each record can be seen as just that: a record of what he got on tape and chose to release at each stage of his career. The albums are discussed in succession, and the body of work is divided into different phases by setting his records in the context of other events as useful guideposts to the times in which the work appears. Dylan's music always has a relation to the times in which it was created, and that relation is at least interesting. Most of the time the relation is critical—sometimes explicitly so; at other times in a more indirect way.

Early on, Dylan refused to be a spokesman or a leader. The implied individualist ethos that sustains much of his work has always struck me as an exemplary creed for artists working in popular forms. Rather than as a person who has answers, Dylan is more important as one who questions, moving restlessly from style to style, song to song, year to year in search of some idea or purpose worth singing about. Sometimes, what he sings is thick with implications, and his fans hear him articulate their own feelings and beliefs; sometimes he sings in a more limited or personal way, and his critics dismiss him for being out of touch. Often, the "I," or what I'll simply call "the singer," of a Dylan song expresses a relation to a woman. Some listeners see these songs as autobiographical expressions of Dylan's own search for romantic fulfillment and his score settling with bad relationships. For me, they are canny, perceptive comments on the possibilities of eros in the times we live through, with Dylan our best minstrel of the songs of romance and resentment, heartache and breakup.

As an artist, Dylan's greatest struggle is not "speaking for" any particular group or generation, but being true to the spirit of Bob Dylan. While that may seem a self-serving goal, my view is that "Bob Dylan" is not a particular individual but rather a series of artistic personae. Bob Dylan, the performer, began as the invention of a young man named Robert Allen Zimmerman in 1960 and became a figure around which many issues and interpretations circulate. Bob Dylan, the songwriter, was a creation of an era, particularly 1962–1963, and of the need for a new voice in an old music, the American folk song. Bob Dylan, the recording star, came fully into his own in 1965–1966 when the demand for and influence of his records became significant. Thereafter came a number of Bob Dylans, through the changing focus of the songs he would write and the records he would make, and there would also be a number of other roles undertaken: Bob Dylan the writer, the actor, the filmmaker, the chronicler, the painter, the symbol, the "grand old man," the wildly uneven performer.

Remaining true to the spirit of Bob Dylan becomes a question of poetics, in its root meaning of poesis, or "making, invention," and a task of performance, of enactment. Bob Dylan, then, is an invention that continually gets reinvented, a work in progress, an ongoing exploration of the possibilities of song and of the collective and individual, public and private, experience of listening to his music and, for Dylan himself, of making music.

At any time, the songs are more important than the hype and the hoopla; they are what endure beyond the times in which they first appeared, and my effort to articulate a context for the work or to read songs in certain ways should not be seen to limit the songs' meanings. Bob Dylan's songs are ever-renewable by performance, both by himself and by the thousands who have performed them professionally, and by all those who learn them for their own pleasure. When, in his song "Forever Young," Dylan says "may your song always be sung," he perhaps expresses his fans' best wish for himself.

Bob Dylan's initial period of making records took place under the influence and expectations of the New York folk scene. Chapter 1 takes us from Dylan's somewhat derivative but striking first album, recorded when he had not yet turned twenty-one, through his earliest albums that, to some minds, forever fixed Dylan in the role of "the voice of his generation," to his change of direction with his fourth album, released in August of 1964.

Chapter 2 covers a brief two years, 1965 and 1966, in which Dylan made three challenging albums that epitomized a new musical style. Dubbed "folk rock" in the press, it is a mix of folk, blues, and rock and roll set to electric guitars and drums, accented by Dylan's signature harmonica playing and filled out with honky-tonk piano and an insistent organ recalling carnival calliopes. This period is the heyday of a number of youthful musical artists who appealed to college students and teens, becoming a force in popular culture and, to some extent, politics. Dylan's trail-blazing, lyrical acuity created new options for popular songwriting that included stream of consciousness and lively satire.

Chapter 3 discusses the period after a motorcycle accident took Dylan out of the public eye. This somewhat mythic year, 1967, finds Dylan recuperating and making music with friends in Woodstock, New York, where he produced a series of recordings not intended for commercial release. The so-called basement tapes mark an important transition point in Dylan's career, while *John Wesley Harding*, released in December 1967, presented to Dylan's listeners a significantly different sound and attitude: spare, quizzical, parable-like.

Chapter 4 covers the period in which Dylan crossed over into country music and pop, with *Nashville Skyline*, *Self Portrait*, and *New Morning*. His break from the rock vanguard felt more dramatically important at the transition from the sixties to the seventies than it does now, but 1969–1973 is an interesting and eclectic period in Dylan's development. It may be that this period interests me more than it does some scribes of Dylan because it's when I first became aware of him.

Chapter 5 begins with Dylan's "comeback tour" of the United States, accompanied by The Band, in 1974. Dylan's return marked a resurgence of interest in how he would live up to his own legacy and a greater involvement with songwriting on his part. *Blood on the Tracks* returns Dylan to critical success with one of his strongest albums. Hanging out again in the Greenwich Village haunts where he got his start fifteen years before, Dylan reconnected with other musicians and put together a barnstorming tour of East Coast cities at the end of 1975 and the start of 1976, the year of the U.S. Bicentennial. The Rolling Thunder Revue was a fitting vehicle for a modern troubadour's lifestyle and inspired a major film project. Part concert diary, part fictional treatment of his own persona, *Renaldo and Clara* was a debacle commercially and critically but a unique film document of the spontaneity and ad hoc energies of the era.

Chapter 6 moves from the world tour of 1978 to the "born again" period in which Dylan joined forces with Christianity. There was little to prepare Dylan's fans for the change in direction: from a searcher, a fabulist and, for some, a Jewish seer, to a preacher for salvation through Jesus Christ. In many ways, this period was the culmination of Dylan as an emblem of his generation: enigmatic and changeable, he could be seen as losing touch, as "the sixties generation" did in the seventies, with his main sources of inspiration. Dylan's version of Christ was much more avenger than Savior, and the songs of the Christian albums contain much apocalyptic denouncing of the contemporary world. For those who still cared, Dylan was again a controversial figure.

Chapter 7 covers the eighties, a period when recording became frustrating for Dylan while he worked with more collaborators than ever before, both in the studio and in concert. The corporatism of this era of rock music was not conducive to the careers of most musical artists who began their careers in the sixties, and Dylan was no exception, though not without some triumphs. This period finds Dylan seeking some form of détente with his own legacy and with the increasingly mainstream status of his chosen profession, as the five-disk career retrospective, *Biograph*, helped make the case that his past was more important than his present.

In the period from 1989 to 1997, discussed in chapter 8, Dylan produced only five new albums, and two of those feature stripped-down renditions of folk-blues classics. *The Bootleg Series Vol. 1–3* supplied listeners with a wealth of gems never previously released and complicated the story of Dylan's recent albums. An award for lifetime achievement and an all-star tribute concert both suggested Dylan's importance would henceforth be retrospective, until *Time Out of Mind*, his noteworthy new album toward the end of the decade, revised any summation of his career.

Chapter 9 discusses Dylan's work in the twenty-first century, which has proved his most successful period since the mid-seventies. The albums he has self-produced, under the alias Jack Frost, have affirmed his command of a wide range of song forms—borrowing from blues, folk, jazz, pop, country, rockabilly—that mostly predate the rock and roll of his own generation. Dylan's stint as a DJ on satellite radio seemed to be both inspired by his interest in earlier music and to inspire his own compositions. *Tempest*, Dylan's thirty-fifth studio album, was released in 2012 to favorable reviews and finds him returning to a storytelling vein he hasn't exercised in some time.

In 1986, at a time when his current work was irrelevant to most critics, and the historical associations of his earlier work were mostly out of step with the conservative ethos of the time, Dylan commented to Mikal Gilmore in *Rolling Stone*:

> All these people who say whatever it is I'm supposed to be doing— that's all gonna pass, because, obviously, I'm not gonna be around forever. That day's gonna come when there aren't gonna be any more records, and then people won't be able to say "Well this one's not as good as the last one." They're gonna have to look at it all. And I don't know what the picture will be, what people's judgment will be at that time. I can't help you in that area. (Cott 2006, 337)

Whether or not the day has come "when there aren't gonna be any more records," this book is an attempt to help us see "the picture," even if "the wheel's still in spin."

I

BECOMING BOB DYLAN
(1960–1964)

On August 28, 1963, Bob Dylan performed before an estimated crowd of 250,000 people as part of the March on Washington for Jobs and Freedom. That same day, Martin Luther King Jr. gave his famous "I have a dream" speech, expressing the hopes of many persons of color in combating a racially biased status quo that had existed for generations in the United States. The march dramatized the growing number of citizens willing to be vocal about civil rights, and King's speech put the issue into memorable oratory, making him a spokesperson for what was then called "the advancement of colored peoples." But why was a young, white, fairly obscure songwriter there, singing his own compositions, at this historic moment?

Bob Dylan was about the age of a college graduate, and had arrived in New York city's Greenwich Village a mere two and half years before as "a complete unknown," to become one of the numerous folkies on the scene. Now, after two albums for Columbia Records, he was performing in a remarkable lineup that included famous names of folk and gospel music like Harry Belafonte and Mahalia Jackson, and was performing beside Joan Baez, a contemporary who was already a major figure in the folk music revival and was becoming increasingly influential, particularly with college students. One song Dylan sang that day, "Only a Pawn in Their Game," was a stirring denunciation of an act of racist violence that killed a young black man, Medgar Evers, that summer in Jackson, Mississippi. Dylan was invited to sing because his songs were becoming reference points for a revitalized leftist folk movement in America.

The march, speeches, and performances in Washington marked the largest manifestation to that date of the Civil Rights Movement, which had been increasingly vocal since Rosa Parks's brave act of civil disobedience in 1955, when Dylan was a teen. After the march, the movement's demands would be given more attention by the administration of John F. Kennedy and gain more importance in the terms of his successor, Lyndon B. Johnson. The march also marked the high-water mark of Dylan's involvement in social issues. Not long after the Kennedy assassination in November 1963, Dylan distanced himself from the "conscience of his generation" tag journalists had conferred upon him.

As Dylan recalled to Mikal Gilmore in 2001, the folk song created an identity for people like himself, "an identity which the three-buttoned-suit postwar generation of America really wasn't offering to kids my age" (424). Identity conferred by a collective purpose was the movement's touchstone. For Dylan, the period of immersion in folk lasted for about three years, from 1960 to 1963. By 1964 his increased celebrity and the changes in his own vision of himself and of the kinds of music he wanted to make would mark the first of many startling transformations in a long and unpredictable career.

WHAT'S IN A NAME?

Bob Dylan began life as Robert Allen Zimmerman, born May 24, 1941, in Duluth, Minnesota, where his father worked as a manager for Standard Oil. In 1946, his parents, Abram and Beatty Zimmerman, moved to Hibbing, Minnesota, after Abe lost his job after contracting polio, which affected his health, and after the birth of their second child, David (Sounes, 23). Robert and his brother grew up in Hibbing, where their father, thirty years old the year Robert was born, worked with his brothers in an appliance store they eventually came to own and run. The Zimmermans were a Jewish American family living in the remote northern Great Lakes area. Hibbing was a mining community on the Mesabi Iron Range made prosperous by the recently ended war's demand for iron. After the austerity of the war, prosperity was reflected in the growing interest in leisure goods, such as the radios and record players that the Zimmerman brothers serviced and sold. Robert discovered, over the airwaves, an exciting world of music he had few chances to encounter locally.

As a teen, Robert's heroes, except for James Dean (the charismatic actor famous for *Rebel Without a Cause*, who died in a car crash in 1955) and some characters in John Steinbeck novels, were almost wholly music makers (Shelton, 28, 45). Young Zimmerman's major early idols can be summed up quickly: Hank Williams, Buddy Holly, Little Richard, Johnny Cash, and Elvis Presley. These were heroes any musically inclined teen might have in those years, each a uniquely gifted artist. Williams and Holly were notable as songwriters; indeed, Bob later named Williams as his favorite, whose songs possessed "the archetype rules of poetic songwriting" (*Chronicles*, 49, 96). Little Richard and Presley were acclaimed for their electrifying performance styles. Performing as a teen with an ad hoc group for Hibbing High's Jacket Jamboree, Bobby Zimmerman's antics at the piano were compared with Little Richard's flamboyant style, and in his high school yearbook the caption under his picture, complete with pompadour, reads "To join 'Little Richard'" (Scaduto, 10–11, 25).

Those first appearances with a band, as well as family reminiscences about little Bobby's performance of "Accentuate the Positive" at four years of age, indicate a joy in performing for people and being the center of attention (Shelton, 32). But enthusiasm for singing and idolizing popular musical entertainers do not necessarily lead to a career in the music industry, much less one as unique and unprecedented as that of Bob Dylan. Even when we add to the mix the old folk, blues, R&B, and more culturally obscure performers—such as Muddy Waters and Howlin' Wolf—whom young Zimmerman heard on the radio (with DJ Frank "Brother Gatemouth" Page broadcasting all the way from Shreveport, Louisiana) we might still be talking about someone who would only go on to be a minor local talent or a DJ.

Unable to jump-start a performing career locally, Zimmerman chose to at least get out of Hibbing. He accepted his parents' idea to enroll at the University of Minnesota, located in the twin cities of St. Paul and Minneapolis. If Bobby Zimmerman had found a course of study at college that engaged him fully, as Abe and Beatty had hoped, there might never have been a Bob Dylan. But by all accounts Zimmerman was an indifferent student, barely going to class, a misfit at the Jewish fraternity where he initially lodged, and a haunter of Dinkytown, the bohemian enclave near the campus where the nonconformity of the recent Beat movement reigned. The Beats' enthusiasm for jazz music as the supreme expression of selfhood had been replaced by a love for folk music. Immersing himself in this locally flourishing ethos, Zimmerman gave up on his adolescent love of rock and roll, or, at least, he gave up on the idea of fronting a band. As Dylan describes it, once he discovered Guthrie's songs he found a calling: "to be Guthrie's greatest disciple" (*Chronicles*, 246). Guthrie was the catalyst for the musical persona that Zimmerman would adopt in his transformation into Bob Dylan.

Early on, Bobby Zimmerman adopted stage names for performing. The first, Elston Gunn & The Rock Boppers, suggests an attempt to create a band by naming it. The name he eventually settled on for himself, Bob Dylan, has been analyzed and explained numerous times. For some, it is an obvious reference to Dylan Thomas, the Welsh poet noted for his popular and visceral style of performance—he toured the United States in 1950 and 1953, dying suddenly in New York on the latter tour. Like others cited as young Bob's heroes, Hank Williams, Buddy Holly, and James Dean, Thomas died young in the midst of much promise and praise. In *Chronicles*, Dylan explains how he toyed with other names, such as "Robert Allen" or "Allyn," variations on his given names. The step from "Allyn" to "Dylan" was inspired by the sound and look of Thomas's name, requiring, to Zimmerman's ear, a shift from "Robert" to "Bob" (79).

The key question about an alias is whether or not it works, that is, whether it produces an association in the mind. As Robert Shelton points out, the name "Dylan," by virtue of Thomas and Sheriff Matt Dillon, on the popular TV series *Gunsmoke*, had immediate associations, but they did not define the name (44). If the name was apt, it was because it allowed Robert Zimmerman to become a one-name entity—Dylan—much like "Elvis." Throughout the period when his fame was building, the name Dylan, somewhat mysterious, not easily ascribed to an ethnicity, became a notation for certain unique aspects of the singer's words, voice, sound, and appearance. To be "dylanesque" became a definable, even an enviable, quality.

As Dylan told Jonathan Cott in an interview in 1978, "I didn't create Bob Dylan. Bob Dylan has always been here . . . always was" (269). If Bob Dylan has "always been here," then the name is more than a name;

it's a role or a spirit, something Robert Zimmerman could inhabit, enact, become. Adopting a name is not simply a matter of hiding one's own name, but of becoming a new individual. Zimmerman, in his early years in New York, tried to elaborate a past that belonged to this character "Dylan." Journalists seeking the facts would often seize upon these fabrications as put-ons, an effort to dupe the public. The more compelling reason for the fanciful biography—which included yarns such as hailing from Colorado or New Mexico, working in a carnival, meeting and playing with legendary figures such as Leadbelly—is that it tells the story of Bob Dylan, not the story of Bobby Zimmerman (Cott, ix). By the time Bob Dylan was accepted as a public figure, Zimmerman had to become Dylan once and for all.

Woody Guthrie had made his mark on history long before Dylan read *Bound for Glory* in 1960. The world of the Depression found in the book, with its romantic evocations of homeless hobos with no possessions, bears comparison with the ethos of *On the Road* (1958), a novel by Jack Kerouac that (for those slightly older than Dylan and on down to the future hippies of the counterculture) offered a vision of the fraternity of the Road, a great American myth of a life of self-discovery, free of mundane constraints and ties to a place. The romantic version of Guthrie's world matched the current romanticism influencing Dylan's generation, but Dylan's interest in Guthrie was not simply a college student's infatuation. "Folk songs transcended the immediate culture," Dylan would write in *Chronicles* (27), and so he undertook to master the acoustic guitar in order to play the songs Guthrie wrote and the songs Guthrie knew. For Dylan, Guthrie's songs of the thirties "were totally in the moment, current and even forecasted things to come" (247). After gaining some proficiency through public performances around Dinkytown, Dylan resolved to go to New York to meet his hero, then in declining health from Huntington's Disease, in a Veterans Administration Hospital in New Jersey.

Dylan arrived in New York in January 1961, immersed himself in Guthrie's circle and became, for all intents and purposes, Guthrie's acolyte. Dylan had found his forte: in performance, he was able to enter imaginatively into the songs, to deliver them with a force and conviction increasingly impressive to those who, like him, were trying to eke out livings as singers of folk songs. Dylan's power as a performer is what impressed the more experienced folksingers of New York's Greenwich

Village. Had he been simply an imitator he would have been politely dismissed. What convinced his elders—like the Clancey Brothers, especially the youngest, Liam; Dave Van Ronk, "the Mayor of MacDougal Street"; Izzy Young, the local maven of the folk scene; and eventually others like the *New York Times* music critic Robert Shelton, Columbia Records executive John Hammond, music promoter Albert Grossman, as well as contemporaries like Joan Baez—was the concentration with which Dylan evoked the fond myth of the ramblin' troubadour, a vagabond in service to music.

In the years since the Great Depression ended, "beat" was no longer applied to the condition of down-and-outers oppressed by a system that had failed them, adrift in an economy in which there was no worthwhile or viable work. The U.S. economy had been rescued by the war effort as well as by social programs, such as the WPA (Work Projects Administration) that Franklin Roosevelt enacted in the period of Guthrie's heyday. In the late fifties and early sixties, "beat" became a badge of honor, the mark of those espousing a life indifferent to material comforts. Much of that critique of materialism was already present in folk music. Folk performers were not trying to get rich like popular celebrities, but sought to give expression to the music they believed in. Bobby Dylan, with his willingness to sleep on people's floors and couches, to live on handouts and what he scrounged playing gigs in Greenwich Village, epitomized the ethos. Later, after Dylan landed a recording contract with a major label so quickly and was becoming a celebrated figure, some would suggest it had all been a pose, a way of aligning himself with the most workable myth to achieve his goals. If there is truth to that idea, it derives from the fact that the "beat ethos"—when no longer an actual economic condition as it was in Guthrie's day—is necessarily something of a pose, using the means of minimal existence, deliberately chosen, to advance a larger cause. For the genuine folkie, the cause is the folk—as opposed to the commercial—tradition or a call to political or social justice or simply to resist the status quo. Such matters occupied Dylan as well for a time, but ultimately the cause he was advancing was his own art.

Dylan spent about six months in Guthrie's circle, paying homage through visits to the hospital and to the home of Guthrie's good friends, where he mixed with an older generation that had seen America go from a period of dire poverty to world-power status. He also became familiar with the belief in song as a force for change—a view he would not have encountered by listening only to Hank or Buddy or Elvis. That the words in a song were important, and not simply important as a statement of emotional intent, was a given for Guthrie. Guthrie aimed always to express a view larger than his own, and that example gave much scope to Bob Dylan's early songs, written somewhat in Guthrie's shadow.

"Song to Woody," one of Bob Dylan's first original compositions in New York, borrows its tune from Guthrie's "1913 Massacre," enacting both an homage to his hero—showing how well he could appropriate the master's work—and a statement of his own status. The song not only acknowledges the debt of the new kid in town, but it also implies that the torch has passed.

"FIXIN' TO DIE" AND HE'S "HARDLY BEEN BORN"

In "Song to Woody," the second-to-last track on *Bob Dylan*, the singer says this world "looks like it's dyin' an' it's hardly been born." Elsewhere on the album, Dylan sings about death in Bukka White's "Fixin' to Die" and in the standard "In My Time of Dyin'" (both very strong performances) and concludes with Blind Lemon Jefferson's "See That My Grave Is Kept Clean." The theme of death is notable for such a young man's album. Part of Dylan's pose—the aura he wanted most to evoke—was as someone more experienced in the ways of the world than he actually was. The key song on that theme is the traditional tune "Man of Constant Sorrow," no doubt chosen because its words of long-lived suffering, with thoughts of release in death, so clearly contrast with the baby-faced artist on the album cover, giving us a long stare that dares us to laugh at his pretensions. Posing as something one is not is part of any singer's birthright: singing the songs as they are meant to be sung, with full identification with the speaker in the song, extends a form of experience to the singer and to the audience as well. When we listen to Dylan, all of nineteen years old and "Fixin' to Die," we share in a projected self-image that leaves Robert Zimmerman behind and opens up imaginative possibilities created by the voice and manner of Bob Dylan, a kid with an unusual voice and the guts to use it.

If one wishes, one can dismiss such identification as wishful thinking and insist that Dylan has no right to an old man's—much less an old black man's—blues (Bukka White served time in a penitentiary, and Jefferson, a blues sensation of the 1920s, was the son of sharecroppers). Such a view is ultimately reactionary and conservative. For what the Civil Rights Movement was arguing for was the common status of humanity, regardless of race. For a young Jewish boy from the Iron Range to take on the persona of an Okie from the Dust Bowl (his Guthrie incarnation), or of a young girl working as a prostitute in New Orleans (in his version of "House of the Rising Sun," lifted from his Greenwich Village mentor Dave Van Ronk, to the latter's consternation), or of a black man in prison, or of a world-weary traveler from Colorado was to make an assertion about shared oppression and about the recognition of shared identity. The lesson learned from hours spent listening to Harry Smith's *Anthology of American Music* was that songs of the American people could include anyone who chose to sing them or to listen.

If listeners would not identify with Bob Dylan's youthful bravado, what was the basis of their refusal? In "Talkin' New York Blues," the other original composition on the album, Dylan characterizes his initial reception in the folk clubs: "you sound like a hillbilly, we want folksingers here." Other write-offs that would continue: Dylan is not musically accomplished, his voice is untrained and unpleasant, and his content is derivative if not an outright theft. And when his real antecedents became known (up to the release of his third album no one knew, at least not publically, the true details of Bob Dylan's background as Robert Zimmerman), he was too middle class for the uneducated vagrant he pretended to be. These were criticisms from those with something to defend. Dylan's appeal was to those who wanted to see the world remade, the criteria altered, to see a young upstart enliven folk music, which was in danger of resting on its laurels or becoming too commercial.

There was money in folk music, or at least a certain kind of folk music. Pete Seeger and The Weavers had had a hit with "Goodnight Irene" in the forties, which gave birth to a folk revival in America, which included popular figures such as Harry Belafonte, Burl Ives, and Odetta, the opera singer who became one of the most successful folksingers in the period preceding Dylan. Hearing her records in a store circa 1958, as Dylan told Ron Rosenbaum in 1978, inspired him to trade his electric guitar for a flat-top Gibson (204). The Kingston Trio took up where The Weavers left off and scored large radio hits, as well as several albums in the top ten simultaneously. Their success may have prompted the National Academy of Recording Arts and Sciences (NARAS) to found a Grammy award for Best Folk Recording in 1960, for the previous year. That year Joan Baez debuted on Vanguard Records and became at once the darling of folk music, singing to large, sold-out halls.

On the one hand, Dylan's ascendancy in the era of more polished folk acts was radical. On the other hand, the championing of Dylan by Hammond and Shelton over older folksingers was, in terms of the purity of the tradition, something of a travesty. Dylan had been playing folk music for all of two years, and his style was largely adopted from countless performers he imitated. Yet his was a take-no-prisoners approach. People would love his style or hate it—in either case they would talk about it, and that is how a name and a reputation get made.

The political aspects of the earlier folk movement of the thirties and forties had come to be seen, by mainstream American culture, as "anti" or "un" American, due to the highly publicized efforts of anti-Communist McCarthyism to purge all leftist sympathies from Washington and the entertainment industry in the mid-fifties. Pete Seeger himself had to endure a forced hiatus in his career due to the taint of "red" associations. Guthrie, while he never joined the Communist Party, did support some of the same leftist programs to which the communists were dedicated. In the early sixties, when Dylan came to town, those antagonisms were still very much alive in the coffeehouses of Greenwich Village where the initial figureheads of the folk movement had sung and played. In assuming the mantle of Guthrie, Dylan might be expected to take on some of the previous generation's political battles.

While *Bob Dylan* is apolitical, there is a strong sense of tragic honor in the album. The songs speak of spirits sorely tried, not by political oppression, but by existence itself and by their place in the world. The two original compositions sketch the outlook of Bob Dylan: his wry observations about a hard-scrabble existence in New York and his salute to Woody, a hero for having endured that kind of life for the sake of experience—the vague "not many men have done the things that you've done." What did Woody do? We would never know from the song, only that he rambled around and knew other singers and other ramblers.

The point of view of both songs—Dylan's perspective on folk music we might say—is the value of individualism, using music to remain outside the snares of comfortable conformism. Implied in this is a young man's dream of remaining free and true to himself or true to the search for himself. Such was the pied piper call that many of Dylan's contemporaries would hear and follow, at least for much of that decade.

Commentators tend to cite the fact that *Bob Dylan* only sold 2,500 to 5,000 copies initially, and that Dylan was regarded by some Columbia executives as "Hammond's folly," suggesting that John Hammond had erred in taking on Dylan. Hammond, a widely respected A&R (artist and repertoire) executive, signed Dylan on the strength of his playing on an album by Carolyn Hester that Hammond produced, of recommendations from others based on Dylan's performances at Gerde's Folk City, and of the impression made on the *New York Times* critic Robert Shelton. The mockery may have been appropriate if one thinks only in terms of sales, but rarely is it mentioned that *Bob Dylan* was nominated for Best Folk Recording at the Grammys, along with Baez's *Live in Concert* and recordings by Belafonte, The Kingston Trio, and The New Christy Minstrels. If only out of respect to Hammond, the boy wonder's nomination indicates that Dylan's debut had not gone unnoticed by the people who count. The album lost to "If I Had a Hammer," recorded by Peter, Paul, and Mary, a new folk group formed by Albert Grossman to cash in on the market The Kingston Trio had captured, featuring a female singer to compete with the success of Baez and others. By the time Dylan completed his second album, he too would be represented by Grossman, and although the song that won the 1963 Grammy for Best Folk Recording was again recorded by Peter, Paul, and Mary, it was written by Bob Dylan. The song was "Blowin' in the Wind," and it reached number 2 on *Billboard*'s chart.

A line in "Talkin' New York Blues," "some people can rob you with a fountain pen," was prophetic of Dylan's ultimate feelings about his relation with Grossman and the setting-up of the publishing company Dwarf Music in 1966 (Sounes, 200–201). Yet in this initial period, Grossman's methods of promotion and his personal financial interest in the songs of Bob Dylan—as recorded by others more radio ready— meant Dylan could not fail to get a hearing. For someone like Dylan, ultimately bound beyond the traditional folk music world, this was of paramount importance. Yet to the people of that world who embraced

Dylan as a strong voice and presence in the movement, Grossman's commercial interests were seen as the driving force behind Dylan eventually "selling out" to rock and pop.

A FREEWHEELIN' SONGWRITER

Recording sessions for Dylan's second album began in April 1962, the month after the release of *Bob Dylan*, continued in July and October, and concluded in April of 1963 (Heylin 1995, 13–14). The length of time signals the intention to better the showing of the first album, and to do that Dylan had to find songs suited to his talent. And that meant writing the songs himself. In that year, Dylan recorded over twenty original compositions, and the progress he made was extraordinary.

On the first album, the two Dylan-penned songs are both in homage to Woody Guthrie: "Song for Woody" is a direct address to the older singer, and "Talkin' New York Blues" is in a form called "talkin' blues," of which Guthrie was a master. Dylan's version recreates the off-the-cuff strumming and talking style that permits the singer to make many seemingly improvised asides. Dylan continued to compose in the form for his second album. "Talkin' Bear Mountain Picnic Massacre Blues" (a comic tale based on a newspaper story about a fraudulent excursion) and "Talkin' John Birch Paranoid Blues" (a send-up of the right-wing political organization), with their genially humorous tone and adlibs, went over well in concert. The elastic nature of the talkin' blues, its capacity for disjointed storytelling and satiric observations, suited Dylan in his earliest period. Neither song made the final cut of the album, but another talking blues, "Talkin' World War III Blues," the best of the three, recorded at the final session in April, 1963, was included (Heylin 1995, 14). Two other comic songs debuted on *Freewheelin'*: "Bob Dylan's Blues," an alternately self-deprecating and heroicizing paean to his own persona, initiates the comic blues songs that continue into Dylan's fifth album, while "I Shall Be Free," a whimsical picaresque romp, introduces a persona common to most of Dylan's early albums and ends the album with a light-hearted self-portrait.

As these songs of irreverent and playful doggerel show, Dylan's closest persona had a common-sense point of view from which to mock hypocrisy. The songs with "a message"—the songs for which *Freewhee-*

lin' is best-known—also aim to speak collectively. In this period Dylan moved swiftly from being a mimic of a folk and blues tradition from the 1920s and 1930s to being a conduit for the voices around him, channeling the concerns of the New Left into songs clear in their conviction, if sometimes vague in their critique.

There are three bona fide classics on *The Freewheelin' Bob Dylan*: "Blowin' in the Wind," "Don't Think Twice, It's Alright," and "A Hard Rain's A-Gonna Fall." In addition to these, each a significant entry in different song genres that Dylan would continue to develop, there is one other that became a staple of his performing repertoire over the years: "Masters of War." The quintessential "finger-pointing" song, its intensity is deadly as it excoriates munitions manufacturers and the military for creating an environment—via the atom bomb—that makes one fearful of giving birth to future generations.[1] The song is the closest Dylan ever comes to the persona of "angry young man," and would be notable if for no other reason. The delivery, and the borrowed tune (from "Fair Nottamun Town," which Dylan learned while on a visit to London to act in a televised play), combine to give stature to Dylan's railing. The singer sees clearly that those who promote war also promote a culture of death, which he answers ironically by longing for the moment when he can stand over their graves.

In contrast to his first album, Dylan does not seem obliged to pretend to be an old bluesman but instead advertises his youth—"you may say that I'm young, you may say I'm unlearned," he challenges in "Masters of War." Most often, the pose on the second album is one of openness. Several songs employ direct address. He tells us of a dream about his oldest friends in "Bob Dylan's Dream," a mournful song about loss of innocence, and he reflects comically, and autobiographically, on his troubles in "Down the Highway" (in which he refers to the extended stay in Italy of his girlfriend—Suze Rotolo, pictured with him on the album cover—while he was making the album). He poses numerous questions to his listener in "Blowin' in the Wind," and, in "A Hard Rain's A-Gonna Fall," asks questions that might be put by Dylan's own father to his "blue-eyed son": "where have you been, what did you see, who did you meet?"

While many have referred to "Hard Rain" as "apocalyptic," the term only fits the song tangentially. The liner notes on the back of the album, written by Nat Hentoff, suggest that the song arose out of the Cuban

Missile Crisis—which occurred in October 1962—and Dylan's quoted comments seem to agree. In fact, the song was written and performed by Dylan a month before President Kennedy made his declaration about the USSR's missiles in Cuba (Heylin 1996, 33). Granted, that situation made Dylan's song all the more relevant and made the song feel more topical. The song does not describe a time after a nuclear holocaust—that's the subject of the witty "Talkin' World War III Blues," which is quite effective at skewering those people all-too-ready to jump into their fallout shelters if a nuclear blast would rid the world of communists. Rather, "Hard Rain" offers glimpses of a world distorted by unsettling, almost surreal imagery that conjures up the mood of "last days." The pageant includes crying clowns, dying poets, a young woman with a burning body, a girl giving away rainbows, a white man walking a black dog, children armed with weapons, and—perhaps one of the more enigmatic images—"a white ladder all covered with water." The "hard rain" may be the start of a second deluge that will finally clear away the hurt and hurtful souls the song describes. The singer suggests that, no chosen one, he will not escape the fate of this world, but will "stand on the ocean until I start sinkin'," while testifying to what he has experienced in visions. It is a song at times wry in its associations, at times sad, and also quite beautiful. The song's poetic images establish a high-water mark for popular song lyrics. As a statement of both dread and defiance, the song accurately captures the feeling of young people facing the post World War II world of nuclear peril.

The most famous song on the album is its opening song, "Blowin' in the Wind," but the delivery here is more subdued and offhand than would be the case once the song became a sing-along anthem at protest rallies. If a "protest song," the perspective is oddly timeless, affecting a relation to eternal things—the roads a man walks down, the seas a white dove flies before finding land (recalling the dove sent out from Noah's ark to find dry land after the biblical flood). A dove is a symbol of peace and the next image protests war, asking when cannonballs will be banned. The setting seems older than our era since cannonballs, if never banned, had become obsolete after the nineteenth century—specifically perhaps for Dylan, the Civil War. If a reference to the Civil War, the image is appropriate since each verse contains a line that may refer to the status of blacks in the United States. In that context, the question would be "how many times must we go to war to settle our differences before we find other means and outlaw war?"

The second verse, with its rhyming emphasis on "sky," "cry," "died," questions our relation to our surroundings. To see the sky means in essence to see, for once, what is too obvious to be missed; this sense is seconded by the cries one needs more ears to hear because one is able to ignore them. The statement that "too many people have died" is an understatement since death claims everyone, eventually, but the claim amplifies obvious facts we don't always see (like the sky) and, coupled with the crying people, points to deaths as casualties related to a cause. To protesters of the Vietnam War, the deaths are the fallen soldiers; to protesters for civil rights, the deaths are killings with no benefit of justice (as, for instance, Medgar Evers). In putting the sky, the cries, and the deaths into relation, the song makes its point. The recurrent question of "how many" gives the song its relentless refrain, but is left to be answered by the wind. Which is to say, not answered at all, since it is clear that one already has looked up enough, possesses enough ears, and should know the death count is too high.

One great talent Dylan developed early is how to end a song. Even if a song contains too many verses, as is sometimes the case, Dylan at his best saves a major statement for the end. In the version of the song on *Freewheelin'*, the most telling questions are saved for last: how long a man must live before he is "allowed to be free." The oxymoron of being permitted to be free (is such freedom real freedom?) poses the problem of freedom as something bestowable by laws. The line, sandwiched between a question about a mountain returning to the sea—an image for the vast length of time for natural change—and a line about refusing to see, arrives as the crux of the lyric, with Dylan's voice giving the question a stirring weight. In the context of political movements, the freedom of the dissident, the protester, the onetime slave, or political prisoner exists as a struggle against those who prevent freedom. The reference to the mountain, then, prefigures Martin Luther King Jr.'s rejoinder in "Letter from Birmingham Jail" to those who preach patience, who claim that the improvement of life for blacks must take place gradually, over many generations, as a mountain is worn down by the relentless surge of the sea.

The economy of the song is striking; its simplicity—the tune is adapted from "No More Auction Block," an old spiritual of the slavery era—is forceful, and its imagery hints at the fatalism of folk poetry in natural symbols, suggesting the wind's indifference to the lack of freedom, the unjust deaths, and the cries of suffering.

Another distinctive aspect of the album is Dylan's skill with romantic songs: "Girl from the North Country," "Don't Think Twice, It's Alright," and "Honey, Just Allow Me One More Chance." In all three, the singer pines for a woman or reminisces about a woman, and in all but the first-named addresses the woman directly. "Honey" is unabashedly playful, suggesting that wooing can be fun, even if one is in ill graces. "Girl" is a stately evocation of a once-upon-a-time love that the singer still feels, hoping the girl he remembers so poignantly remembers him as well. And yet the description is deliberately generic—she had long hair, was a "true love," and the singer would like her to have a warm coat in the cold north (which he is clearly not returning to any time soon). "Girl" leaves us with the vision of both the girl and her lover when they were young and untried by the dark nights and bright days the singer has lived through since.

Finally, the strongest, "Don't Think Twice" is the quintessential "it's time to move on" song of Dylan's generation, building from the masterful songs of hurt feelings Hank Williams wrote. The lyrics capture a regret "Girl" articulates but, rather than seen from a distance, here it is presented in lines addressed to the lover herself. The singer has made up his mind to go and gives his reasons. The refrain, "don't think twice, it's alright," might be sincere, but it might also be disingenuous. At one point, he admits he wishes she would do something to try and change his mind, but then the refrain cuts that thought off with a feeling of "you won't anyway and it's just as well." The two songs, "Girl" and "Twice," present us with a lover who leaves, not without regrets and, once he's safely gone, evoke a memory he hopes to preserve. Both songs suggest a young man more concerned with his "precious time" than with the women he is recalling.

Dylan's ability to express a nuanced relation to women had a great influence on the songwriters of his generation. At times dismissive, at times seductive, acerbic, chastened, charming, lyrical, even mystical, the attitude toward women and romantic love in Dylan's songs is complex. In both songs, the theme of "woman versus girl" is sounded. The "true love" in "North Country" was only a girl, while the lover in "Don't Think Twice" is, to the singer, "a woman," though he was told by others that she is "a child." This difference gets reworked further in one of Dylan's signature songs "Just Like a Woman," but for now it is enough to note the need for more experience, so that we might say the roads one must walk to become a man—a key question in "Blowin' in the Wind"—are calling away from any settled relation to a lover. In that context, the question might be: "How many girls must one man have?" There is a touch of the playboy in Dylan's outlook at times—the men's magazine *Playboy* and the empire it founded in which males could be catered to by a bevy of beauties, began in 1953, the year Dylan turned twelve, so that his adolescence, as it was for most men born in the 1940s and 1950s, was marked to some degree by the magazine's insistence on women as interchangeable figures of pleasure (it's interesting, in that light, to note that Dylan's future wife, Sara Lownds, worked for a time at the Playboy Club in New York). In "I Shall Be Free," Dylan imagines President Kennedy calling him up for advice on spurring growth. Dylan's answer is a list of foreign movie actresses, all noted for their voluptuous figures: Bridget Bardot, Sophia Loren, Anita Ekberg. "Country'll grow," Dylan deadpans.

The Freewheelin' Bob Dylan easily outperformed its predecessor. It cracked *Billboard*'s Top 25 and reached number 1 in the UK. With this album, Bob Dylan achieved a musical identity he would have a hard time living down.

THE WINDS OF CHANGE

Around the time of his second album, Dylan became known as a songwriter willing to take on the issues of the day. *Freewheelin'* provides an antiwar song, "Masters of War," and another, "Hard Rain," that was interpreted as a protest against nuclear armaments, and yet another, "Blowin' in the Wind" that was seen as both antiwar and pro–civil rights. The album includes "Oxford Town," a sarcastic treatment of the need for federal troops when the first black student at "Ole Miss," James Meredith, attempted to attend class. As well, "I Shall Be Free" contains a satiric aside on the Jim Crow South: the singer says a can of black paint fell on his head; he went to wash the paint off, "but had to sit in the back of the tub," a reference to the segregationist practice of making blacks sit in the back of the bus.

The racist practices of the Jim Crow South were a target for several of Dylan's songs (though he had not yet traveled to the Deep South). His earliest effort was "The Death of Emmett Till," recorded April 1962, and based on the trial of two white men accused of killing Till, a black teen visiting Mississippi from Chicago in 1955, for his remarks to a married white woman. The case caused a great outcry when the killers—who admitting kidnapping Till but not killing him—were acquitted, then later admitted the murder in a *Look* magazine interview. The failure of justice provoked much press and is considered instrumental in the first Civil Rights Act of 1957. Dylan's song is rather clumsy and heavy-handed, but shows him trying to move from the case—the song is very inexact about the details—to the larger theme of racism and the Ku Klux Klan. In 1963, two further incidents of racial violence spurred Dylan to respond in song: the killing of Medgar Evers, leader of the NAACP, and one of the local black investigators of Till's death, in Jackson, Mississippi, in June 1963, inspired "Only a Pawn in Their Game," recorded in August; and a random act of violence by William Zantzinger resulting in the death of a middle-aged maid in Baltimore in February 1963 inspired "The Lonesome Death of Hattie Carroll," recorded the following October. Both songs appear on Dylan's third album, *The Times, They Are A-Changin'* (Heylin 1995, 23–24).

Both "Pawn" and "Hattie Carroll" employ the tactic of stepping back from actual incidents to allow the singer to condemn the larger social construct of racism. As the saying goes, "society is to blame"—such is the moral of "Pawn." The killing of Evers, according to the song, is the result of whites learning from childhood that blacks are inferior and that, if whites use violence against blacks, the law will protect whites from punishment. Dylan's lyrics indict a nameless "they"—at first, meaning white Southern politicians but eventually including everyone who permits racism to continue. "Their game" is to suppress the fight for equality and to enforce racial privilege legally.

"Hattie Carroll" is very specific about the crime that inspired it: the killer is named (though his surname is altered, intentionally or not, from Zantzinger to Zanzinger), and at each stage of the narration—with details about Carroll's life of servile labor ("she just cleaned up all the food from the table") or about her employer's life of privilege, or about his blow with a cane when she failed to serve him swiftly enough—the singer repeats the refrain that it is not yet time for tears. The tears should fall, the song concludes, only when we learn that Zantzinger received for "penalty and repentance," a mere six months sentence. The song finds pathos in its rendering of the social injustice of wealth and poverty (the depiction of Carroll's labor resonates with images of slaves and masters from pre–Civil War Southern plantations), then inflates to an epic inclusiveness in its rendering of the "blow from a cane that sailed through the air and came down through the room, doomed and determined to destroy all the gentle." For all that its heart is in the right place, the suggestion that Carroll's death itself should not be grieved, but rather the meager punishment the crime received, barely escapes becoming a sanctimonious rhetorical gesture.

Lest we think that economic deprivation was a theme fit only for Woody Guthrie's Dust-Bowl ballads of the thirties, *The Other America*, Michael Harrington's groundbreaking account of poverty in America, published amid much attention in the spring of 1962, demonstrates the relevance of songs like "North Country Blues" and "The Ballad of Hollis Brown." The first is told by a woman, daughter of a miner, sister of a miner, wife of a miner, who realizes that the mining life is over for her offspring. In the song, the miners' impoverishment is due to their wages being undermined by cheaper labor in South America, a telling glance at labor practices. "Hollis Brown" is an even more grim story of tragically bad luck befalling a subsistence farmer. Both songs are highly dramatic portrayals of "lives of quiet desperation," to use Thoreau's phrase. Harrington's book argued that prosperity in America is largely an effect of education and that those left behind on the farm or in dwindling communities built upon occupations grown obsolete have not been brought into the same quality of life as their contemporaries. Like Harrington's book, both of Dylan's songs focus on the white working poor, with "Hollis Brown" attaining an archetypal status through the song's relentless repetitions and driving rhythm, and "North Country" achieving a plainspoken portrait, starkly beautiful as the photographs of Walker Evans.

The themes of racist violence and of grinding poverty relate to the very "times" to which the album's title alludes. In the period when Dylan wrote and recorded these songs, the administration of John Kennedy was beginning to turn—too slowly for some—to domestic issues such as civil rights for nonwhites and the lack of federal support for America's working poor. With the stand-off over Cuba behind him for the moment, Kennedy seemed ready to enact domestic policies to which Dylan's third album provides something of a Greek chorus. Two key songs on the album herald the need for change: "The Times, They Are A-Changin'" and "When the Ship Comes In."

From *Freewheelin'* through *Blonde on Blonde*, Dylan albums begin with a song that could be said to epitomize the theme of the record; released as singles, the lead songs are able to stand for the album in an immediate way. "The Times, They Are A-Changin'," unlike "Blowin' in the Wind," was not covered by other recording artists at the time. The song readily associated Dylan, as its singer, with the theme of political change. The song's didactic tone—addressing in turn "people," "mothers and fathers," "writers and critics," "senators and congressmen"— and its willingness to sound like a prophet of old, invoking a coming flood and cribbing from the Bible ("the first one now will later be last"), indicate that Dylan was straining for big statements. That said, there are lines in the song that have considerable aphoristic force—"don't speak too soon for the wheel's still in spin"—while other commands, such as telling members of the older generation to "get out of new [road] if you can't lend your hand," have the force of youthful challenge. Many found in the song a voice for what they would like to say, with the assumption that the contemporary moment was changing more rapidly than was true for previous generations. Whether or not this was so, there was certainly a more developed media to capitalize on slogans and million-dollar phrases. Dylan's song weds a timeless perspective to a youthful outlook. Ancient and modern at once, like the best forms of folk wisdom, the song continues to resonate as "the waters," in one form or another, continue to rise. Like a prophet raised on the Bible, Dylan seems to see the apocalypse in terms of water and a flood. Indeed, "When the Ship Comes In" also makes emblematic use of the sea, though here the anticipated ship, a sort of Noah's ark, is sent to rescue those who have kept the faith. Both songs imply or envision punitive ends, possibly apocalyptic events, for indifferent, unhelpful, or malicious behavior.

The powerful indictment of war-mongering on *Freewheelin'* is extended and deepened by "With God on Our Side," apropos of the Kennedy administration's increase of support to the Vietnamese in their battle with the communist Viet Cong. The singer leads the listener through a history lesson of U.S. military engagements to arrive at the then-current arms' race with the USSR, as the Cold War provided most of the rationale for U.S. involvement in Vietnam. In the song, each successive war is invoked as a lesson every American school child is taught, even if, as with World War I, "the reason for fightin' I never did get." At the close, Dylan proposes the notion that, if God were truly on our side, there would be no more wars. This idea is set up by a surprising verse in which the singer ponders the question of "whether Judas Iscariot had God on his side." The most obvious meaning of the verse is that the United States is being betrayed by those it trusts to defend it, but there is an implication that some acts sanctioned by God—the betrayal of Christ—may be a betrayal of values commonly held. The song was first performed at the Town Hall concert in New York in April 1963, and then twice again at the Newport Folk Festival in July 1963, both times with Joan Baez. "With God" is the kind of song for which Dylan was highly praised in the folk movement: somewhat formulaic, the song manages to convey a challenging sense of values, even of insight, while maintaining a plainspoken, "everyman" pose.

Times also continues the more personal songs that marked the second album so strongly. The wistful, nostalgic sentiments found in "Girl from the North Country" and "Bob Dylan's Dream" are continued, in even more succinct and poetic fashion, in "One Too Many Mornings," sung with a simple but affecting delivery. The song offers one of Dylan's first self-conscious comments on his status as a "spokesperson": "everything I'm sayin' you could say it just as good." The song has the tone of one who realizes he has wasted too much time, but here the blame falls on the times themselves moving too fast. There is simply an ache in the world that the singer is trying not to be overwhelmed by. In place of the slightly bitter but shrugging "Don't Think Twice," Dylan this time offers "Boots of Spanish Leather," a song that, like "Girl," takes its tune from a traditional arrangement, and expresses the pain of realizing, through messages sent from a traveling lover, that a love is over.

What is lacking on *Times*, as compared to *Freewheelin'*, are songs of humor and charm. The album is very earnest, at times strident. Dylan's grasp of detail has greatly improved, but nowhere on *Times* do we find the imagistic reaches of "Hard Rain." And in place of the off-the-cuff explorations of his comic persona so well represented on *Freewheelin'*, we have the somewhat defensive "Restless Farewell" as a send-off.

Dylan wrote the song late in the recording process in response to a smear article in *Newsweek* that tried to expose him as a phony and a plagiarist (Shelton, 138–39). The article did not do any real damage to Dylan's career but, as a personal attack, seemed to require a response. Not only did Dylan close the album with "Farewell"—mentioning "the dust of gossip and the dirt of rumor"—but he also included "11 Outlined Epitaphs," printed on the back of the album and continued as an insert. In this free verse ramble, which begins with Dylan "blindly punchin' at the blind," Dylan becomes more cagily autobiographical than in the earlier "My Life in a Stolen Moment," mentioning the "legacy visions" left by the town he grew up in—"it was a dyin' town"—and his wish to have "lived / in the hungry thirties" like Guthrie, who is named as "my last idol" because, as the first idol Dylan met face to face, he was able to see him as a man with his own reasons for what he did and said, "an' every action can be questioned." In one passage, Dylan specifically expresses his dissatisfaction with magazines and the kinds of "rumor tale" used to coerce an artist's cooperation. The album and its liner poem indicate a young man beginning to take himself rather seriously.

During the making of *Times*, Dylan was proclaimed "the crown prince of folk music" at the Newport Folk Festival in July 1963. He appeared with Baez, its reigning queen, and performed as her special guest at several of her concerts. Baez was quite smitten by Dylan and also believed strongly in his duty to write the songs they should be singing to their audience. They were a couple to some degree at this time, almost perforce as folk royalty, though Dylan continued his increasingly volatile relationship with Suze Rotolo as well. The importance of Baez and the folk movement for Dylan in this period cannot be overstated. Baez, herself a very irreverent character, was approached in performance with great reverence, her audience hanging on her every word. Dylan's performances, now lifted from the gritty folk bars of New York and Cambridge and placed in concert halls beside Baez, inspired the same intense listening. Another influence at this time was the senior folk star Pete Seeger who was instrumental in having Dylan take part in political events, such as the SNCC (Student Nonviolent Coordinating Committee) rally to register black voters in Greenwood, Mississippi, in July 1963. Thus, with these two major folk icons as mentors/collaborators, one a spokesperson for the veritable Old Left, the other a star to the New Left, Dylan found himself dubbed repeatedly "the voice of a generation."

The third album was finished by October 1963 but not released until January 1964. By that time, Dylan's comfort with his "folk conscience" mantle was unraveling. On November 22, 1963, John F. Kennedy, the thirty-sixth president of the United States, was assassinated in a motorcade in Dallas, Texas. The entire country reeled from the surprise of the attack. Those for whom Kennedy's election in 1960—in a very close and contested race against Richard M. Nixon—was a victory for youthful vigor could not help seeing great hope and energy wasted in a shocking moment of violence. Less than a month later, the Emergency Civil Liberties Committee bestowed the Tom Paine Award upon Bob Dylan for his civic-minded songs. In his acceptance speech, Dylan revealed "another side" indeed.

A SINGULAR FIGURE

Accepting the Tom Paine Award in December 1963, shortly following the Kennedy assassination and the public mourning it inspired, Dylan went off on a tangent that aimed to be timely but was perceived as an outrageous provocation. In criticizing the assembled members, albeit jokingly, for not being young and not having hair, Dylan seemed out of sorts with the fact that he was not addressing his own generation (some of his friends who came to the event with him were not let in, apparently). If Dylan had ever wanted to appeal to an older generation, here was an opportunity, but he went the other way. It seems as if he strove to offend those honoring him to convince them that he was not what they assumed him to be. In the song "Motorpsycho Nitemare," recorded in June 1964, a traveler wants to offend a farmer whose hospitality makes him uneasy, so he shouts "I dig Fidel Castro and his beard." A calculated offense to a patriotic American, the line recalls Dylan's speech at the awards dinner: to strike a sufficiently "weird" note, Dylan mentioned Cuba and claimed he could see some of Lee Harvey Oswald in himself. Viewed sympathetically, the statement might indicate that, far from a saint, Kennedy represented a political establishment that might cause someone very frustrated to turn to violence.

Whatever his intentions, Dylan's comments inspired considerable outcry, to say nothing of fewer donations to an organization that would honor someone as confused as Bob Dylan. Frustrated by his inability to make his point, Dylan published a verse statement in *Broadside* in January 1964, but again failed to get his idea across. The real problem was the idea of himself as a "spokesperson" for anything but his own views, which in all honesty he perceived as being in flux and not resolved even on something so obvious as the view one should take of a presidential assassin. We should not take Dylan's speech and his letter-poem, and certainly not the award nor the assassination, as causes of his move away from the so-called protest movement. Rather, Dylan was trying to lodge a protest against his assumed role within the movement. In the winter of 1963/1964 the symptoms of Dylan's restlessness with his public role were manifest—first announced in "Restless Farewell" and its boast to "not give a damn."

Key to the changes in Dylan's image, outlook, and output at this time is the fact that he spent time away from Greenwich Village. He took a cross-country road trip with some friends, that great getaway that fuels *On the Road* as well as countless student odysseys after graduation. Dylan at the time was approaching twenty-three and can be thought of as equivalent to a graduate student. He had "graduated" from his intensive apprenticeship to the folk song movement and its practitioners. In becoming a celebrated figure, he was moving into the "journeyman" phase of acquiring an art. It was time to stop writing the kinds of songs those around him required and to write songs as the artist he was becoming. Already the tag "poet" had been thrown at him, both as a comment on what made his song lyrics different from other writers, and as a means to gain his lyrics more serious attention. Though such claims are always fraught with literary assumptions, Dylan was self-consciously developing a new idiom, both with his lengthy, free-form verse pieces on the back of his albums and with songs more expressionistic in their imagery.

The manner of the songs for the fourth album, *Another Side of Bob Dylan*, was inspired by the use of marijuana. One aspect of the influence of a poet like Arthur Rimbaud, the visionary French poet of the mid-1800s whose poems impressed Dylan, or Rimbaud's Beat descendants such as Allen Ginsberg, Michael McClure, Lawrence Ferlinghetti, all of whom Dylan met in this period, is some acquaintance with "the disregulation of the senses." This phrase, from an important letter Rimbaud wrote at sixteen, describing the means of becoming the kind of poet he intends to be ("a seer" or *voyant*), is generally taken as a license for forms of intoxication to induce a visionary state, such as through hashish and absinthe (Rimbaud's substances of choice) or, in the sixties, marijuana, and hallucinogens like LSD or psilocybin.

The changed state of mind produced by such substances can perhaps best be observed by looking at *The Other Side of the Mirror*, Murray Lerner's film of Dylan's appearances at the Newport Folk Festival. In 1963, Dylan is the darling of the folkies, dressed in denim and plain shirt, looking like Woody Jr. In 1964, the month after recording his fourth album in one all-night session, he is dressed in black, looking like the hipster he was becoming. He debuted "Mr. Tambourine Man" at the afternoon workshop session, a song that was a leap well beyond anything he had recorded to that point, suggesting the state of reverie associated with smoking marijuana. Certainly, this was a very different kind of song—implying a different singer and a different kind of audience—than straight-forward tales like "North Country Blues" or soapboxes like "With God on Our Side." While performing the latter with Baez at Newport in 1964, Dylan seems to have diffculty keeping a straight face, typical of the random hilarity of the stoned.

Meanwhile, the year 1964 saw developments in three themes Dylan had tackled on his second and third albums—increased awareness of poverty, antiwar agitation, and civil rights issues. In January, President Johnson declared his "War on Poverty," and in March announced that his administration would increase military assistance to South Vietnam, which inspired the first protests against the war by students—marches were held in New York, San Francisco, Seattle, Madison, and Boston. Casualties in the undeclared war would top 1,000 by mid-summer. In February, the trial of the killers of Medgar Evers, in Mississippi, ended in a mistrial because of the jury's inability to pronounce a judgment, and in June three civil rights workers were murdered by Klansmen there. July brought the passing of the Civil Rights Act of 1964 and race riots in Harlem. Clearly, Dylan's early songs remained more timely than ever. But 1964 saw an important event of another kind: The Beatles' first number one song—"I Want to Hold Your Hand"—topped U.S. charts in February, the same month the band from Liverpool played *The Ed Sullivan Show* (while Dylan was on his cross-country jaunt), and by April, the height of "Beatlemania," The Beatles boasted the top five songs on *Billboard*'s Hot 100. With the cute, quipping personalities of "The Fab Four" a key part of their celebrity, the idea of youth trying to change the world met the idea of youth playing the world for laughs.

The songs on *Another Side of Bob Dylan*, released August 1964, half a year after *The Times, They Are A-Changin'*, indicate how swiftly Dylan, who wrote most of the new songs while visiting Europe, was changing, removing himself from the New York scene and its associations. The only topical references on the album are challenges to Muhammad Ali (addressed by his given name, Cassius Clay), who had become the Heavyweight Champion of the World by beating Sonny Liston in February, and to Barry Goldwater, a conservative dedicated to taking the country back from the liberals, who became the Republican presidential nominee in July, and a joke about the Russians getting to heaven first, a reference to the current "space race" to the moon. The album's stand-out tracks show the extent to which Dylan was writing hit songs beyond the confines of folk: "It Ain't Me Babe," a signature song for Dylan, was a country hit for Johnny Cash and his wife June Carter Cash in 1964, and a Top Ten pop hit for The Turtles in 1965. "All I Really Want to Do," the album's opener, was a hit for Cher in 1965, and The Byrds, who became recurring "folk rock" interpreters of Dylan's songs, recorded a truncated version of it, as well as "My Back Pages" and "Chimes of Freedom," two of the new songs that indicate Dylan's move to a more deliberate poetics.

A notable change from the previous album is *Another Side*'s return to the off-the-cuff humor of *Freewheelin'*. Dylan is in good spirits in the opening track, "All I Really Want to Do," an upbeat tune memorable for the yodeling "doooooo" on the chorus. The song presents a somewhat more genial Dylan, laughing at the idea that anyone would try to "be like me." Side 2's first track is even more light-hearted, a sustained comic narrative—a traveling salesman joke—in which the singer runs afoul of a farmer and his daughter, who at first reminds the singer of the glamorous women in *La Dolce Vita* (such as Anita Ekberg) and then of Alfred Hitchcock's *Psycho* (both films date from 1960). With outrageous rhymes—"I heard something jerkin' and there stood Rita looking just like Tony Perkins"—the song is a combination of an off-color joke and a sketch about a young person's nonconformity and leftist sympathies, with a witty pop culture hipness.

Other songs on *Another Side* present somewhat chastened versions of Dylan's self-image: in the piano-based "Black Crow Blues," he says he feels "out of touch"; in the rousing "Spanish Harlem Incident"—a good example of the path of excess that Dylan's lyrics are willing to tread at this point, revelatory in small lyric touches—he wants to know if he's "really real"; in "I Shall Be Free No. 10," he mentions a friend who stabs Dylan's image with a Bowie knife and pretends "to barf" at the mention of Dylan's name; and in "To Ramona," a heartfelt offer of psychic advice to a young girl having a hard time dealing with people who make her feel "you must be exactly like them," he ends with the admission that he might need some help himself, "maybe some day, baby."

The kind of "help" advocated is belief in one's own convictions. "My Back Pages" describes a growth toward greater youth. We might infer that, at twenty-three, Dylan had discovered, in youth culture, a feeling of camaraderie based on a shared indifference to the exhortations of "good and bad" professed by the old guard leaders he had mocked at the Paine Award dinner. Any adherence to political slogans is undermined by the singer's sense that teachings are not to be trusted, and the crusading of his earlier period has come to seem romantic and self-important. The song's lyrics are not always as graceful as they might be, but there is a strong sense of an individual voice, very much Dylan's own diction and structure, that makes the song feel genuine despite its somewhat ponderous conceits. Much more nimble is "I Don't Believe You (She Acts Like We Never Have Met)," a song so deft in its quick rhymes and bouncy rhythm, it feels like a catchy pop song. It tells of a girl who, though a passionate lover the night before, now acts like she never met the singer; the song registers a common enough experience in the era of fleeting romantic encounters, and its mocking, sing-song quality makes the song a more shrugging dismissal than "Don't Think Twice." If "she" can be made to stand for Dylan's fans, the song also effectively creates the "cold shoulder" his turn to rock and roll will receive in some quarters.

"I Don't Believe You" can be bookended with "Ballad in Plain D," an autobiographical song that tells, in an at times naked and at other times overwrought way, of the final breakup with Suze Rotolo. Despite the snipes at Rotolo's sister, depicted as a "parasite" and a meddler, the song manages at times to be compelling—Dylan candidly admits his own lies and confusion and his continued admiration for the girl he loved. The song's conclusion, while perhaps self-congratulatory in its imagery ("I'm a poet and I know it," Dylan quips on "I Shall Be Free No. 10"), captures the odd prison house of Dylan's career: "Are birds free from the chains of the skyways." At this point, stars like Dylan and The Beatles were anything but free, becoming figures of intense identification and fascination, increasingly hounded by fans and media, to say nothing of steered by the pressures of management.

The two most important songs on *Another Side* differ rather drastically from each other. "Chimes of Freedom" is a key transitional song. Rarely performed by Dylan after this period (his performance of the song at the Newport Festival in 1964 can be considered definitive), the song occupies a space between the songs of social ills—such as the antiwar songs "Masters of War" and "With God on Our Side"—and songs of poetic, even metaphysical, reverie, such as "Gates of Eden" (recorded for the next album). "Chimes" might be compared to "Hard Rain," but is not as successful, reaching a bit too earnestly after big statements; at the same time, it provides an inspiring evocation of a storm of thunder and lightning. A bit self-consciously "visionary" (as if Dylan were assigned to "write a visionary poem"), the song has its adherents, though my sense is that, still under Guthrie's influence, it overreaches in trying to be a consolation for "every hung-up person in the whole wide universe."

Finally, the last track, "It Ain't Me Babe" is impressively spare. Its mood takes something of the "fare thee well" of "Don't Think Twice" and combines it, subtly, with the "don't ask me for answers" themes of "Restless Farewell," "One Too Many Mornings," and others: the woman addressed in the song has to understand that the singer will not dedicate his life to her. This might be insufferably egotistical if it were not for the fact that the song is conjuring something only too common: the "all or nothing" aspect of most romantic attachments—which can include attachments to causes and group projects. The feeling of being stifled, of having to shut down one's own aspirations and aims for the sake of a false ideal, is what makes the song compelling and the "no, no, no, it ain't me babe" chorus, which is, in a sense, an honest admission of defeat, so liberating. While the song seems to articulate male detachment from courtship rituals, it can also be sung by a female as a defiance of the role of patient helpmate to masculine self-regard.

On Halloween of 1964, Dylan performed at Carnegie Hall, accompanied on three songs by Joan Baez. The concert, which would eventually be released as volume 6 in the *Bootleg Series*, demonstrates how strong Dylan's performing repertoire was at this time. Early signature songs like "Hard Rain" and "Don't Think Twice" are mixed with songs of social commentary, such as "Hattie Carroll" and "Who Killed Davey Moore?," a disquisition on the death of a boxer, together with songs not yet released, like the impressionistic "Mr. Tambourine Man" and mind-bending songs more oblique in their critique of contemporary culture like "It's Alright, Ma (I'm Only Bleeding)." The set also includes the talking blues numbers about the John Birch Society and World War III, as well as some of Dylan's more recent romantic songs, the passionate "Spanish Harlem Incident" and the playful "I Don't Believe You." Baez is on hand for the high-minded "With God on Our Side," the romantic longing of "Mama, You've Been on My Mind," and the go-your-own-way kiss-off "It Ain't Me Babe."

The set is much like the shows Dylan would play in England in the spring of 1965, but by then he would have a new record out with an entire side of songs accompanied by electric instruments. On that tour, documented in a film by D. A. Pennebaker released as *Don't Look Back* in 1967, Dylan brought along Baez and then never invited her on stage. The neglect was a cheeky slap in the face to the woman who had been a mentor, a muse, a lover, and a collaborator and indicated not only that the romance with Baez was over, but also the romance with the folk movement that still enthralled many of Dylan's fans. "It Ain't Me Babe" conjures up all this with the sense that anything that is not "me" at the moment must be dropped. And Dylan's old friends and fans took the challenge personally. As Irwin Selber wrote in an open letter to "Bob" in *Sing Out!*: "Your new songs seem to be all inner-directed now, inner-probing, self-conscious—maybe even a little maudlin or a little cruel on occasion" (McGregor, 67). The fear was that Dylan cared now only for himself and a "handful of cronies."

Bob Dylan was well on his way to ending his folk career, at least for a time. *Another Side* made it clear that, if Dylan had significance now, it was as an innovator in contemporary song, not as a composer of songs for rallies. The album, released the day after the U.S. Congress passed the Tonkin resolution, permitting the president to conduct military actions against North Vietnam at his own discretion, was toothless in terms of the wider world around it. And *Another Side* did not sell as well as its predecessor, perhaps indicating that Dylan had moved away from his old fan base without having won a new one. That situation would soon change.

NOTE

1. During the making of his fourth album in 1964, Dylan, speaking to Nat Hentoff, characterized such songs as "finger-pointing songs": "You know—pointing to all the things that are wrong" (Cott 2006, 16).

2

ELECTRIC DYLAN
(1965–1966)

For many, the moment that epitomizes the next phase of Dylan's career is his appearance at the Newport Folk Festival in July 1965. Generally referred to as the moment "Dylan went electric"—to the consternation of many folk fans in the audience—the concert has become a common reference point. One version is that Dylan stepped onto the stage as an iconoclast to douse his listeners in an electric assault, to dismiss dramatically the folk song movement. That is the negative view. More positively, the set proclaimed his belief—shared by some of the best songwriters of his generation—that rock and roll could be a form of serious musical expression. For many of Dylan's initial fans, rock and pop were not artistic at all, but only commercial drivel sold by the recording industry to "the masses." Thus for some, and they tended to be vocal fans and critics at the time, Dylan at Newport blatantly advertised his decision to "sell out" (Sheldon, 210–11). For others, rock was "where it's at," and any attempt by Dylan to restrain his vision to the folk song would be retrograde. Scaduto quotes Dylan saying, "My words are pictures and the rock's gonna help me flesh out the colors of the pictures" (211).

In retrospect, it is obvious that Dylan had taken the folk song as far as he could. It would be up to other songwriters in that genre to work through the challenge he presented. Dylan was in pursuit of a different form that, in some ways, did not exist yet. The idea that rock and roll could be literate, that it could involve imagery and flights of imaginative association, was exciting and very much of the moment. Those receptive to that idea found in Dylan the perfect scribe to lead the way. A five-man electrical combo in California, led by David Crosby and Jim (later Roger) McGuinn, adapted one of Dylan's more introspective tunes to the three-minute hit-making playlists of AM radio. Released in April 1965, "Mr. Tambourine Man," as recorded by The Byrds, took a Dylan song to number 1 on the pop charts and jived in a timely fashion with its author's own ambitions. Dylan's "Subterranean Homesick Blues," an electric single released in March, had barely penetrated the Top 40.

Interestingly, The Byrds' LP, *Mr. Tambourine Man*, released by Columbia in June 1965, included McGuinn's electric reworking of "The Bells of Rhymney," a tune Pete Seeger had adapted into a folk classic. Thus was "folk rock" born. The point is that even if Dylan had not "gone electric," his songs were being turned into pop songs in any case, and even folk songs by artists like Seeger were being transformed into the sound the youth market craved. Though he began his career as a solo folk song–singing performer, Dylan saw clearly that artists and audiences interested in a melding of folk and rock were in the emerging vanguard.

For those who knew nothing of young Robert Zimmerman's infatuation with Little Richard and Buddy Holly, the change could be blamed on The Beatles. The music of the band from Liverpool, whose first album appeared in England in 1963, began to flood American radios in 1964. Each of their albums contained a mix of styles mostly derived from American R&B, country, and occasionally a bit of Tin Pan Alley. Their sources were very much the music of Dylan's youth, back when he fronted a rock group. And The Beatles' original compositions were meeting with tremendous popular and critical success. The group swiftly became the darlings of their generation. What is more, The Beatles were listening to Dylan: George Harrison recalled listening to *Freewheelin'* during the band's European tour, and Lennon found in Dylan's lyrics the wherewithal to be more personal in his songwriting. Simply put, the era we are now discussing—1964 through 1967—was unprecedented as a watershed period for rock music. Two of the most influential artists associated with the sixties—Dylan and The Beatles—produced in this brief period truly landmark recordings that have stood the test of time as significant albums.

"THEY'RE ALL PROTEST SONGS"

The other issue, apart from whether they should be electric or acoustic, is the subject matter of the new songs. Nothing could have prepared Dylan's fans for the assault of "Subterranean Homesick Blues," a blast of fast-paced Chuck Berry–inspired R&B. Released on March 8, 1965, the song hit the airwaves in the United States the day after "Bloody Sunday"—a violent clash between civil rights protesters and state troopers in Selma, Alabama—and the very day the first American combat troops—3,500 marines—arrived in Vietnam. The two fronts were forming in what newly elected President Lyndon Johnson had declared, in his State of the Union address in January, would be a "Great Society": a war in support of South Vietnam against the Communist Vietcong, and "a war" in support of civil rights and equality for nonwhites in the United States. Dylan's single, while not addressing any particular issue, directs a volley of words, delivered at breakneck speed, at a world that feels more and more overwhelming: "I'm on the pavement, thinking about the government," the song says early on, and proceeds to rush through various glimpses of street life, with gestures of warning: "Look out, kid, they keep it all hid"; advice: "Don't follow leaders, watch your parking meters"; and cryptic observations: "You don't need a weatherman to know which way the wind blows." All the earnestness of Dylan's earlier songs has been burned away by the background jabs of an electric guitar against a rollicking beat. Out front, riding the sound, Dylan's words create a new kind of street poetry, bouncing with a rock rhythm more infectious than the jazz rhythms favored by the Beat poets of the previous generation. The song is catchy, danceable. As with a speeded-up film, one catches only some of it the first time through, but repeated listenings bring the torrent of words into focus. Unlike the abbreviations of longer Dylan songs that The Byrds would specialize in, "Subterreanean Homesick Blues" is complete in itself. Dylan anatomizes the world from the viewpoint of the young and hip in two minutes and twenty-some seconds.

Bringing It All Back Home, the album that "Subterranean Homesick Blues" kicks off, was released at the end of March and can be considered a poem for the Great Society. Daniel Kramer's cover photo is a remarkable document in itself. Previously, album covers were fairly staid: photographs of the artist, perhaps done as a treated photo or a painting. Dylan's two previous album covers were black and white photographs of him alone; his second album, in color, showed him on a street in the Village with his girlfriend clasping him. *Bringing It All Back Home* shows Dylan in the midst of what looks like a collage strewn about him in an arranged way: *Time* with the president on the cover; an album by his friend Eric von Schmidt, as well as albums by hip comedian Lord Buckley, by Lotte Lenya, a performer of Brecht songs, and by Robert Johnson, the great blues guitarist; *Another Side of Bob Dylan*; a fallout shelter sign; and various objets d'art. The edges of the photograph blur in a circle around Dylan who glares at the viewer, stroking a cat, a screen magazine open on his knee. Behind him a thin, angular woman in red (Albert Grossman's wife Sally) reclines on a chaise lounge against a mantelpiece. The setting has been identified as the Grossmans' house in Bearsville, New York. Fitting, since the Grossmans' estate became a refuge for Dylan once his popularity made walking the streets of New York City more stressful, and much of the album was composed there. The title of the album suggests that the world—represented by the elements of the collage—has invaded the singer's "home," and that the "it" in the title is virtually anything and everything he might have on his mind. More packed with references and poetic flights than ever, the songs fulfill the cover's promise.

The first side of *Bringing It All Back Home* contains three songs that became additions to Dylan's performing repertoire for quite some time: "Love Minus Zero/No Limit," "She Belongs to Me" (the B Side of "Subterranean"), and "Maggie's Farm" (also released as a single). Like "Subterranean," the latter is a fast-paced blues. Delivered in a frenetic whine, the song reviles an established bourgeois family: Maggie's father, like a government official, keeps the National Guard around his door; Maggie's mother, "the brains behind Pa," lies outrageously about her age and lectures the servants. The singer, with "a head fulla ideas drivin' me insane," is an under-appreciated worker, tired of living off the largesse of fat cats. Dylan chose the song to open his first electric show at the Newport Folk Festival in July, suggesting perhaps that his apprenticeship to the folk song was a kind of Maggie's Farm—"they say, 'sing while you slave,' but I just get bored."

"She Belongs to Me" sketches a complex relation to a woman who is also an artist. The lyrics at times suggest a somewhat servile perspective on the man's part, but the tone evokes fascination and, considering the title, pride in the relationship. Male and female relations as a shifting ground of pleasure and pain, of forms of psychic give-and-take, inform Dylan's searching approach to romance in this period. "Love Minus Zero/No Limit" shows what Dylan can do with the love song when truly inspired. The song goes beyond "She Belongs to Me" in its worshipful attitude toward a woman, though this time the observations about her—"she knows too much to argue or to judge"—suggest less a fellow artist and more a muse figure, tenderly evoked as "like some raven at my window with a broken wing." Dylan's lyricism can be both sharp: "banker's nieces seek perfection, expecting all the gifts that wise men bring" and elusive: "in ceremonies of the horsemen even the pawn must hold a grudge." The "dylanesque" is not only a matter of aphoristic comments—such as "don't ask me nothin' about nothin', I just might tell you the truth"—but also of cryptic, memorable phrases.

The longest song on the side, "Bob Dylan's 115th Dream" is a hilarious fantasia about the discovery of modern America, with the singer "riding on the *Mayflower*," helmed by Captain A-rab. The song revisits the kind of picaresque encounters Dylan serves up in "Talkin' World War III Blues" but with even more bite—including take-offs on The Beatles as depicted in *A Hard Day's Night*, references to Jesus, Captain Kidd, funeral parlors, jails, pay phones, hot dog stands, crêpes Suzette, Moby-Dick, and, obscurely, "the Pope of Eruke." The song commences with Dylan solo on acoustic guitar, only to be interrupted by gales of laughter. "Ok, take two," producer Tom Wilson says, and Dylan begins again, joined at once by his rock band. The song ends with the appearance of Columbus and his three ships, as though America were still to be discovered. "Good luck!," the narrator says to the explorer.

"Subterranean" and "115th Dream" frame the side well: both are rapid-fire take-offs of a vividly hyperkinetic America, rock and roll cartoons of the craziness of modern life. Both have the flair of drug humor—with "Subterranean" mentioning "mixing up the medicine," a "bust" in early May, and "plants" (wire-taps) in the bed. The album's second side, solo acoustic except for a second guitar on the first track and a bass guitar on the final track, is comprised of four of Dylan's truly stellar songs of this period, two of them somewhat "druggy," and each a remarkable step beyond the songs on *Another Side*.

"Mr. Tambourine Man" is in many ways the signature song of Dylan's transition from conscientious folk song writer and wry commentator on topical issues to the bard of youth culture. Though personal in its immediate reference, with Dylan commenting on his own morning-after state—"my hands can't feel to grip, my toes too numb to step, wait only for my bootheels to be wandering"—the song's address to the tambourine man becomes the listener's address to Dylan himself as well. He becomes, effectively, the one who will play a song for us, leading us, like "the ragged clown behind," to the beach and a vision of a liberated dance by the sea, free of "memory and fate" but also of the moment itself. "Let me forget about today until tomorrow," the last line, expresses a yearning to be oblivious to the present. Dylan had won plaudits for the topicality of his songs but here envisions a telling flight beyond the constraints of "today." That said, the song is incredibly timely in striking the pose that would unite his contemporaries seeking not simply thrills in marijuana and drugs, but a "raised consciousness."

"Gates of Eden," in its evocation of an altered state, takes up from the mood of "Tambourine Man"; the song is bound to make more "sense" if one is stoned while listening to it. In fact, the initial verses are so tangled in syntax and imagery that parsing them in any straightforward fashion makes one feel like a "Mr. Jones"—a phrase that would soon, thanks to "Ballad of a Thin Man" on the next album, come to be synonymous with anyone unhip. To "dig" "Gates of Eden," in a sense, is to be comfortable with lines like "the truth just twists / Its curfew gull just glides"; figures such as "the motorcycle black madonna two-wheeled gypsy queen," her "silver-studded phantom," and a "gray-flannel dwarf"; and pronouncements such as "there are no truths outside the gates of Eden." The imagery at times may be incoherent, but that is part of the deliberate effect. Unlike most lyricists, Dylan uses words as associative patterns. Rather than tell a story or flesh out a melody with words of emotive phrasing, Dylan's lyrics become incantatory—meaningful for the state of mind they create and evoke. The song aims not simply to tell about what transpires either within or outside the gates of Eden but to approximate an Eden-like trance. If one is "inside" where there are truths, where there is no sin, where it does not matter "what is and what is not," then one can grasp the song; if one is "outside," the song seems empty rhetorical flourishes with little or no meaning. Dylan himself can rarely give this song its due—but on the album he delivers a hypnotic performance.

The first two songs on side 2 present an inward-turned poetry. Both suggest a state something like meditation, produced by and producing "skipping reels of rhyme." The rhyme skips even livelier on the third track, "It's Alright, Ma (I'm Only Bleeding)," but here the stance is one of the most penetrating in Dylan's career. Dylan throws darts, and almost every one strikes a bull's-eye. The song is a caustic statement of values, positioning the singer against a barrage of false positions—the "he or she or them or it" that try to override the individual. Poking fun at "old-lady judges" who, "limited in sex," attempt to push "fake morals" and at those who pursue security above all or who obey authority they do not respect, the song also takes shots at advertising, false preachers and teachers, and "the masters who make the rules."

The furor over Dylan's comments about Oswald at the Tom Paine Award dinner perhaps inspired the reflection about being guillotined if his "thought-dreams" were made public. In any case, the position taken in the song is not of someone protesting in the name of some party or cause but of one willing to be a pariah and outcast because of his skepticism and satirical outlook. "It's life and life only," he shrugs, suggesting that the will to die for a cause does not mean so much if one does not take life too seriously to begin with. Addressing the final line of each chorus to "ma," each time rhyming with the final line of each of the three previous verses, the song reminds us of the litany of encounters in "Hard Rain," though this time in a lockstep rhyme scheme. Here, the threat of an apocalypse is not brewing, and the "blue-eyed son" is on the attack, reassuring "ma" that "it's alright." All the pressures of the world he describes can be met if one has enough resolve. His only defense and his only weapon are words, but now, with the words of "My Back Pages" in mind, he chooses not to preach. If the song rallies us, it is because hearing the symptoms of the crass, self-serving media culture of America denigrated with wit and spite is liberating—to a degree.

In case some listeners had not grasped that his fifth album marked a signficant change in direction for Bob Dylan, the final song, "It's All Over Now, Baby Blue" offers four verses that comment on endings. The first line, "you must leave now, take what you need, you think will last" shares some of the sense of end times of "Hard Rain," when only what is necessary might survive. Saints "comin' through" might make us think of angels at the end of time, particularly as we are told to "look out." The second verse seems to restart the song, suggesting that the highway is unsafe, and one should take only what has been acquired "by coincidence." Essentials, it seems, are stripping away, the sky is folding, and in the third verse, the carpet is moving. The third verse includes the idea of being left behind by a lover and of remaining stuck in place as "seasick sailors" and "empty-handed armies" go home. And so the final verse more emphatically insists on departure, leaving behind "stepping stones." The power of the last verse is in its sense of necessity: something calls and you must go. To remain is to be an anachronism in clothes one has already shed, and to be numbered among the dead who have no choice but to remain. Sung with a mournful, brooding delivery, the song is not gleeful—this is no moment "when the ship comes in"— or even particularly hopeful. The mood is reminiscent of Rimbaud's at the close of *A Season in Hell*, a feeling of something still to come, while an important period—a "season"—is ending.

As Dylan moved beyond topicality to more eternal and agonistic perspectives, *Bringing It All Back Home* captured the irreverence of hip defiance. Bursting with a sharp rock and roll attack on one side and offering poetics never encountered before, the album was an oddity, a hybrid album by an original. It might be expected to stand for a year or more as a definitive statement. Why should Dylan release another album before he could top this one? But top it he did, six months later, heralded in July by one of the greatest rock songs of his—or anyone's— career.

AN UNLIKELY HIT

Simply, "Like a Rolling Stone" is one of the greatest rock songs ever produced. And, in its time, one of the more unlikely radio hits. At just over six minutes, the song is almost twice as long as most Top 40 songs, and, given Dylan's vocals and the song's voluminous words, its success is surprising. In a sense, Dylan's music does not really belong on AM radio. Unlike The Beatles or The Rolling Stones who produced hits regularly, Dylan's recordings are generally too idiosyncratic. In fact, the song climbed to number 2, demonstrating the appeal of the song's unique sound. "Like a Rolling Stone" hit a nerve.

From the opening line's "once upon a time" to the final line of the last verse, "you've got no secrets to conceal," the song's attitude toward the addressee is not simply dismissive but at pains to describe her state. The song addresses "Miss Lonely"—characterized as a debutante from a good background who has been slumming and "scrounging" in a world of bohemians and their mind games. The jibes at her condition feel more merited than mean-spirited, with a combined subtlety and ferocity. While unmasking Miss Lonely's delusions, the song implies the need for such delusions.

The "finest school" and the "pretty people," along with cryptic characters like "Napoleon in rags" and "the mystery tramp," have contributed to a chaos trying to pass as a person. After all the deals and the secrets and all the attempts to pawn what there is to pawn, Miss Lonely can only hope to salvage herself as a "complete unknown," a rolling stone. Songs that celebrate a down-and-out condition—like Roger Miller's stellar "King of the Road," released in January 1965—often have a kind of shrugging grandeur that negates their pathos, and "Like a Rolling Stone" uplifts while tearing down, or tears down to be uplifting. As a rock attack, the song's unique kick is in suggesting that, ultimately, rock music itself will sustain us in our hour of need. Against schooling, social class, profession, and other affiliations, rock offers a different kind of belonging. Thus the song's message is timeless. It is not a song one relives nostalgically, like many hits of yesteryear, but rather one that always testifies to what it represents. And so it is one of Dylan's most often performed songs. People go to a Bob Dylan concert to celebrate the role Dylan's peculiar version of rock and roll has played in shaping their lives. Few songs attest to that allegiance better than "Like a Rolling Stone."

How can one feel bad when responding to the chorus's demands of "how does it feel?" Dylan first wrote a true chorus—rather than simply a refrain—on "Mr. Tambourine Man." On "Rolling Stone," the chorus becomes the hook, with the drums carrying the song as Dylan varies the rhythm of the words each time to create a shifting emphasis. The uplift of the chorus suggests that, however badly one may have managed one's life, relationships, and ambitions, life still feels pretty good. This is what rock and roll blues are all about, and "Like a Rolling Stone" is a definitive track in the genre, an anthem.

The song hit the stores five days before Dylan's closing appearance at the Newport Festival. One might have thought that Dylan's fans would be eager to see and hear him perform this amazing and unprecedented song. Perhaps some, perhaps many, were. But the version of the show that has come down in history stresses those who felt assaulted by the song—and its distorted volume. Part of the outcry was a reaction to not being able to discern the words—always a key element for Dylan's listeners (Sounes, 184–85). Rather than a voice crying in protest against the System, Dylan appeared to be simply a hip recording artist trying to sell records.

"Like a Rolling Stone" did sell, and many concluded that Dylan "sold out"—chose a more commercial music and found his niche. Such a view is frozen in history, trying to hold onto a moment that was already over. As Dylan sang in the song that ended his set, solo on acoustic guitar, it was time to "strike another match, go start anew." Those who were first turned on to Dylan and his music by "Rolling Stone" were responding to someone who grasped that there was "no direction home" and found a common bond in that. Dylan's protest now, one might say, was not simply against the powers that be, which might be changed by political change, but rather against the modern condition itself. The "folk" had to meet the "masses," many of them teens who were being raised to be either managers or workers or cannon fodder.

The song also takes aim at the legions dedicated to pop bohemianism, those thrilled by the glamour of disaffected stars of youth culture. Such attraction gave rise to a battery of hangers-on in the orbit of pop artists like Andy Warhol. Dylan aims his derision at those who live a life of cultural vampirism, sucking their sustenance from the buzz of stardom. And yet, the song is not simply contemptuous, for without "the complete unknowns"—which every star was at some point—how could the stars be stars?

ROCK'S FIRST MASTERPIECE ALBUM

Released at the end of August 1965, *Highway 61 Revisited* can be called the first rock masterpiece. The only other album in the running is The Beatles' *A Hard Day's Night*, released in July 1964, the first album composed in its entirety by John Lennon and Paul McCartney. The comparison is instructive about what we value in mid-sixties rock. The Beatles album is a collection of infectious songs, memorable for their arrangements and melodies. Working closely with producer George Martin, The Beatles set the standard for what a rock record should sound like, and no other recordings quite matched theirs. Their influence on the pop song was unparalleled in this period. *Help!*, the album The Beatles released in August of 1965 in conjunction with their second feature film, clearly showed Dylan's influence in its merging of rock and folk, and in more subjective lyrics in two of Lennon's compositions in particular. And one reason that *Highway 61 Revisited* presented even more of a challenge than *Bringing It All Back Home* is that Dylan, aided by his new producer Bob Johnston and fluent musicians, notably Al Kooper, Mike Bloomfield, and Charlie McCoy, greatly improved the textures of his songs, giving each a distinctive sound as did The Beatles on their albums. The influence between The Beatles and Dylan worked both ways.

Highway 61 Revisited contained the most adventurous lyrics of any rock songs to date, and was also the most sophisticated album Dylan had yet made in terms of its production and instrumentation. Indeed, if one compares the album to a folk-rock classic like The Byrds' *Mr. Tambourine Man*, featuring four Dylan compositions from 1964 presented with electric instruments and Beatlesque harmonies, Dylan's version of rock is much more edgy, bluesy, and diverse. Full of pointed verbal barbs as well as some of Dylan's most sustained imagery, the songs of *Highway 61 Revisited* became reference points for Dylan's contemporaries. For a year, from summer 1965 to summer 1966, Dylan was at the pinnacle of his talent and "the King of the Cats" for rock songwriters.

Four of the songs, namely the title song and tracks 1, 2, and 4, match up with songs on the previous album, all versions of Dylan's trademark blues romp. Like "Subterranean Homesick Blues," "Like a Rolling Stone" (discussed in the previous section) kicks off the album with a torrent of words and a fast-paced attack. If "Subterranean" is a tongue-in-cheek warning about the kinds of perils the world offers, "Rolling Stone" is a cautionary tale of someone who has let the world rob her of status and identity. "Tombstone Blues," the second track, like "Rolling Stone," contains a full chorus, this time based on a Woody Guthrie lyric, and the verses feature some of Dylan's densest lyrics to that point. With its chorus about a core family unit, "Tombstone" can be compared to "Maggie's Farm," though here we are no longer in a bourgeois setting, but are rather faced with a hard-scrabble way of life, with mama and papa shoeless and foodless in factories, alleys, kitchens.

The cast of characters is vast for a five-minute song, with Dylan throwing off sketches comprised of a colorful name and a few bits of information. Some of the names are famous: Ma Rainey, the blues singer, together with Beethoven, a giant of Romantic music, in a "bed roll"; Jack the Ripper, one of the most notorious serial killers in history, sits "at the head of the Chamber of Commerce"; Gypsy Davy, from a song Woody Guthrie sang, adapted from an old ballad known as "Black-jack Davy," now no longer steals a well-to-do wife, but rather "burns out the camps" of the gypsies, with his "faithful slave Pedro"; "Brother Bill," who wants to enact a scenario out of Cecil B. DeMille's biblical film *Samson and Delilah*, may be a reference to Billy Graham, the most famous TV evangelist of the day; elsewhere John the Baptist appears, alternately praising and questioning, "the Commander-in-Chief" who calls the sun/son "chicken," rather than "yellow." This seems a carica-ture of President Johnson's increase of the draft to make more sons go fight in Vietnam. (Interestingly, the federal penalty for burning a draft card—an act of protest draft-age men were engaging in more frequent-ly—was ratified the day after *Highway 61 Revisited* appeared, so that a young male listener at the time might well make the connection.) Dy-lan's lyrics, rather than directly engaging the issue of war, as in "With God on Our Side," now take for granted a nation at war, in which patriotism is perverted by questionable motives and arbitrary power. Dylan mocks those exempt from the war—"in the old folks' home and the college"—hinting that both institutions are likewise remote from what's happening. The prickly song careens through an American land-scape where only the street-smart and hip have a chance of maintaining sufficient cool to remain unfazed. The singer ends by addressing a "dear lady," wishing he could write a melody that would be soothing, a conso-lation for "useless and pointless knowledge."

The two songs closest to love songs on *Highway 61* show a concern with how romance colors one's own existence. *Highway 61*'s track 3, the archly titled "It Takes a Lot to Laugh, It Takes a Train to Cry," builds from the feeling of vulnerable exposure found in the earlier "One Too Many Mornings," creating a sense of extremity which, in "Lot to

Laugh," produces a great seductive cry: "I wanna be your lover, baby, I don't want to be your boss." The song, a mellow shuffle appropriate to the singer's claim to be "up all night," varies some lines from "Solid Road" by Brownie McGhee and Leroy Carr, but, as usual with Dylan's borrowings, the words are twisted to his own mood. "Lot to Laugh" is elastic and vibrant like a far-off train whistle, an indication of how Dylan can take staples of the blues tradition and make them sound old and new at once.

In "On the Road Again" on the previous LP, Dylan mocked a woman's family and their living arrangements—including the butler and the mailman—asking "how come you don't move?" In "From a Buick 6," we might imagine we are on the road with the couple who now constitute a world unto themselves. Arguably, the only nonessential song on the album, "Buick 6" is mainly memorable for its chugging riff and its off-the-cuff sketches of its particular muse: "she walks like Bo Diddley and she don't need no crutch." The refrain says that even if the singer "falls down dyin'" she would "put a blanket on the bed"—a glance at the role of woman as nurturer rather than femme fatale, while also cleverly underscoring "fatale."

A recurring metaphor on *Highway 61 Revisited* is the carnival, and "The Ballad of a Thin Man," the first-side closer, evokes the sinister side of the circus metaphor. With a brooding aura, the song conjures up a world of circus geeks, sword swallowers, one-eyed midgets, and other misfits. Into this setting ventures the obtuse and unsuspecting Mr. Jones, who is berated for not knowing what's going on, or indeed what the cryptic utterances and actions of these characters mean. The singer addresses the song to Mr. Jones, and unlike the address to Miss Lonely, the contempt drips from Dylan's voice, establishing him as the master of the musical put-down. Like "Masters of War" there is a clear sense of outrage against the person addressed, but the sins of Mr. Jones are much less threatening and much more common. A scapegoat to all those he meets, Mr. Jones is burdened with a cluelessness that is endemic, Dylan suggests, among professional commentators—those who "prophesize with [their] pens" and pretend to knowledge of subcultures they have not truly penetrated. "Thin Man" throws jibes such as "you're very well-read it's well known" and "with great lawyers and scholars you've discussed lepers and crooks," suggesting a member of the intelligentsia, judgmental and secure in a certain milieu, but derisively out of his element. Aping the cry of an outraged authoritarian, Dylan intones with wild irony at the close: "there *oughta be a law* against you comin' around." The song became a staple of Dylan's tours in 1966 and 1974 and continues to be a crowd pleaser, its target seeming to be outsiders who just don't get what Dylan represents to his fans.

"Queen Jane Approximately," another song addressing a woman, opens side 2 and feels a bit like a blending of "She Belongs to Me" and "It's All Over Now, Baby Blue." Here Dylan speaks to Queen Jane much as he does Baby Blue and Miss Lonely, summing up her situation, mentioning her mother, father, sister, and a host of surrounding characters, including flower ladies, advisors, clowns, and bandits. The mention of her children who will "start to resent" her suggests a mother, perhaps older than the singer himself. The situation described, in which Queen Jane is "tired of herself" and her "creations" and "sick of all this repetition," suggests a strong woman in crisis, facing a loss of belief in family, art, and the kind of social activities in which ladies of a certain status thrive. Again, Dylan saves his best line for last: "when you want somebody you don't have to speak to, won't you come see me"; the singer seems to be offering his services as a young man able to pleasure the body if not heal the soul. The interplay of piano and background organ creates an off-kilter honky-tonk quality that would be developed to greater effect on *Blonde on Blonde* to create a trademark sound— both boozy and bluesy—for Dylan's meditations on women.

Dylan's signature style of picaresque song lyrics had been evolving since "Talkin' New York Blues" told of his early adventures in the city. Next came a fantasy of the city after a nuclear blast on "Talkin' World War III Blues," followed by an extended pop joke in the travel song "Motorpsycho Nitemare," then the crowning achievement, "Bob Dylan's 115th Dream," his fifth album's fantasia of a voyage of exploration. As with the discovery of America in "115th Dream," "Highway 61 Revisited" features amorphous vignettes full of Dylan's trenchant humor, though this time there is no first-person perspective. Each verse tells a new story, united to the others only by a refrain indicating something will take place or has taken place on Highway 61. The title references the U.S. Route running from Dylan's birthplace, Duluth, Minnesota, down to New Orleans, parallel most of the way to the Mississippi River—the great inland waterway so dear to the ghosts of American history, whether of Huck Finn and riverboats, of slaves fleeing the South, or (to those traveling from the East) of the sense of entering the West by crossing "Old Man River." Rather than a song as long and sprawling as the highway it commemorates, Dylan keeps it quick, moving in just over three minutes from the biblical Abraham to the staging of "the next World War" for an audience on bleachers.

The opening shows Dylan irreverent with purpose: God's command that Abraham "kill me your son"—Isaac in the Bible—earns from "Abe" the rejoinder, "Man, you must be putting me on." In the context of the enforced sacrifice of sons with the escalating draft and the war in Vietnam, the song and God's threat, "the next time you see me comin' you better run," resonate, particularly when we consider that Highway 61, at the time, ran from New Orleans to the Canadian border—flight to Canada being a favored escape for draft evaders. A high-pitched sound identified on the credits as a "police whistle" further emphasizes the song's "take-it-on-the-lam" overtones.

In addition to "Like a Rolling Stone," three songs on *Highway 61 Revisited* are unprecedented: "Thin Man," and the final two tracks on side 2. The first, "Just Like Tom Thumb's Blues," could be the flip side of "Mr. Tambourine Man": a song about being on the street—in this case Juarez at Easter time—in an altered state. But rather than the footloose and dreamy feeling of being high in "Tambourine Man," "Tom Thumb" recounts a state of paranoia and psychosis. Women are not to be trusted; fortune and fame are taking their toll. The singer needs "another shot" but doesn't have the strength for it, and seems to regret "hit[ting] the harder stuff." The song ends with a classic Dylan farewell: "I'm going back to New York City, I do believe I've had enough." The drawn out syllables of "had e-nough" sum up the sense of distress and resentment. The vocals tell the tale themselves, as this strung-out blues is one of the most engagingly sung of Dylan's career thus far.

Reminiscent of "Gates of Eden," in that each verse ends with a reference to its titular place, "Desolation Row" marks a decided advance on the earlier song. Accompanied by bass and Charlie McCoy's lyrical fills on guitar, Dylan presents an epic song, over eleven minutes long, that never falters, providing sketches of a series of encounters, adventures, and observations abounding in sad and satiric imagery. In terms of its consistency and coherence, "Desolation Row" sets the bar for Dylan's more visionary lyrics.

The song opens by telling us "the circus is in town" and in another verse we are told a carnival is taking place on Desolation Row—described with the panoramic flair of a Hieronymous Bosch painting. The recurring reference to the place keeps it before us as a nebulous space through which the figures described pass or to which they aim. The opening verse places the singer in Desolation Row, looking out, and the final verse places him somewhere where he "cannot read too good" and requests that any letters sent to him be mailed from there. The final verse, then, suggests a speaker who has traced the world of Desolation Row, from "postcards of the hanging" sold there to a letter received, implicitly not from there. In between, we meet with, possibly, the "people that you mention" in the letter, but only after the singer has changed all their names.

The names given are ripe with associations, as figures found in popular culture (Cinderella, The Phantom of the Opera), in history (Casanova, Einstein, Robin Hood, Ezra Pound, T. S. Eliot), in literature (Romeo, Ophelia, The Hunchback of Notre Dame), and in the Bible (Noah, the Good Samaritan). Most of these characters inspire an entire verse encapsulating them in a brief narrative: Romeo accosts Cinderella and is asked to leave; Ophelia has become an "old maid" at twenty-two, her eyes "fixed upon Noah's great rainbow." Much of the song's effect depends on the skill with which Dylan creates these brief scenarios.

"Desolation Row" is also a good example of one of the major artistic features of Dylan's lyrics: their unpredictability. As one listens to the song (and appreciating it requires listening to it as it is sung rather than reading the words off a page or screen), there is a tension to see how the next line completes or extends the line one has just heard. Unlike Dylan's fast-paced songs that overwhelm with a torrent of words, "Desolation Row" moves at a walking pace, sustained by the careful embellishments on guitar and the tempo of the rhythmic bass. The structure of each twelve-line verse puts considerable weight on the fourth and eighth lines, the lines that rhyme with the second and sixth lines respectively. In effect, the tension to be resolved is how the rhyme will complete each quatrain. Into the third quatrain Dylan packs, for each verse, a summary or a comment, often adding a detail, while conveying musically both the sense of inevitable return (each verse ends with the words "Desolation Row," rhymed with the preceding line) and the sense of incompleteness. There is always another verse to follow, until the penultimate verse is followed by a harmonica break, and after the break the final verse acts as a coda for the song.

The rhyme lines are, as it were, the load-bearing supports in each verse, in most cases registering a significant or surprising detail. In the first verse, for example, the second line tells us the passports are being painted brown, an odd detail that hangs in the air until the fourth line tells us "the circus is in town." The weight of the declaration, simple and direct, seems to be a comment on all that has come before and on all that will follow. Next, to illustrate the circus, we are told the "blind commissioner" is in a trance with one hand "tied to the tightrope walker." Then the rhyming line, "the other is in his pants," arrives with inevitability (hearing what's "on the other hand" is perfectly natural) and with a smirk: worse than being caught with your pants down is being caught with your hand in your pants. The song picks its way carefully through each verse in the same pattern, so that Cinderella's smile is rhymed with "Bette Davis style," and Romeo's demand and its riposte stand in rhymed relation. Elsewhere there are fanciful rhymes—"iron vest" and "lifelessness," "Notre Dame" and "expecting rain"—as well as emphatic rhymes that almost seem to take action: "world inside of a leather cup" and "blow it up."

More than previous Dylan songs, "Desolation Row" invites an allegorical reading. One might suppose the meaning of the song would be arrived at if one could ascribe precise meanings to the characters mentioned. If Einstein is "disguised as Robin Hood," we might give thought to what the genius of theoretical physics and the heroic bandit have in common and why he is accompanied by "his friend, a jealous monk." The specificity is beguiling, but at the same time—unlike allegory—there is a sense that the designations are arbitrary or at least not intended as moral qualities. The song wanders through familiar names in unfamiliar relations, creating situations where "the lover" may be represented by both Romeo and Casanova, the beloved, perhaps by Cinderella and Ophelia; "altruism" may be represented by the Good Samaritan and by Robin Hood, though the latter is only a disguise for Einstein. There are also wry associations, for instance when the radical rallying song "Which Side Are You On" becomes the cry of those wishing to adjudicate between Neptune, or the ocean, and the *Titanic*. While one might want to give precise meanings to such images, the fitful symbolic dimension is more associative than allegorical. Dylan, in a way quite unique in the history of songwriting, has developed an imagistic style of writing that seems to tell stories by using arresting images, but refrains from making statements. One would be hard-pressed even to say what the theme of the song is. "Desolation Row" seems both a promise and a threat, a source of despair though at times perhaps an escape from it. One can liken it to other broad concepts—like America, Hollywood, or a phase of artistic production—without exhausting the aura that makes it so beguiling.

The United States at the time of the release of *Highway 61 Revisited* was still grinding its way toward civil rights—President Johnson signed the Voting Rights Act into law, ending provisions that kept blacks from voting in Southern states; five days later, on August 11, the Watts area of Los Angeles exploded in riots, showing how racial tensions through-out the country could tip into violence at any point. Johnson also made moves to escalate his other "wars": the "war on poverty" gained major legislation with the creation of Medicare and Medicaid at the end of July, while two weeks later the first significant land battle occurred in Vietnam. In other words, it was a period of high liberalism, with John-son seeming to believe that the government was mandated to improve the lot of the poor, to improve the social standing and political voice of nonwhite citizens, and to save South Asia from the threat of Communist rule. In this period, white male college students, many of whom would become vocal against the war as the decade wore on, were well poised to enjoy a level of prosperity that no previous generation of Americans had enjoyed in such large numbers. And many of Dylan's staunchest fans were among their number.

No longer responding to particular events, Dylan's music was itself making history. In a mere two years since the recording of *The Times, They Are A-Changin'* the times had changed remarkably, with Dylan now an artist with a built-in grasp of blues-based tunes to go along with his sense of folk phrasing and diction. The message was in the music itself, and his image-packed lyrics, pacing themselves to more frenetic or dreamy rhythms, offered a concentrated response to what it felt like to be, perforce, among the "confused, accused, misused, strung-out ones and worse," as "Chimes of Freedom" puts it. Unlike the more topical songs of his earlier period, the songs of *Bringing It All Back Home* and *Highway 61 Revisited* are more amorphous in their themes. The earnestness of the early songs has been replaced with wry humor and bizarre but literate allusions, while Dylan's voice, often both frail and strident in his solo recordings, had become a husky whine with an elastic sense of rhythm, much imitated. The explosion of interest in such matters as the space race between the United States and the USSR; the anxiety surrounding international hostilities in the nuclear age; the struggle for equal rights for all; the great appeal among youth of the "invasion" of British rock bands; and the increasing sophistication of television and televised advertising created an era in which even commercial radio was pushed beyond the banality of a hit parade. With the increasing numbers and power of FM radio stations (stereo broadcasts began on FM in 1961), alternative culture would find its musical niche: AOR (album oriented rock) favored long songs like "Desolation Row" that could not be played on AM radio stations.

Born in 1941, Dylan was positioned to be one of the immediate elders of those born in the "Baby Boom"—which refers to the spike of births in the United States that began in the mid-1940s, peaking in 1947, but not declining to below the number of Depression-era births—the first great trough of the twentieth century—until about 1967. Thus, the "followers" for Dylan and his contemporaries in 1965 were those aged twelve to twenty-one, born in 1944–1953—a very large demographic. The Beatles, with their televised cartoon program in the mid-sixties, had more outreach to the grade-school set, but Dylan's music would become a rite of passage for more literate teenage rock enthusiasts well into the seventies and beyond. Received and studied as a poet by many of his listeners, Dylan's great contribution to rock in this period remains as a milestone and as a challenge for all subsequent rock artists who aim, by age twenty-five, to make a name and a mark that will last.

"I WOULD NOT FEEL SO ALL ALONE"

In November of 1965, Bob Dylan married Sara Lownds, a twenty-six-year-old woman with a four-year-old daughter from a previous marriage, Maria, whom Dylan adopted. In January 1966, after a series of concerts in California, featuring solo and electric sets, and a few weeks before beginning sessions in New York for his seventh album for Columbia Records, Dylan became father to a son, Jesse Byron. Not yet twenty-five, Dylan's songwriting skills had reached full maturity and he would begin to turn away from life in the limelight, hard to do due to his records' increasing influence. But first came a series of landmark concerts in the United States in February and March, in Australia in April, and in Europe and England in May. Columbia Records recorded a number of the shows, and a bootleg recording of the Manchester show on May 17, 1966, was released unofficially and illegally. Known as "The Royal Albert Hall concert" (on the last date of the tour Dylan played two shows at the London venue), the recording became a key collector's item for Dylan completists. Officially released as volume 4 in Columbia's *Bootleg Series* in 1998, the concert was notorious for a heckler shouting "Judas!" at Dylan just before the band launched their final song, "Like a Rolling Stone."

As recounted at length in Robert Shelton's *No Direction Home*, the reactions to the tour with The Hawks have to be among the oddest in music history (251–56). Here you have people paying to see shows featuring a singer playing his most recent material, material derived from brilliantly innovative and fairly popular records. The noisy response goes beyond the occasional shouted challenge or request typical of live shows; there are periods of aggressive clapping before most songs in the electric set, indicating an impatience with the show or a desire to disrupt it. At one point, Dylan commences a string of nonsense utterances until the crowd becomes quiet then concludes "if you only just wouldn't clap so hard." The enthusiastic applause that meets this statement indicates that the "silent majority" at the shows were not in sympathy with the heckling. Indeed, the shout of "Judas!" meets with some laughs and an initial volley of applause, but only a small contingent endorses the lame witticism. The genuine applause after the songs shows the audience is mostly appreciative. Dylan's comment "I don't believe you, you're a liar!" seems to be in response to something not quite audible on the tape that is said after the Judas comment.

In any case, the historical view of the concerts is that Dylan and The Hawks met almost universal abuse wherever they played and that the press of the day wrote off the concerts as misguided provocations designed to antagonize. It is hard to believe. Anyone who cares about rock music—with "ears to hear," as it were—would have to esteem these shows as the forefront of the form. However, one should bear in mind that rock concerts at this time—such as The Beatles' show at Shea

Stadium in August 1965—were generally met by long, protracted wails and screams from teenage girls. The conviction that one should make some kind of noise during the songs and certainly during the silent bits between songs seemed to be widely accepted at rock shows, as opposed to the utter silence during Dylan's acoustic set. It should also be kept in mind that rock music at this volume and with this degree of attack was far from commonplace. Dylan and The Hawks created together an unprecedented sound, with swirling organ, a rhythm section like a madcap rockabilly band, piercing guitar from Robbie Robertson, and in front of it all Dylan's lambent vocals, stretching syllables, elongating vowels, enunciating or slurring with a stoned cadence as he leveled lines like psychic bombs at the audience.

Though bootleg recordings of the concerts would be much sought after, this would not be the last time Dylan's fans would be unhappy with his live performances. In fact, the experience of hearing and seeing Dylan play live can seem an exercise in perversity, for rarely does an entire audience hear the version of Dylan they most want or expect to hear. One could say that Dylan makes a point of disappointing his fans, though that view—certainly held by some, at every phase of his career—is gainsaid by the many dedicated fans who swap tapes of his shows and compare versions of his songs with almost religious fervor. On the 1966 tour, Dylan sounds inspired, but during the acoustic set at times he sounds tense, brooding, or sloppy. Solo, he performed songs not yet released but destined to become classics: "Visions of Johanna" and "Just Like a Woman," as well as giving spacey renderings of some of his greatest songs, which were at most only two years old: "It's All Over Now, Baby Blue," "Desolation Row," "Mr. Tambourine Man." In the electric set, the three best rock songs on *Highway 61 Revisited*—"Just Like Tom Thumb's Blues," "The Ballad of a Thin Man," and "Like a Rolling Stone"—were featured, together with moody evocations of formerly acoustic songs—"I Don't Believe You" and "One Too Many Mornings"—and a powerhouse version of the song on the first album learned from Eric von Schmidt, "Baby Let Me Follow You Down."

For many, Dylan was still the singer-songwriter of his first four albums, a singular voice armed only with a guitar and harmonica weaving hypnotic spells of sing-song poetry. Dylan with The Hawks was entirely different. To accept the uniqueness of Dylan's music and stage presence at this time was perhaps too much to ask of audiences enraptured with the early albums. The speed of Dylan's transformation may be inevitable only in hindsight. The other view that comes with hindsight is how challenging this period was in Dylan's own development: in the midst of the tour, on breaks in February and March, he recorded in Nashville the greatest album of his career and a signature record in a period not lacking in landmark albums. The Beach Boys' masterpiece *Pet Sounds* was released at that same time, as was *Freak Out!*, Frank Zappa's groundbreaking debut album with the Mothers of Invention; in December, The Beatles released what many consider their finest effort, *Revolver*. The year 1966 was a banner year for rock, and *Blonde on Blonde* was one of its milestones.

For the first time in Dylan's recording career the overall sound of the album is as important as the individual songs. This is the era when the long-playing rock album began to have a status as "a work," rather than as simply a collection of songs. *Blonde on Blonde*, due to the excellence of the musicians Bob Johnston assembled in Nashville, weaves fascinating musical interplays, edging toward a country honky-tonk atmosphere made carnivalesque by Dylan's familiar organ and harmonica sound. The effect suits perfectly the dense, druggy aura of the album. After the raucous opening track, with its brass-band ambiance and chortling background voices, and its cry that "Everybody must get stoned!" *Blonde on Blonde* maintains a smoky late-night feel, suitable for the first gray light of pre-dawn, as related by Sean Wilentz in his essay "The Sound of 3:00 A.M.: The Making of *Blonde on Blonde*" (2011, 105–28).

While every Dylan album has at least a few songs focused on romance, this is his first to fix on women in almost every song. The opening song does not mention women directly, but its title, "Rainy Day Women #12 & 35," is a cryptic phrase that sets the tone of the album's effort to catalogue women as types—women, we may assume, are the "they" who will stone you, etc. Several of the songs are concerned with wooing a woman, as in "I Want You" with its buoyant and high-spirited propositions; others chart an entire relationship, as in the emotional meltdown of "One of Us Must Know (Sooner or Later)" or the wry kiss-off of "Most Likely You Go Your Way and I'll Go Mine." Dylan had worked similar material before, but the songs on *Blonde on Blonde* show the effects of the previous two albums—the confident poetics of *Bringing It All Back Home* and the ability to lay bare the psyche found in key songs on *Highway 61 Revisited*, together with the latter album's phantasmagoric effects. Such elements combine on *Blonde on Blonde* in songs like the slow, mellow "Temporary Like Achilles," a sleepy elegy that, like the "scorpion that crawls across your circus floor," has a considerable sting. As does "4th Time Around," a funny and mordant take-off on The Beatles' "Norwegian Wood (This Bird Has Flown)"; Dylan's song, where a girl finesses the singer only to receive a wry comeuppance, mimics the madrigal-like sound of the Lennon/McCartney tune.

The songs on *Blonde on Blonde* could be called misogynist in their relentless focus on how women preserve an advantage through a host of romantic clichés. Dylan's songs archly puncture such images, as for instance the caustic and flippant "Leopard Skin Pill-Box Hat." Compare that song to any of The Rolling Stones' many attempts to flay the pretensions of the modern girl on the make ("Who's Been Sleeping Here," "Cool, Calm, Collected," "Stupid Girl") to see how much more trenchant Dylan's perspective is on male anxieties and the stress of maintaining one's cool with a chosen female. Dylan's songs abound in caustic observations in keeping with the outlook of earlier songs like "If You Gotta Go, Go Now," and for instance in "Pledging My Time": "they sent for an ambulance and one was sent / somebody got lucky, but it was an accident."

Because we know that Dylan "got lucky" in finding a wife with whom to start a family—a woman he later acknowledged as a key inspiration for the album's final track, the sprawling "Sad Eyed Lady of the Lowlands"—the women on *Blonde on Blonde* may be a catalog of the many unappealing relationships Dylan had encountered. But not all songs here are dismissals of vain women; the key songs that evoke how women can haunt are "Visions of Johanna," "Just Like a Woman," and "Absolutely Sweet Marie." The point is not whether or not Dylan had relationships with actual women like those in the songs but that his imagistic songwriting now addresses the theme dearest to the pop song: love and its vicissitudes.

"Visions of Johanna" is a moody masterpiece, a song that epitomizes the album in its ghostly, strung-out feel. The setting, unlike Dylan's more phantasmagoric masterpieces like "Gates of Eden," "Thin Man," or "Desolation Row," is fairly concrete: an urban space with lofts, museums, and trains, where friends, lovers, and other strangers hang out with small talk, country radio, and coughing heat pipes. Louise and her lover are present while Johanna is absent, though present as a haunting vision that drifts in and out of the singer's mind. A muse figure who, with "her cape of the stage," has been identified with Joan Baez, Johanna can be said to be the occasion for a meditation—on desire, infinity, and the sorts of rambling topics that T. S. Eliot, in "The Love Song of J. Alfred Prufrock," characterized by: "In the room the women come and go / Talking of Michelangelo." The comparison is instructive, for Dylan's song has much in common with Eliot's poem; both use an associative, almost stream-of-consciousness technique, letting the words and images impell themselves across the mind in what Eliot likens to images in a magic lantern show. Dylan name drops the Mona Lisa rather than Michelangelo, but the target is similar: high-culture commentaries that creep into a scene of dilettantes and artistes.

As verse, "Johanna" is amorphous: the rhyme pattern for each stanza should be AAA, BBBB, CC, but after the first verse, the third line of each subsequent stanza is much longer, demanding a caesura that feels like a line break, so that the AAA pattern, while still present, almost gets broken. And in the third stanza, the BBBB section is comprised of very short lines. The variation helps to create the fluid, unpredictable nature of the lyrics, giving them an off-the-cuff, spoken quality. Finally, in the last of the five stanzas, the BBBB segment extends to five lines (six in at least one recording of the song) before the CC couplet, creating a stanza of ten or eleven lines rather than nine. The irregularity demonstrates the difference between song lyrics and poetry; since these words are not intended to be read off the page, the variations are a part of the performance, with Dylan able to draw out lines or cut them short in his vocalizing. On *Blonde on Blonde*, "Johanna" receives a masterful performance, with the musicians finding a way to flesh out the amorphous moods of the song. Musically, the song is a step beyond the lovely but simple embellishments of the more straightforward structure of "Desolation Row." "Visions of Johanna," more furtive and grand in its playing, is full of arresting images such as "the ghost of electricity howls in the bones of her face," and telling lines like "we sit here stranded though we're all doing our best to deny it."

"Just Like a Woman" closes side 2, and is one of Dylan's most traditionally structured songs, with a memorable chorus and an emphatic bridge. In the version on *Blonde on Blonde*, "Woman" also boasts a lovely musical coda, one of the more fully realized instrumental passages in Dylan's recordings. The sentiments of the song—concerning Queen Mary, a character reminiscent of Miss Lonely and Queen Jane, though only addressed in the bridge and the final verse and chorus—conjure up a woman who has, in some ways, the upper hand. As the singer seethes at the end, "I was hungry and it was *your world*" before enunciating a list of characteristics, this time in second person: "you *fake* just like a woman. . . ." The venom at the end of the song is not the tone throughout, however. The more general mood is sad, muted, with the great opening line, "Nobody feels any pain / Tonight as I stand inside the rain," suggesting an irony aimed at oneself as well as at the object of desire, with "her curls, her amphetamine, and her pearls." The song is so elusive in its dominant statement, it cries out to be interpreted, and it has been, by a variety of singers such as Richie Havens, Nina Simone, Joe Cocker, and Dylan himself in, to date, five officially released live recordings. The main point of the song seems to be that even a grown woman can be demanding and vulnerable in ways that suggest "a little girl."

"Absolutely Sweet Marie" is one of the lesser known great songs of this period of Dylan's work. The song cranks along, up-tempo, almost swing style. Dylan's vocals are engaging, and Sweet Marie, the addressee of the song, seems to be someone the singer enjoys pursuing—there are many plaintive questions fired at her, always culminating in the refrain "so where are you tonight, Sweet Marie?" There are also two bridges, at one point bearing the eminently quotable line: "to live outside the law you must be honest" and its often forgotten punch line: "I know you always say that you agree—alright, so where are you tonight, Sweet Marie?" Like "Achilles" and "4th Time," "Sweet Marie" takes aim at many romantic conventions, at the images that have distorted women's reality, but also at the kinds of disguises women hide behind when it suits them. The song concludes with memorable images and an evocative delivery: "Now I stand here looking at your yellow railroad / in the ruins of your balcony." The stresses on **yellow railroad** (with great euphony in yel-rail, low-road) and the drawn-out syllables on *ruuuins* and *baaaalcony* highlight a poetry that few singers could conjure. With *Blonde on Blonde* Dylan invents a performance style uniquely his own, with phrasing that makes the listener very aware of the words and their interrelations, creating verbal effects that completely overwhelm the usual indifference to lyrics in rock songs, but also making the words become sound in stirring ways.

Another major song on the album, "Stuck Inside of Mobile with the Memphis Blues Again," in the vein of "Tombstone Blues" and "Highway 61 Revisited," features a series of bizarre observations ("people just get uglier and I have no sense of time") and inconclusive encounters ("she said 'your debutante just knows what you need, but I know what you want'"). Like "Rolling Stone," the song's chorus flings out an insistent question, "Awww, mama, can this really be the end?" The song epitomizes the vocal style of *Blonde on Blonde*: each time the refrain comes around, Dylan finds another way to shift emphasis, seeming each time to reach for "an end" he doesn't find. One might be indefinitely stuck in Mobile (the joke of being stuck and "mobile" is coy). Typical for Dylan songs of this period, the cast of characters is numerous, including Shakespeare, the Ragman, the Rainman, the Senator, the Preacher, Mona, Ruthie, and Grandpa. Unlike "Desolation Row," most of the characters are noted by their roles or occupations, rather than by names famous from another source. Likewise, the song is much less grand in its conception, describing the kinds of losing situations common in traditional blues songs, dressed up in Dylan's characteristic wordplay and a delivery both insouciant and bemused.

Finally, the epic track of *Blonde on Blonde* is "Sad-Eyed Lady of the Lowlands," one of Dylan's most sustained lyrics, with the title figure tying the whole together, arguably more fully than a place name like "Gates of Eden," "Desolation Row," or "Highway 61," can. However, that very coherence adds a certain redundancy to the piling up of verses—five in all, but each consisting of two quatrains, AAAB, each a question, followed by a chorus that addresses the lady in the full title phrase, then follows with another quatrain, AABB, ending with a two-part question. Dylan packs much into the long lines of the song, as he does in "Johanna," in many ways the song's companion piece, but here the elasticity of lines and delivery are held in check by a metronomic rhythm. In fact, the song feels somewhat like being on a treadmill, moving forward in time but always returning to the same question. The musicians on the track provide much of the fluctuation from verse to verse; sometimes the guitar steps forward more, sometimes the organ's Wurlitzer-like tones are more strident or more subtle, and Dylan's vocal, as usual saving the best for last, lets us know when we reach the end with his forcefully enunciated concluding line, "With your *saint*like *face* and your *ghost*like *soul* / Oh, who among them do you think could destroy you?" This is followed by a shift as Dylan lifts his voice in finality in the last chorus.

The song is a meditation, we might say, on the female principle as Dylan perceives it, in terms that are deeply personal but also at times stunningly evocative, not only in the words themselves, which are rather baroque in their unfurling lines, but also in the delivery. For instance, Dylan's voice on "with the child of the hoodlum wrapped up in your arms" is incredibly sorrowful, seeming to wrap up the Lady and the baby in a protective mantle. Or listen to the little tremelo in his voice on "into your eyes where the moonlight swims," seeming to conjure the light playing across her eyes. Though without a dedication on the album (this is the first Dylan album without liner notes), Dylan, in "Sara," a later song addressed to his wife, says he wrote "Sad-Eyed Lady of the Lowlands" for her, his recent bride and the mother of his child, admitting what seems undeniable about the song: that it was written and sung with someone in mind, a figure much more tangible to his emotions than the composite addressees of many other songs. We might suppose the "Sad-Eyed Lady" is the muse of his poetry, and his engagement with her an endless quest to unburden himself of his "warehouse eyes" and "Arabian drums." As the song consists only of questions for the Lady, one feels how plaintive and yet willful his need for an answer is. "Was ever woman in this manner wooed?" we might well ask.

Major events in world news at the time of the album's release include the inauguration of Mao's Cultural Revolution in China (the "May 16 edict"), a new development in the attempt to create a communist state that had considerable ramifications for leftist politics while also raising fears that China might intervene more directly in the Vietnam War on the side of North Vietnam. In the United States, a march of protest against the war with demonstrations at the White House ended at the Washington Monument and, on May 16, Dr. Martin Luther King Jr. gave his emphatic speech denouncing the U.S. policies in Vietnam. In early June, James Meredith, a civil rights activist, was killed in Mississippi. The issues Dylan had once raised his voice to critique were still very much an ongoing concern. Though it would be hard to imagine a Dylan album further removed from the issues of the day than *Blonde on Blonde*, such albums would be forthcoming shortly. In fact, there was a timely event that *Blonde on Blonde* could be said to engage with: on June 30, 1966, the National Organization for Women was formed, thus bringing politics into the bedrooms of America and into the depiction of women in all areas of culture, including popular song.

All of Dylan's albums contain songs of romance, songs fraught with the problems of communication between the sexes, songs that consider male representations of women as objects of desire. Many of his songs use direct address toward a woman, a rhetorical gesture that makes the song feel personal. After *Another Side of Bob Dylan*, with the knock-down-drag-out, affair-ending song "Ballad in Plain D," the poetic flights of "Spanish Harlem Incident," and the heart-felt outreach of "To Ramona," the view toward women began to stress the need for imaginative interpretation, as with *Bringing It All Back Home*'s "She Belongs to Me" and "Love Minus Zero/No Limit." On *Highway 61 Revisited*, the direct address to a woman had become a feature of characterization, describing the psychic subterfuges by which women live and shape their lives. On *Blonde on Blonde*, the scale tips toward psychological warfare, the wounded longing and unanswered tenderness of eros. While whining about women (or men) for being hard-hearted, indifferent, promiscuous, or clinging is a long-standing blues tradition, the songs on *Blonde on Blonde* infuse such clichés with a newly vital diction. Dylan's skill at venomous put-downs became legendary, but his emphasis on how women "fake" and "ache" and "make love" and "break" showed a nuanced feel for the feminine struggle to please, love, and compete with men in male-dominated contemporary society.

Dylan's status as a father and a married man would come to dominate his attention in the years immediately ahead, and the inauguration of that period can take as its date July 29, 1966. Dylan was in an accident on his motorcycle that caused him some injuries—their severity has been debated, with exaggerated claims of near death finally boiling down, in the most recent biographical accounts, to minor injury and a much desired rest from the road (Shelton, 259–60; Sounes, 219–21). The accident was reason enough for Dylan to cancel his scheduled tour. He would be off the road for eight years. But because Dylan and his manager Albert Grossman had a considerable work ethic, Dylan, now living with his family in Woodstock, New York, near his manager, spent his time working with The Hawks, who had been hired for the tour, on demos of songs others might record. With this withdrawal from public performance for an extended period for the first time since 1960, the early—and for many the major—phase of Dylan's career came to an end.

3

RURAL GLORY
(1967)

FROM A BASEMENT IN WOODSTOCK

Beginning with his accident in July 1966, Dylan's performing career took a long hiatus, and in August The Beatles completed their final U.S. tour at Candlestick Park in San Francisco. Still under a cloud in the United States because of John Lennon's "we're bigger than Jesus now" remarks in March, The Beatles ceased touring in favor of intensive studio work, beginning in November of that year and culminating in June 1967, with the release of one of the most highly respected and influential albums in the history of rock music: *Sgt. Pepper's Lonely Hearts Club Band*. Dylan, in contrast, withdrew to the Woodstock area and, beginning in March 1967 and continuing through the summer, recorded not in a state-of-the-art four-track facility as The Beatles did at Abbey Road Studios, but in the houses he and his friends lived in, particularly the basement of the house known as Big Pink, where Rick Danko, Garth Hudson, and Richard Manuel of The Hawks were living. The tapes they made were intended at most as demos, and indeed, a number of the songs were recorded by other artists such as Manfred Mann, Fairport Convention, and The Byrds. But, as the five CDs-worth of music that has become available on the Internet makes apparent, there was also a great deal of taping of good-natured performances of songs from a wide range of sources. These recordings are low in profes-sionalism and high in spirited interplay. Loose, almost impromptu, including at times false starts and unfinished endings, the songs cannot even be called "rough mixes." In many cases the recording itself is barely demo quality. And yet these "basement tapes" had an influence that runs counter to rock's mainstream and the emergence of psychedelic music, a genre that can best be attributed to the twin wonders of marijuana and multi-track recording.

A figure who gained considerable publicity in this period was a former psychologist at Harvard, Dr. Timothy Leary, a proselytizer for the intellectual and spiritual use of a chemical called lysergic acid diethylamide, or LSD. A psychotropic drug originally developed by the U.S. military for interrogation purposes, LSD, or "acid" in street parlance, could, in Leary's view, produce states of sensory awareness, mental introspection, and revelatory self-knowledge unavailable by natural means—except perhaps through bodily deprivation and meditation as in certain ascetic cults and religions. Since the mid-sixties, the use of marijuana by those Dylan's age and younger had increased steadily into the early seventies.[1] Beyond marijuana, de rigueur among most college students, LSD began to enjoy a hip currency celebrated by author Ken Kesey and his followers in what they called "Acid Tests" in San Francisco. By 1967, the mainstream media knew about LSD, and by the time its possession was outlawed in 1968, it had become the gateway for the intrepid to experience a "higher consciousness."

The recreational use of drugs produced audiences geared for two kinds of music, both somewhat exploratory and experimental: on the one hand, long, free-form jams—"acid rock"—that came to be epitomized by a San Francisco band first known as The Warlocks and then as The Grateful Dead and, on the other, layered recordings with surprising manipulations of sound and tape speed, using echo, reverb, distortion, and found recordings in methods smacking of the practices of avant-garde music. Simply put, rock music was moving toward hard rock through a stress on the sonic properties of instruments in live performance—loud feedback, drum solos, crescendos, and "trippy" interludes, all following one another in extended improvisations. Meanwhile, pop music was moving toward a greater sophistication in recording practices by layering tracks so as to create novel soundscapes. At this time, almost every major recording group produced an album with a more or less psychedelic sheen, with arrangements referencing everything from Baroque music to vaudeville to campy show tunes, all to vary the palette of the basic rock song. The Beatles had ridden to greatness on three guitars—lead, bass, rhythm—and drums and artful harmonies, but they had also become adept with instruments outside that basic range, including string arrangements, sitars, tambla, harpsichords, and flugelhorns. Though in Dylan's single released in March 1966, he had accompanied his cry "Everybody must get stoned!" with the sounds of a lopsided marching band and raucous partyers, his recordings after *Blonde on Blonde* remained aloof from the druggy tendencies of the period.

The songs officially released from Dylan's Woodstock sessions will be discussed in chapter 5, as the recordings were not made available by Columbia Records until 1975, after Dylan and The Band's successful U.S. tour in the winter of 1974. Dylan's home-style recordings were mostly unknown until 1968 when Jann Wenner, the editor and founder of the nascent rock magazine *Rolling Stone*, published an open letter calling for the release of the tracks Dylan had recorded in Woodstock. A selection of songs on a demo acetate, sent out to artists who might be interested in recording them, had been leaked and in 1969 was bootlegged on a compilation with Dylan performances from as early as 1961 and as recent as Dylan's appearance in May 1969, on *The Johnny Cash Show*. Called "the great white wonder" or "little white wonder" because of its all-white cover and labels, the bootleg made some of the Woodstock recordings available to anyone determined to find them.

The songs themselves, in the unprofessional, underproduced versions that have come down to us, feel like off-the-cuff inspirations in very collegial enjoyment of American music. Dylan, the former folkie, and the band members—Canadians with a love of old blues and bluegrass and "hillbilly" music—join together to play songs by the likes of Johnny Cash, Ian & Sylvia, Hank Williams, and others. The Dylan originals created in this environment tend toward three to four minute songs with often a standard format of three repetitions of verse/chorus. The lyrics supply imagistic vignettes that could be considered the "down home" version of the urban carnivalesque Dylan had explored on his previous three albums, abounding in non sequiturs and in jokey, homey diction, with refreshing and playful absurdity. Some are a bit racy, but the general feel is childlike—the kinds of nonsense songs children often recite off the top of their heads, generally guided by rhyme. In the midst of the throwaways are surprising gems that ring with an aged authority. Just as for some, Dylan's early folk songs seemed as if they had always existed, the Woodstock songs seem not to be the work of one man but of an entire region. Dylan and his companions create a ballsy, backwoodsy version of Americana, filled with homespun oddity, inspired silliness, and cryptic drama. What one hears in prototype is the working out of the third great transformation of Dylan's music in less than a decade.

"ONCE UPON A TIME..."

In March 1967 Columbia Records, with no new Dylan recordings to release, put out *Bob Dylan's Greatest Hits* (Dylan's contract was undergoing negotiation, with defection to another label possible). Such repackaged LPs commonly summarize a popular artist's output, and Dylan's *Greatest Hits* is significant as the first time the different phases of Dylan's career appear together on the same disk. Opening the album with "Rainy Day Women #12 & 35" emphasizes the most recent version of Dylan's music over his folk period. Only three tracks from the preelectric albums are included: "Blowin' in the Wind," "The Times, They Are A-Changin'," and "It Ain't Me Babe" present a quick summary of the second through fourth LPs, and sound dated in 1967. The first side ends with "Like a Rolling Stone," which arrives with the punch of the authentic Dylan, or at least the version of Dylan by now more familiar to most purchasers of the album. The second side opens with "Mr. Tambourine Man," making the album worthwhile for containing two major statements from the fifth and sixth LPs on one disk. The side also includes a Top Ten single by Dylan, released in September 1965 and not included on any previous LP: "Positively 4th Street," a song that shows Dylan at his most truculent, putting down a would-be friend described as the most self-serving and envious of hangers-on, the kind of figure that Dylan, in his hip fame, has to distance himself from—the worst thing someone can be is "a drag." Unlike other "put-down songs" like the needling "Ballad of a Thin Man," "4th Street" feels deeply personal, a song—somewhat like "Ballad in Plain D"—that aims to give Dylan's perspective on a relationship gone bad. The album ends with "Just Like a Woman," its placement making the song, along with "Rolling Stone," "Rainy Day Women," and "Mr. Tambourine Man," one of the most readily identifiable Dylan tracks of the time.

The Grammy-winning cover of the album became iconic: Rowland Scherman's silhouetted photograph of Dylan's head in profile, with spotlights dancing in his coruscating locks, and on the back is another close-up, in high contrast, of Dylan playing harmonica on his 1966 tour. At the lower left of the back cover are images of all seven Dylan albums in reverse order, from left to right, the three electric albums posed above the four acoustic records, so that one looks at first the wild-haired rock bard of *Blonde on Blonde*, and moves backwards to the capped kid of *Bob Dylan*. The implied question might well be: What will he become next?

In 1967, Dylan's electric albums continued to be seminal for an impressive explosion of creativity in rock music; the blending of folk and rock on his mid-sixties albums was only the start, but it was an influential start. The late sixties gave rise to a variety of new genres, such as rock versions of British folk in Fairport Convention; new fusions of jazz, rock and white soul in Blood, Sweat and Tears, and Chicago; new acid rock-tinged versions of the blues in Led Zeppelin; in the super group Cream, featuring Eric Clapton; in Janis Joplin with Big Brother and the Holding Company; and in the exploratory music of The Grateful Dead and Jefferson Airplane. An early version of both art rock and New York punk arrived with The Velvet Underground's first album, produced by pop artist Andy Warhol and featuring a stony-voiced German chanteuse known as Nico, the urban grit and literary pretensions of songwriter Lou Reed, and the avant-garde tendencies of collaborator John Cale. Frank Zappa, a brilliant composer and guitarist, spent much of his time lampooning the trends of rock while also creating idiosyncratic experimental works difficult to classify. Los Angeles produced its versions of psychedelia in The Byrds' experiments with various styles on their albums of 1967, in the progressive work of Arthur Lee's band Love, and in the Brecht-meets-Dionysus stylings of The Doors. It was also the era when any number of new songwriters, who might once have gone the folk circuit as Dylan did, thought nothing of immediately recording with session men to produce a "soft rock" sound.

Jimi Hendrix's debut album, *Are You Experienced* was released in England in May 1967 and, released in the States that summer, became influential for its unique electric guitar sound. Hendrix loved Dylan's music; he covered "Like a Rolling Stone" at his breakout performance at the Monterey Festival in June 1967, wrote Dylanesque lyrics—as in his haunting song "The Wind Cries Mary"—and in 1968 released an enduring version of a new Dylan song, "All Along the Watchtower," with multiple guitars creating a dense, moody texture. Comparing Hendrix's version to Dylan's stripped-down original on *John Wesley Harding* provides a clear contrast of Dylan's late sixties recording style with that favored among most of rock's vanguard. When asked by Jann Wenner what sound he was going for when he recorded *Harding*, Dylan pointed to "the sound Gordon Lightfoot was getting" (157). As "soft rock," versions of that sound became a radio staple of the early seventies.

Dylan was moving toward country music, but before arriving there with his ninth album, he produced one of his most enigmatic and challenging records. While many find the lyrical complexity of his midsixties albums baffling, the simplicity of *John Wesley Harding* makes the album, in some ways, harder to interpret and more uniquely timeless.

"NOTHING IS REVEALED"

The album that Dylan made in Nashville late in 1967 with Charlie McCoy and Kenny Buttrey, the main session men from *Blonde on Blonde*, is remarkably different from the latter LP. *Blonde* is steeped in a druggy, late-night urban setting, filled with observations about or directed at an assortment of women and delivered with a voice and persona won from hard performing. The songs' lines stretch to accommodate whatever material Dylan wants to pack into them, giving a convincing sense of the "head full of ideas" referenced in "Maggie's Farm." In the interim between *Blonde* and *Harding*, Dylan began working in shorter songs, more contained but all over the place in terms of their content. *Harding*, in contrast, is filled with short stories; most of the songs consist of three verses and focus on a major character or a single situation. The economy of the songs is impressive—though potentially mystifying for fans looking for more of what the previous albums had taught them to expect. The new album seemed a return to his folk base, and that was welcome enough to send the album high up the charts.

In Dylan's career, the switch from folk to rock was indeed dramatic, but as we have seen, the tendencies toward the latter were already in play due to the directions both folk and rock were taking. The attraction of rock for an artist as out in front as Dylan should not be surprising, but it is unlikely that a fan of *Freewheelin'* in 1963 could have predicted *Blonde on Blonde* three packed years later. Similarly, little would have prepared a fan of the latter, in a year and a half, for *John Wesley Harding*. What is more, the most influential rock at the time was still responding to what Dylan had achieved on his three rock albums. For Dylan to switch to such spare arrangements was in some ways—particularly for the greater numbers of listeners his rock albums attracted—a perverse and even conservative gesture. Given how influential this change also became, it could be said that Dylan was as much in the vanguard as ever. *Harding* was seconded by the first and second albums by The Band, in 1968 and 1969 respectively; by The Byrds' switch, in August 1968, from psychedelic rock to country rock in their trend-setting *Sweetheart of the Rodeo*; and by The Rolling Stones' move from the psychedelic indulgence of *Their Satanic Majesties Request* in December 1967 to *Beggars Banquet*, their best album yet, released in November 1968, which includes country rock, an old blues spiritual, and "Jigsaw Puzzle," an overt attempt to write a Dylanesque lyric. Early in 1969, The Beatles, disillusioned with the process of overdubbed recording that had dominated their disks since 1966, commenced sessions for their intended next album by returning to live-in-the-studio recording. The psychedelic era was short-lived. Dylan's work of 1965–1966 contributed to its origins, much as his work of 1967—both the bootlegged and the official releases—contributed to its demise.

John Wesley Harding is a striking album for any period, but the time of its release makes it even more portentous. Out of the public eye for about a year and a half, Dylan seemed to suddenly emerge as if from a wilderness, bearing cryptic messages. The front cover showed him accompanied by a trio who looked nothing like rock musicians, and Dylan's bearded visage brought to some minds the image of a Talmudic scholar. Formerly, Dylan's liner notes, or back cover musings, only indirectly referenced the album itself—as when *Highway 61 Revisited*'s stream-of-consciousness prose referred to its songs as "exercises in tonal breath control"—but on *Harding*, Dylan presents a vignette about Three Kings (associated with the three kings or wise men who sought out the infant Jesus) seeking illumination about "Mr. Dylan's new album." Tongue in cheek, the story sends up those who seek deep meaning in song lyrics, while also seeming to play into such ponderings.

The album lends itself to an allegorical interpretation, its songs including figures such as the Joker and the Thief, the Watchtower, a Wicked Messenger, a Lonesome Hobo, a Landlord, the Immigrant, the Drifter, as well as slightly more individualized characters such as Frankie Lee and Judas Priest, together with the seemingly historical Tom Paine, St. Augustine, John Wesley Harding—though Dylan adds a "g" to the famous outlaw's name. The album is comprised of twelve songs and it is tempting to read it as a narrative, with each song a chapter in an ongoing tale, and also as a song cycle, corresponding perhaps to the months of the year. Though there are few, if any, deliberate narrative links between the songs, *John Wesley Harding*, whether continuous or not, seems to ask to be read as all of one piece. Rather than a collection of whichever current songs Dylan chose to release, *Harding* seems to offer twelve parts of a single statement.

The view of a record as a single work had become prevalent with the release of The Beatles' *Sgt. Pepper's Lonely Hearts Club Band* in June. The album, with its introductory song and reprise, seemed to suggest an unusual degree of integration for the entire album. The impression is not fully sustained, but it is true that previously The Beatles LPs were issued in rather different versions in the UK and the United States. With *Sgt. Pepper*, all versions of the album were identical in their arrangement of songs. Dylan's albums had already enjoyed a consistency of presentation, but on all previous LPs there were songs that might have been included or excluded. As with *Sgt. Pepper*, the songs on *John Wesley Harding* seem to accept no additions, subtractions, or substitutions. Both albums conjure alter egos—Sgt. Pepper's band, the gunslinger Harding—to establish a space separate from the respective artists responsible for the records. In Dylan's case, the album is less focused on his own persona than previous albums were, and current events and personal experience less directly invoked.

"John Wesley Harding," the opening track, conjures a hero of the West, rather than the actual outlaw: a man "always known to lend a helping hand" and "never known to make a foolish move." The parallel is instructive: grand generalities—"never known," "always known"—surround Harding. In fact, the lyrics of the song are a tissue of vague assertions—"soon the situation there was all but straightened out"—that leaves the listener uncertain of what exactly Harding is noted for: "no charge held against him could they prove." Perhaps, but that is not the same as saying he is innocent. Hardly a portrait of Harding—whether Hardin or a composite gunslinger—the song's simplicity almost masks its ambiguity. We are entering a world informed by tall tales that make larger-than-life heroes out of so many figures of American history. The delivery of the song is relaxed, almost casual. Rather than expanding into a lengthy story song as Dylan's audience might expect, the song barely introduces Harding before concluding, and yet, strangely, it does not feel incomplete. Dylan's evocative harmonica, suggestive of a life on the trail, takes up most of the song. We are given a miniature of Harding, something we can look at in various lights until perhaps we can begin to see what he was like.

A more familiar historical figure plays a part in the second track, and we might begin to think the album will be a tour of American types. "As I Went Out One Morning" locates itself "around Tom Paine's." Dylan, we might recall, was the recipient of the Tom Paine Award in 1963, which evokes an association that might be fortuitous, but that draws us into the song as a possible allegorical reflection on Dylan's own experience. The song relates how the singer one morning spies "the fairest damsel that ever did walk in chains." Just how fair is that? As in the previous song, the wording is direct but also oddly aslant. In any case, the woman, who he believes means to do him harm, pleads with him not to send her away. After at first dismissing her, he tells her he will "secretly accept" her and "together we'll fly south." Tom Paine "himself" runs up and commands the girl "to yield." He then apologizes to the singer: "I'm sorry for what she's done." It is odd that such a deliberate narrative, in which the action is clear and the statements straightforward, should be so cryptic. We find ourselves in the land of parable. Even more than in the previous song, the context is undefined. We might expect the damsel to invite our sympathy; if so, the males—the singer and Tom Paine—fail to resolve her distress. The singer's certainty of the harm she intends, contradicted by his acceptance of her, is deliberately ambiguous. We might align her with temptation—an Eve-like figure who seduces the singer from his proper path, which is restored to him by Paine, a figure for right action. We can see Paine as liberating the singer from the chains the damsel seeks to entrap him with. They might be the chains of the flesh, the chains of pride, even the chains of matrimony. We sense there is no end to such interpretive substitutions. The song itself, with its eerie harmonica accompaniment and its prodding, loping bass, is full of portent that leaves us hanging. The song's ending—a brief harmonica coda after Paine's apology—is particularly successful. "What she's done" might be nothing more than getting past the singer's defenses, but in any case it seems the damage is already done. Like a myth, the song is a foundational tale, a story of how some state of affairs came to be—indeed, as with the biblical tale of the fall into sin in the Garden of Eden, the story is best understood as a fall from grace.

Continuing such religious-mystical associations, the next song, one of the best on the album, introduces the figure of St. Augustine, "alive as you or me"—Dylan borrows the phrase used to describe a dream of Joe Hill in the famous song about the Swedish-American activist who, after death, becomes an eternal figure for the struggle of workers against bosses. St. Augustine, in the dream the song recounts, is alive but in misery for the state of humanity. The singer dreams he himself is of the mob that "put [the saint] out to death"; as with "Morning," the singer speaks from a position of guilt, as one who commits an act that compromises him and, here, leads to anger and terror when the dream ends. The pathos of the final line, "I put my fingers against the glass and bowed my head and cried," is striking; it is a line of stark beauty, and the first person delivery gives it a directness that is truly moving. Here we have someone awoken from a dream, leaning against a mirror or window (I tend to favor the latter—as in, "I've been up all night, leaning on the windowsill") and shedding tears over a dream. The meaning of the dream may be the guilt of having joined those who killed the saint.

St. Augustine, of course, was not actually put to death, but this is a dream after all. What does it mean to kill St. Augustine? The answer to that question might well fill a small treatise: as with the damsel in the previous song, or indeed Tom Paine himself, St. Augustine could stand for many things: the Church; the historical St. Augustine who, in his *Confessions*, admits to his own venial failings before finding the true faith; or the eminent preacher of the *City of God* whose teachings above all promoted the idea that reflection upon God's will was the best procedure for any human activity. In the song, St. Augustine, who claims the people are without a martyr to call their own, seems to take on that role himself. As in "With God on Our Side," the question seems to be whether those who put Jesus or St. Augustine to death are doing something sanctioned by God. At the very least, the implication of the dream seems to be that the singer—in accepting the damsel and putting the saint to death—has turned from the path he should be following, whether a path of righteousness or of creative purpose or of something else. Here, the harmonica coda is longer, more elegiac, creating a sense of consolation.

We begin to see that the introduction of John Wesley Harding at the outset was a means of suggesting good and bad as shared characteristics; Harding extends a helping hand with a gun in it. He may not be innocent but no case against him wins. The theme of guilty association becomes prominent. Each song, until the final two on the album, in some way describes a struggle for self-definition that includes a sense of failure, compromise, missed chances, or wrong choices.

The struggle is placed in a starkly apocalyptic context in "All Along the Watchtower." Beginning with a memorable opening line—"'There must be some kind of way out of here,' said the Joker to the Thief"—the song consists of two verses of exchanges between the named figures and then concludes with a verse that places the scene in an ancient setting, recalling, as is well known, verse 21 from the book of Isaiah in the Bible. The call to "watch in the watchtower" comes as part of a "grievous vision" that includes a chariot with a couple of horsemen and ends with the fall of Babylon and the destruction of its idols. The comments of the Joker to the Thief—names that suggest untrustworthiness, continuing the theme of guilt and duplicity—place him in contrast to "businessmen" and "plowmen" he maligns, figures for industry and farming. The Joker positions himself outside such involvements, suggesting that his world—he speaks of "my wine" and "my earth"—suffers from the activities of such men. The lines struck an immediate chord with the counterculture seeking an alternative to the corporatism that dominated American life. The Thief, who speaks kindly, chides the Joker and those who "feel that life is but a joke." The rhyme of "this is not our fate" with "the hour is getting late" is chilling.

What the duo's fate should be is not stated, and the comment may be hopeful: there are alternatives, "some way out of here," but the mention of the hour creates more anxiety. As a reply to the Joker, the line implies that all the latter said might be a joke or false. The final verse jumps, like a film cut, to a different scene; we may infer that the "two riders" (who appear in Isaiah as well) are the Joker and the Thief, approaching the watchtower, where "princes kept the view." There are also women and "barefoot servants"—description is minimal but conveys the biblical sense of exact but inessential detail. The most quizzical is the "wild cat" (a "lion" in Isaiah) that growls "outside in the distance" where the two riders approach as "the wind began to howl." One implication is that the two riders are arriving at the watchtower under evil portents. Do they bring destruction, or are they seeking asylum? If we suppose that the two riders are the Joker and the Thief, arrival at the watchtower, where there seems to be some degree of order, could be the "way out" they crave. And yet the song does not convey a happy solution; like most of the songs on *John Wesley Harding*, it seems like a parable harboring some darker meaning, a meaning that might be too awful if stated outright.

The comical narratives Dylan composed up through his fifth album come to mind with "The Ballad of Frankie Lee and Judas Priest." While lacking the off-the-cuff jabs of the talkin' blues and the jokey incidents of "Motorpsycho Nitemare" or "115th Dream," "The Ballad" is written in a wry, tongue-in-cheek manner similar in spirit to the narrative on the album's back cover. Indeed, the character the Kings consult about the meaning of the album is named Frank. They say they understand he's "the key." As such, he might be a reference to Frankie Lee in the song. It seems a stretch to consider them the same person (Frankie Lee dies in the course of the song, so, unless he gets resurrected . . .), but there is at least a tease in the idea. The story of Frankie Lee and Judas Priest can also be seen as a continuation of "Watchtower" with Frankie as "the thief" (he's offered a wad of cash and hesitates to take it) and Judas Priest as "the joker" (his comments in the song suggest that he is toying with Frankie), but the world this song inhabits seems light-years away from the mood of "Watchtower." The singsong delivery is playful in the manner of a nursery rhyme or a folk ballad for children. The story, ostensibly a cautionary tale with a moral ("one should never be where one does not belong") or two ("don't go mistaking paradise for that home across the road"), shows how Frankie—a figure for needs ("needed money one day") and desires (he loses control when faced with a house full of women)—is overcome by his own greedy enjoyment of the pleasures of the flesh. Judas Priest—a wonderful name suggesting how the anointed of God can also be a traitor—extends charity and teachings to Frankie, but also seems to ensnare him. In the end, the "little neighbor boy" who bears away Frankie's body while concealing his own guilt, states "nothing is revealed." The singer's offer of two morals seems a way of robbing the boy's comment of its finality, and yet that comment seems to bear more weight, for it illustrates the attitude of the album. Or rather, the boy's comment, in relation to the singer's moral, makes clear the interplay of definite statement and the more esoteric or allegorical meanings implicit in the songs. In form, with its narrative verses punctuated, like "Desolation Row," with two harmonica solos, "The Ballad" resembles Dylan's earlier songwriting. Indeed, the moral is the first direct address on the album and immediately brings to mind—though with an unusual drawl—the early Dylan's tendency to make didactic claims.

"Drifter's Escape," side 1's final song, also narrates straightforward action that carries a variety of meanings, depending on how one reads the principal figures in the tale. The Drifter is similar to the Thief as his time "is not long" and, like most of the principal figures so far, he does not "know what I've done wrong." The judge speaks to the Drifter and possibly to Dylan's listeners when he says "you fail to understand . . . why must you even try?" A *deus ex machina*—here a bolt of lightning—strikes and "knock[s] the courthouse out of shape." Everyone but the Drifter kneels to pray—he escapes. The song is the closest to blues so far on the album, with the opening line, "Oh, help me in my weakness," positioning the song in the genre of earlier songs like "Maggie's Farm" or even "Bob Dylan's Blues." Unlike those songs, however, "Drifter" offers a satisfying tale in which piety—hypocritical piety, perhaps—loses, and feckless determination triumphs. Or, if not exactly triumphs, at least escapes punishment. How cheered we are by this outcome will be based on whether we feel this is something of a kangaroo court, with the lightning perhaps a sign of God's wrath, or whether we believe in the rectitude of the judge, in which case the Drifter availing himself of a chance occurrence for escape becomes another thing he does wrong. As with Harding, able to escape punishment because no crime could be proved, the Drifter eludes what may, after all, be justice.

And on that ambiguous note the first side ends.

Dylan opens side 2 playing expressive barroom-style piano as he croons a song addressed to his "Dear Landlord." The imagery of the Drifter's trial continues with the line "please don't dismiss my case"; on the whole, the song takes a stance against a possible oppressor—whether landlord, boss, or other figure of authority. The opening plea to not "put a price on my soul" has led some interpreters to see the song as addressed to Dylan's manager Albert Grossman; while such one-dimensional readings are too reductive, it may be that Dylan's dissatisfactions with his management fuels the situation of the song. Indeed, Dylan's critics and audience might also be said to put a price on his soul in their deciding to endorse his music or not. The line about agreeing not to underestimate one another puts the song on a reasonable footing, as does the comment that suffering from a heavy burden makes no one "unique." The song is one of Dylan's more gracious direct address songs in that it seems not to be trying to one-up the Landlord as much as get along with him. The "Landlord" could be "the Lord," to whom one owes one's soul or could be a profane figure to whom one owes a debt. The idea of telling God not to put a price on one's soul is striking: a statement we might imagine Adam making after the Fall or Christ in Gethsemane or on the cross.

Indeed, side 2 of the album is filled with characters who carry burdens of guilt even more clearly than those on side 1. The inexact nature of the sins in "As I Went Out One Morning," the dreamed guilty act in "St. Augustine," and the Drifter's doubts about his crime are all put to the side by "I Am a Lonesome Hobo," where the singer, in the guise of the Hobo, admits to a host of crimes: bribery, blackmail, and deceit that, in the example in the second verse, sounds like bearing false witness against his brother—an act specifically forbidden by the Ten Commandments. The lonesome Hobo has been identified with Cain, as the biblical figure who killed his brother and was forced into a life of wandering rootlessness. Indeed Cain-like, the Hobo, like Coleridge's Ancient Mariner, seems to wander about telling others to avoid his fate. What is interesting is that he doesn't exhort his listeners to be faithful and true, but rather tells them "to live by no man's code"—a surprising line when it is delivered as a code to live by. At the same time, the Hobo demands that we hold our judgments for ourselves—which returns us, in tone, to the commandment at the end of "Landlord" about not underestimating one another. Here, we should refrain from all judgment of others except as it applies to ourselves: "judge not lest ye be judged." The sentiment would seem to extend to the judgmental figures of side 1.

"I Pity the Poor Immigrant" is a strikingly original song, and also a deeply moral one. Dylan's delivery of the song is indeed gently pitying, and the slow, sleepy pace of the melody makes the song feel much longer than it is. The suffering of the Immigrant seems interminable, but not unmerited—he "uses all his power to do evil," and cheats and "lies with every breath." The singer, in one of the most ringing statements, attributes to the Immigrant a condition of existential fear and hatred: "Who passionately hates his life and likewise fears his death." Such misery, we begin to suspect, applies to many who are "immigrants" in the widest possible sense: we know not where we come from nor where we are going. The song continues to escalate, pointing out the meanness of the Immigrant's existence, denying him consolations— his gladness will pass, his visions "must shatter like the glass," recalling "the glass" against which the dreamer of St. Augustine placed his fingers. We might suppose that the dream of St. Augustine was indeed one of the visions that will shatter, leaving a wholly fallen, profane world— or, to borrow a line from "Gates of Eden," "leaving men wholly totally free to do anything they wish to do but die." The most disturbing aspect of "Immigrant" is that the speaker, who refers to himself at one point, bears such an ambiguous relation to the main character. The Immigrant falls in love with wealth and "turns his back on me." We might suppose we are hearing the voice of God (perhaps the Lord/Landlord) who judges the Immigrant for forsaking Him.

The first three songs on side 2 establish a moral and metaphysical context that deepens what were only hints on side 1. We might begin to expect the side will culminate in a direct statement of faith or of despair. In any case, the second and third songs, while still using what are almost double entendres as we saw on side 1, are bleaker and more stringent. That tendency breaks with the fourth song, corresponding to "Watchtower" on the first side. The portentous nature of the album is well represented by "The Wicked Messenger"—who comes "from Eli" (whether a place or short for Elijah) and seems to be the kind of off-kilter biblical prophet that the conclusion of "Watchtower" might have prepared us for. Unable to speak without flattering, the Messenger uses his thumb to indicate who sent for him (we are not told) and uses written messages to communicate. His message "The soles of my feet, I swear they're burning" is both cryptic and comic. It is also a double entendre since "burning souls" would indicate the damned. Has the Messenger come to condemn rather than flatter? Does he condemn by flattering? We cannot be sure. The final verse—introduced by a jokey parallel of the changing seasons (falling leaves) and a biblical miracle (parting seas)—tells us the people confronted the Messenger with a message of their own: "if you cannot bring good news, then don't bring any." In one sense, this is the climax of the album we have been following. The tendency to become more condemnatory—as with the Landlord, the Hobo, and the Immigrant—is here halted. The Messenger will not judge nor tell us who will be judged nor how. Despite all our sins, all our faults, all our guilt, we want to hear only good news. And this brings to an end Dylan as a prophetic voice in song for at least three years.

The next song delivers good news: a strutting little tune that would be perfect for Elvis Presley, "Down Along the Cove" seems to depart entirely from the logic of the previous songs. It arrives as a great breath of relief, a laying down of the onerous task of struggling with the question of existence. And yet the song, with its repetitions in which the singer exults that he sees his true love "comin' my way" and spies "his little bundle of joy" (which might be the woman or their child), repeats twice "Lord have mercy, honey." In most cases, such invocations in a gentle R&B song like this would not be taken seriously. The expression simply means "holy cow" or something along those lines: a merging of "holy" language with a profane locution. But in the context of *John Wesley Harding* and the train of associations we've been following, the call for "mercy" is suggestive. The true love between the singer and his lady is a form of mercy, something coming from above, so to speak. We have turned a corner. There is some value to existence besides misery and crisis and a feeling of guilt that, the Judeo-Christian tradition teaches, is the result of our first parents' original sin. There is the joy of love. Some might see the "little bundle of joy" as the Christ child.

The album ends with a song well on its way to being the kind of country ditty that Dylan's next LP offers. "I'll Be Your Baby Tonight" is laid-back, mellow, offhandedly seductive. It is a great love song of settled bliss for a couple staying home, shutting the lights and drawing the shade with, in the bridge, an audacious rhyme of "moon" and "spoon" that comes from nursery rhyme, from the world of hackneyed rhymes and to some listeners suggests the easy-going ineptitude of Dylan's change in mood. The line "bring that bottle over here" is a suggestive invitation for a night in bed with a woman and a bottle, and with the refrain "I'll be your baby tonight," includes the idea of a baby bottle, nursing, and other such activities (like baby making). The song is casually ribald, and with its insinuating harmonica and drawled lengthening of "yoourrrrr" the performance recalls earlier songs like "It Takes a Lot to Laugh" and "Temporary Like Achilles." Now, we might say, the singer has come through the dark night of the soul that *John Wesley Harding* was shaping up to be. He and his lady have decided to "go play Adam and Eve."

In October, shortly before the recording of the album began, Woody Guthrie passed away. Dylan was immediately interested in a public tribute to his early mentor and model. On January 28, 1968, Dylan joined Judy Collins, Tom Paxton, actors Will Geer and Robert Ryan, Guthrie's son Arlo, and The Hawks (billed as The Crackers), among others, for a tribute concert, Dylan's first public performance since 1966. His set consisted of Guthrie tunes "Ain't Got No Home," "Dear Mrs. Roosevelt," and "Grand Coulee Dam." Here was the first public evidence that Dylan was still able to perform—was not "a vegetable" or amnesiac after his accident, nor strung-out on hard drugs—and it's fitting that his appearance should bring him back, with full-throated, mature delivery, to the songs of the man he began his performing career emulating. Neither he nor the former Hawks were what they had been two years previously. The wildness was gone, and so were the "boos." It must have seemed as though Dylan had returned to the fold.

Was this a farewell or a taste of things to come? No one knew for sure, least of all Dylan himself.

NOTE

1. As summed up by J. Slaughter: "Fewer than one million Americans had tried cannabis by 1965; by 1972, twenty-four million people had smoked marijuana at least once, eight million people were using it regularly, and at least half a million people were consuming it daily" (420).

4

"TAKE ME AS I AM"
(1968–1973)

THE YEAR ALL HELL BROKE LOOSE

In October of 1968, Dylan's friend and fellow musician Happy Traum, together with John Cohen, interviewed Dylan for *Sing Out!*, the folk music publication that had followed his early career closely and published denouncements of his "liaison with the music trade's Top Forty Hit Parade" in the mid-sixties (Young, 93). Traum questions the distance between the early Dylan and his more recent work, specifically mentioning "Masters of War" as a "black and white song. It wasn't too equivocal. You took a stand." Dylan replies that "thousands and thousands of people" wanted that song, "so I wrote it up." The comment sounds a bit disingenuous, as if the act were facile, yet Dylan makes a clear distinction: then, there was "this force which is needing all these songs"; now, "my insight has turned into something else" (Cohen and Traum, 137).

The "force" that demanded the songs was largely the people of his circle. As a young man, Dylan listened to what those around him, in the politically conscious milieu he occupied, were saying. He then found a way to say that in a song. To be a conduit for a collective demand is certainly worthwhile, and it made Dylan's early recordings and performances a reference point for many. The insight offered in his most recent album is "something else," something, we may infer, more personal, inner-directed, and better able to confront questions not timely but timeless. The above section on *John Wesley Harding* suggests some of Dylan's new insight: the trials, the blame, the guilt, and the sense of judgment, of trying not to "make a foolish move," are all overcome by the discovery of love—personal, individual, fulfilling love. Dylan, at the close of *Harding*, becomes publically a lover, a man who finds the meaning of life in the woman by his side and their "little bundle of joy."

That said, it is important to note that these particular times were fraught with even more turmoil than were Dylan's younger years. The year all hell broke loose, 1968, is in many ways a watershed year for both countercultural and mainstream politics. In that year, largely in response to the lack of faith in his leadership within his own party, President Lyndon Johnson did not seek reelection. The Democrats' policies—the war in Vietnam abroad and the war on poverty at home, together with efforts to pursue changes in civil rights—were meeting with opposition, both on the right and on the left. LBJ's withdrawal from public affairs could be said to be a blow to the moderate liberal position that had dominated the country since the New Deal. The assassination of Robert Kennedy, after he had successfully begun to steal the fire of the antiwar campaign from Eugene McCarthy in the run for the Democratic nomination, ended hopes for a candidate who might bridge the more radical and more moderate wings of the political left. Hubert Humphrey, as Johnson's vice president, seemed nothing more, to the radical left, than business as usual, which meant the old guard Democrats' rule of the party.

Thus the voice of dissent became more extreme, departing from electoral politics and moving from marches to riots and not only in the United States. In Paris, "May '68" is known as the time when students went to the barricades to protest the regulated nature of higher education in France; they came close to forming a revolutionary movement in unison with workers disgruntled by layoffs and plant shutdowns. In eastern Europe, the attempt of the Czech young to join the countercultural youth movements in Europe were forcefully repressed by Soviet tanks in the streets of Prague. Meanwhile, in China, Mao's Cultural Revolution was unseating the professionals in the name of a radical-communist changing of the guard such as had not been seen since Stalin's ruthless reshaping of the USSR in the fifties. Totalitarian repression was becoming the hallmark of the left. In the United States, 1968 was also marked in blood: in addition to the murder of Bobby

Kennedy, there was the assassination of Martin Luther King Jr., and Malcolm X, a spokesman for a more militant black politics, was also shot down.

The economic difficulties that would escalate in the seventies first became visible in this period. In some ways, the situation in the United States simply demonstrated the falling off of the high production and general prosperity of the first twenty to twenty-five years of postwar rebuilding. Other developments that affected the young listeners of rock music—in addition to escalating war, the draft, campus unrest, social inequalities, and dissatisfaction with the corporatist cast of American prosperity—included the outlaw status of their drugs of choice. The clash with authorities over political freedoms for minorities and for freedom from the draft extended to the freedom to use prohibited substances like marijuana and LSD. "Authority that they do not respect in any degree," to use Dylan's words, seemed to the young repressive and arbitrary in its power. "Freaks"—the self-label of drug users—could join "queers" and "brothers" as terms used to designate members of subcultures and minorities with grievances against the "straight, white" mainstream. The living emblem of "the pigs" was the Republican nominee, Richard M. Nixon, a former McCarthyite, vice president under Eisenhower, and self-proclaimed spokesman for "the silent majority," who became president elect in November 1968.

Because of songs already four or five years old like "Masters of War" or "The Times, They Are A-Changin'," Dylan still remained a voice for youth in this period, as "the battle outside" was truly "ragin'." Songs like "It's Alright, Ma (I'm Only Bleeding)" spoke to a widespread search for alternatives to the middle-class American Dream. For many young listeners—born in the fifties—Dylan's songs were already in place as anthems for a rite of passage from mere entertainment and the ideals of the parental generation to music that accorded with youthful discontent and the collective search for new values. Ironically, as Dylan became a private man committed to his family, the image of him as an advocate of radical assaults on the status quo became more widespread than ever. In his withdrawal from the public, Dylan provided little current information to counteract the image of him still prevalent from the mid-sixties: a youthful seer, a far-out hipster, an electric poet. The so-called Woodstock Nation celebrated a form of cultural anarchy that found some of its antecedents in Dylan's music, so that his life at this time was

beset by the consequences of his earlier work. A "force" was still needing songs and was still demanding he write them.

WOODSTOCK AND NASHVILLE

> This was just about the time of that Woodstock Festival, which was
> the sum total of all this bullshit. And it seemed to have something to
> do with me, this Woodstock Nation, and everything it represented.
> So we couldn't breathe. I couldn't get any space for myself or my
> family, and there was no help, nowhere. I got very resentful about
> the whole thing, and we got outta there.
> —Bob Dylan to Kurt Loder (301)

Mike Wadleigh's documentary film of the Woodstock Festival, held
August 15–18, 1969, in the town of Bethel, New York, about sixty miles
from the town of Woodstock (where Dylan and his family resided at the
time) gives a good idea of what the "Woodstock Nation" Dylan speaks
of was like. The political turmoil of 1968 helped create a more audacious form of "be-in" than was practiced in 1967. The mood of the
young was to seek change, not as a political process, but as an altering of
consciousness, a "new society." While the more extreme notions about
what would be required to reinvent modern life were not shared by all,
some sense that the forces of urban and suburban modernity—the gas-
oline-fueled behemoths, the air-conditioned office blocks, the conform-
ist tract housing, the assembly-line production of not only appliances
but of foods enhanced more and more by chemicals, the commercial
colonization of the Far East as the never-never land of cheap labor and
goods—were unsustainable. Books such as Rachel Carson's *Silent
Spring* (1962) created a dramatic sense of the abuse of nature by modern life. Variously, there were "back to nature" movements and outcries
that equated the U.S. standard of living with the use of the Bomb, the
most destructive device yet invented, and with the forms of genocide
and enslavement that played an important but rarely acknowledged part
in the nation's history. The provocative and attention-grabbing few
urged others to become either a terrorist against the forces of oppression—as in the Weathermen collective—or "a freak": someone who
refuses to live by the rules of civil society. The boundaries of consciousness and selfhood, this view went, could be dissolved by sacramental

use of marijuana and psychotropic drugs. Along with those boundaries would be lost the compunction to possess and to repress. And for those who had gone beyond drugs, there were any number of mystical systems of thought floating around. The "Woodstock Nation" was primed for statements from a seer—and Dylan had become, along with The Beatles and a few other mainstays of the rock pantheon, one of the seers, his lyrics and his persona adaptable to any number of interpretations; his "put downs" and "put ons" were inspired surreal clowning, and his withdrawal from the spotlight left him open to wild speculations about his intentions. Consider the comment made to Dylan in 1969 by *Rolling Stone* editor Jann Wenner, a fairly plugged-in guy, we would imagine: "the expectation of your audience—the portion of your audience that I'm familiar with—feels that you have the answer" (149).

Much of this might be what Dylan has in mind as "the sum total of all this bullshit." But to put the zeitgeist in perspective, let us take a moment to consider some of the events of 1969: Richard M. Nixon was sworn in as president on January 20, 1969; ten days later The Beatles played publically for the first time in three years. The impromptu concert was on the rooftop of the office block that housed their company, Apple Records, in London, and was filmed for the movie they were at work on, which would be released in 1970 as *Let It Be.* The afternoon was in fact their last performance as The Beatles, but few fans would have assumed that at the time. The appearance seemed to herald a return to the public arena, the kind of gesture that would give new hope to those who still wanted to believe in the spirit of the mid-sixties. The Beatles, with their use of drugs to spur their creativity, had been pied pipers to a certain degree, leading large numbers of the young to seek meaning in their works via "enhanced states."

Lennon, newly inspired by the artistic conceptions of his wife Yoko Ono, began to perform a self-styled radical celebrity: from May 26 to June 2, John and Yoko held a "Bed-In for Peace," meeting with press and some notable guests as they held forth, guru-like, in wry commentary on how raising awareness was largely a matter of the will to question and to depart from social norms. Not unlike the do-it-yourself informality of Dylan and The Band's "basement tapes," an impromptu recording of "bed-in tapes" yielded a song, "Give Peace a Chance," that called upon Nixon to end the war in Vietnam. In fact, the first troop withdrawals took place in July, but the bombing of Cambodia (secret as far as the U.S. press was concerned) had commenced in March, as Nixon attempted to win the war with fewer U.S. soldiers at risk.

Contrast Lennon's activities with those of Bob Dylan, another alleged counterculture guru. On April 9, the same day that students at Harvard (led by the increasingly militant Students for a Democratic Society [SDS]) seized administration buildings to make demands, Dylan released his sunny *Nashville Skyline*, delivering romantic songs in mellow croons and jaunty honky-tonk. That same month saw the standoff of Berkeley students with police over an empty space the students and locals had christened "the People's Park" (an incident with similarities to what occurred at Zucotti Park at the Occupy Wall Street protests of 2011–2012), which led to the death of student James Rector. When, in May, a memorial for the fallen student was held on Berkeley Plaza, Governor Ronald Reagan, taking a cue from his president's activities in Cambodia, bombed the students—albeit with tear gas rather than explosives. Meanwhile, Dylan performed on June 7 as part of the debut of *The Johnny Cash Show*. Cash, an iconic figure of country music, had been friends with Dylan since they met at the Newport Folk Festival in 1964, and Cash had been vocal in support of Dylan when others maligned him for abandoning the folk movement. A duet between the two singers, covering Dylan's early song of lost love "Girl from the North Country," appears as the first track on *Nashville Skyline*.[1] From the point of view of rock and youth culture, Cash was a figure of the country music establishment, a form of music noted for its appeal to conservative tastes in America, such as the desire for a segregated South. Which is not to say that Cash was not a liberal but rather to indicate the extent to which Dylan, at this time, should not be identified with the more radical voices and intentions of folk and rock but with at best liberal, middle-of-the-road Americana.

In June, the Weathermen, willing to employ terrorist tactics for their ends, disrupted a meeting of the SDS, signaling the extent to which students in America were either apolitical or militant. The moderate middle ground was being eroded. At the end of June, the famous Stonewall riots upon a police raid on a gay bar in San Francisco sent up a call for a new kind of radicalism, one based on sexual rights. In July, *Easy Rider*, a cinematic exploration of counterculture figures, drug running, and motorcycles became a standard-bearer for the "new Hollywood," as many young viewers flocked to what, by industry standards, was simply a low-budget exploitation film, complete with de rigueur nudity and acid trip. In December, The Rolling Stones took part in a free concert at Altamont Raceway in California at which a black man was murdered by a member of Hell's Angels, a California motorcycle gang. The dark side of the "peace and love" movement, ostensibly expressed at the Woodstock Festival in August, was observable not only in the violence at Altamont and the violence that ends *Easy Rider*, but also in the killings masterminded by Charles Manson, a deranged acid guru whose sway over a rag-tag collection of strung-out dropouts persuaded them to "revolution" via multiple murders on August 6 in California. The supposed source of Manson's inspiration were songs on The Beatles' so-called White Album (aka *The Beatles*), released the previous November.

Earlier, on July 20, 1969, Apollo 11 landed on the moon and the world received transmissions in which a human, Neil Armstrong, set foot on the surface of the earth's satellite. The moonwalk was considered a U.S. victory in some quarters, but for others it was an empty one: such technological superiority was not leading to surrender in Vietnam. The second landing of the year, on November 19, was overshadowed by the release on November 20 of photographs from the My Lai massacre, showing the results of a U.S. battalion gone berserk that killed the entire population of a defenseless village in Vietnam. The dark side of U.S. military efforts, the violence and psychosis lurking in those distorted by drugs or by tensions in our society, and the psychic costs of the Woodstock generation's celebration of unlicensed freedom were becoming all too obvious as the sixties ended. The feelings came to a head in the "Days of Rage" riots by the Weathermen-led SDS to "bring the war home" at the Democratic Convention in Chicago. To some commentators, the war effort in Vietnam was costing the United States its soul, and that very soullessness was emblematized by the pointless effort to colonize a dead rock trapped in Earth's orbit.

All this had nothing to do with Bob Dylan, who had recorded in Nashville songs in which, "my oh my, I dig my country pie," and that turned the stark youthful truth of his "Girl From the North Country" into a sentimental country ditty. Clearly, Dylan had no interest in pop rock's quest for inner peace, as suggested by The Beatles; nor in hard rock's celebration of amoral sensuality, as suggested by The Rolling Stones; nor in the folk movement's search for values, as epitomized by his former lover and comrade Joan Baez (married to Tom Hayden of SDS, a jailed draft evader); nor even in his own previous efforts—via folk rock, the genre he had helped create—to satirize the absurdities of the moment or to articulate a collective vision, even if cryptically. Rather, he put together an album that's little more than a showcase for an entirely new singing voice, with music played by first-rate Nashville session men (the album's instrumental, "Nashville Skyline Rag," was nominated for a *Country* Instrumental Grammy). In a world seemingly coming apart at the seams, Dylan had loosened up and recorded his first "just fun" album. Like Dylan, other musicians and songwriters were finding new inspiration in country music perhaps as a way of aligning with the values of a nation whose populace believed in their God-given right to pursue individual wealth and happiness above all. On *Nashville Skyline*, regardless of the state of the nation, Dylan sounds safe and content, his days as a firebrand, visionary, poet who "accepts chaos" done. For that, many would never forgive him.

The album yielded one of Dylan's last Top Ten songs for several years: with its mellow croon, "Lay Lady Lay" sounds like no previous Dylan song, indicating that the master of the mercurial had remade himself yet again. The song is a mature love song, expressing a man's claim that his lover can "have [her] cake and eat it too." Other lines, like "his clothes are dirty but his hands are clean," express the old formula— see Tim Hardin's "If I Was a Carpenter"—of a common workingman trying to seduce a classy woman through a promise of pleasure ("whatever colors you have in your mind, I'll show them to you and you'll see them shine"). The song is remarkable among Dylan songs for its unabashed sensuality. In terms of the sexual revolution, the song's popularity suggests that, though conservative, a man who knows how to "pitch the woo" in a manly if sensitive way is still a valuable commodity. Barbara O'Dair, who was twelve when she first heard the song, describes the singer as "commanding and kind, benevolently paternalistic" (80).

Other songs show Dylan stepping out with the band and having fun ("saddle me up a big white goose, strap me on her and turn her loose"), while perhaps trying to inhabit the songwriting stable of his hero Hank Williams ("Tell Me That It Isn't True" and "One More Night" are both Williamsesque). Besides the hit, the standout track is "Tonight I'll Be Staying Here With You," a jaunty, seductive jolt of country honky-tonk—"Throw my ticket out the window / Throw my suitcase out there too." Both "Lady" and "Tonight" are radio-friendly songs, either on country stations or the adult "easy listening" stations becoming prominent as the World War II generation moved toward middle age and Dylan's approached thirty. *Nashville Skyline* is a far cry from the lengthy phantasmagorias of mid-sixties Dylan, as many of the songs recorded in Nashville seem almost like covers of popular songs. Indeed, Dylan, with his voice almost unrecognizable, became with this album a different recording artist, distancing himself from the work that had made his reputation. Recording covers of others' songs would be the default position for his next two projects as original songs were not flying off his pen.[2]

"THROW THAT MINSTREL BOY A COIN"

Nashville Skyline, with its more developed country sound, was not an anomaly in the music world even if it might be a surprise to Dylan's rock fans. The musicianship on the record is superb, and the songs, which lack for the most part the characteristic oddities of Dylan lyrics, are more accomplished as musical compositions. In his interview with *Sing Out!* in 1968, Dylan admitted that, were it not for contractual obligations, he might not "write down another song as long as I lived," a perhaps honest indication that he no longer had much to say (124). In part, this was due to his remove from the kinds of scenes that inspired his writing in favor of family life, his home, and a more relaxed, even retiring, pace; but it was also the case that he no longer seemed to identify with a particular audience. In turning from folk to rock, Dylan antagonized one audience, but found another eagerly waiting; the rock audience still embraced his music in the late 1960s, but he turned from its expectations without finding another ready audience. Country music in the United States had heavily policed borders. Recording in Nashville with Nashville session men did not make you "country." Even figures as veteran to the scene as Johnny Cash, Willie Nelson, and Waylon Jennings all experienced periods of ostracization for not hewing to the country music codes. All three became "outlaw" figures within country, and Dylan, from that point of view, was simply an outsider, even a poseur. Indeed, Dylan's next live appearance would be as the headliner at the Isle of Wight rock music festival in August 1969, which he played for the money and to escape Woodstock at the time of the "Peace, Love, and Music" festival.

Dylan's dalliance with country should be given some context. At Christmas 1968, Elvis Presley's "comeback special" for NBC aired, bringing into the living rooms of America a musical icon whose career had been reduced to mindless Hollywood fluff for years. The special was an eye-opener for those who, like Dylan, had admired Elvis in his early career. Elvis's return to glory included the release of *From Elvis in Memphis* in June 1969, a few months after *Nashville Skyline* and during the period when Dylan was working toward his next album. Meanwhile, Johnny Cash (like Presley one of the artists whose career had originated at Sun Studio in Memphis) produced two strong live albums recorded in prisons in 1968 and 1969 after years of middling studio recordings and landed a weekly television variety show on ABC, debuting in June 1969. On the first show, Dylan appeared as a guest, performing solo and with Cash. With psychedelia in retreat, 1968 also saw the debut of new musical artists such as Creedence Clearwater Revival, who combined elements of rock and country to produce a string of Top Forty hits, as well as Neil Young and Joni Mitchell, two new songwriters with distinctive voices and searching lyrics, and Gram Parsons, who made influential records that tapped the country roots of rock and roll, as did the early albums of The Band, the new name for Dylan's old backing band. Young, Mitchell, and CCR were all guests on *The Johnny Cash Show* in its first season. Parsons steered The Byrds toward country music on 1968's *Sweetheart of the Rodeo* and also, through his friendship with Keith Richards, played a part in The Rolling Stones' greater feel for country on the string of great LPs they produced from 1968 to 1972.

All of which is a way of saying that Dylan's next album might have been a crossover classic, as the rock vanguard and exciting new bands were embracing country, thus "catching up" to Dylan's records of 1967 and 1969. Instead, his idiosyncratic double LP called *Self Portrait* was not quite at home anywhere and would be for many the ugly duckling in Dylan's catalog. Derided on its release in June 1970, *Self Portrait* finds Dylan, a year shy of thirty and out of touch with rock, trying on the sappy arrangements of Easy Listening radio (including backup singers reminiscent of Elvis's Memphis LP), while also searching for the blues roots that fueled his best work. Given Dylan's statement to *Sing Out!*

that he was "content to play just anything I know" (124), it is not surprising that the album includes covers of some of his contemporaries: originals by Gordon Lightfoot and Paul Simon, as well as songs Joan Baez and Ian & Sylvia made popular. Some of the choices are curious—such as Dylan's duet with himself on Simon & Garfunkel's hit "The Boxer" (included on *Bridge Over Troubled Water*, the Grammy-winning Best Album of 1970 and the best-selling LP of 1970, 1971, and 1972)—as if Dylan were trying to show he could be both Simon *and* Garfunkel. The recording has to be among a handful of the most inept of Dylan's career—as Greil Marcus succinctly put it, "Jesus, is it awful" (*Dylan* 19). Middling as some of the studio work is, insult is added to injury with the cover of "Like a Rolling Stone" from the Isle of Wight concert, backed by The Band. There, Dylan flails his own legacy alive.

It would be hard to imagine someone performing the song with less feel for its dynamic. Dylan flubs lines in a laughable manner and seems to be groping for what the song might be saying. Only at the end of the last verse does he seem to get the song under control. As a live performance for those who were there, it may have been acceptable, particularly in the excitement of this rare appearance at a big outdoor festival in Britain that rivaled the giant Woodstock festival in New York that same month. Placed on the album as an official release (certainly the concert was bootlegged in any case), the song stands as an embarrassing contribution to the "self portrait." We might say, as Dylan himself has argued in *Chronicles*, that he was deliberately trying to estrange an audience that had become too invasive, too demanding, and too crazy (113–23). And yet there is no reason to think that he deliberately sang the song badly at the show. Rather, hearing the tape of the show, he chose it for inclusion on the album where it seems a send-up of whatever he once was. The irony is that this version was cheered by the audience. No "boos" as in 1966. You don't boo the newly risen messiah.

Self Portrait sparked controversy as the first album by Dylan that neither fans nor critics could admire. The sense of what Dylan "owes" his fans hung heavy over the reception of the album in its day. Today, the album is best seen in the light of Dylan's comments to Cameron Crowe in the mid-eighties: "a lot of stuff that was worse was appearing on bootleg records. So I just figured I'd put all this stuff together and put it out, my own bootleg record, so to speak" (21). As with any bootleg, official or otherwise, there is a range in quality—*Self Portrait* showcases the perils of Dylan's under-rehearsed, one-or-two-take method once he moves from his own songbook to others' tunes. Rather than drop what doesn't work, he elects to include it. Nothing on the album is burning to be released, though "Copper Kettle" and "Living the Blues" would have made a great single. Still, the album has its fascination, with throwaways like "Days of '49" (just short of definitive), "It Hurts Me Too" (which has the feel of some of the covers in the Woodstock recordings), and the novelty of Dylan as a middle-of-the-road Nashville singer: "Blue Moon," "I Forgot More Than You'll Ever Know," and "Take Me as I Am." The latter song, written by Boudleaux Bryant, can be heard as a wry comment to his disappointed fans: "If you cannot overlook my faults, forget me. / Take me as I am or let me go." As a "self portrait," the album presents a Dylan, somewhat lazy, somewhat foolish, even vain—the album seems like a quintessential vanity project—but it also shows him to be unpredictable as ever with, as they say, "his own way with a song." But Elvis's recent success with his Memphis album is instructive: key factors are the choice of material, the arrangements, and primarily the performances. Elvis reestablished his rock and roll, pop, and country credentials; Dylan seems to aim at a similiar range of styles. With an arranger and producer better able to adapt to Dylan's requirements than Bob Johnston proved to be, the album might have been more successful.

The year of *Self Portrait* is the year in which The Beatles broke up, with Paul McCartney announcing what was already a de facto split in April 1970. On May 8, Apple Records finally released the controversial and never satisfactorily completed "live in the studio" LP, *Let It Be*. It is worth noting that two of the most influential recording artists of the sixties, The Beatles and Dylan, did not manage to make the transition to the new decade unscathed. At least, the notion that both could do no wrong was diminished by the reception of these records. For The Beatles, it was the end as a group; the songwriting team of Lennon and McCartney went their separate ways and produced idiosyncratic, personal LPs in this period. For Dylan, the early seventies was a time of transition.

The day after *Self Portrait* was released, Dylan, despite misgivings, journeyed to Princeton University to receive an honorary doctorate. The event furnished him with a new song that would be included on the album he had begun before *Self Portrait* was finished and wrapped up in August. *New Morning*, released in October 1970, managed to rein-state Dylan in good critical graces. With its short and direct songs, the album is closer to *John Wesley Harding* in its feel, but the intervening work on *Nashville Skyline* and *Self Portrait* helped make Dylan's sing-ing voice a more expressive instrument. Singing some of the tracks with a cold gave Dylan's voice a husky, intimate quality. The mellifluous croon of *Skyline* and the Nashville songs on *Self Portrait* is gone, and the vocals are warm and expressive, never cloying.

The songs include "If Not For You," which ex-Beatle George Harri-son covered on his popular solo album *All Things Must Pass*; released in November 1970, Harrison's album remained number 1 on the U.S. chart for seven weeks early in 1971, showing the commercial command of "the quiet Beatle." Dylan's version of "If Not For You" did not chart and the songs on *New Morning*, for the most part, did not become part of Dylan's performing repertoire. In general, the songs showcase Dy-lan's vocals, and the album thrives on its understatement. "Day of the Locusts," inspired by the Princeton ceremony, is amusing in its comic touches: Dylan hopes the pieces of a young man's exploding head won't fall on him and sums up, "sure was glad to get out of there alive" with full-throated emphasis. On "Went to See the Gypsy," which has some of the compressed allegorical feel of *Harding*, Dylan quotes laconic di-alogue from an encounter (popularly regarded as an account of an al-leged brief meeting with Presley around this time that Dylan denies): "How are you? He said to me. I said it back to him." "If Dogs Run Free" is borderline doggerel (pun intended?) given a comic, "cool jazz cat" delivery, complete with scatting from Maeretha Stewart and a sotto voce "get it baby" from Dylan at the fade. The title track is uplifting with graceful background organ courtesy of Al Kooper, who did the lion's share of work on the album, complementing wonderfully Dylan's enthusiastic singing: "this must be the day when all of my dreams come true," he exults. "Sign on a Window" is possibly the best track on the album, as it seems almost off-the-wall enough for "basement tapes," but rather than being merely quizzical, it offers an end-of-youth reflection: "have a bunch of kids who'll call me Paw—that must be what it's all about." "Me Paw" rhymes charmingly with "Utah," as the singer ima-gines living out west, fishing from a stream.

New Morning, particularly with songs like the title track, "Locusts," "Time Passes Slowly," and "The Man in Me," creates a sense of idyllic pastoral. The singer on *New Morning* is not looking for "some kinda way out of here," but seems to have found a place where he belongs— "we walk beside rivers and sit beside fountains"—where, at album's end, he can reflect upon the "Father whom we most solemnly praise." Much of the spiritual striving of the sixties, which led some to drugs, some to various religious disciplines, some to psychological and sexual experimentation, and some to political causes and rallies, was in service of the ideal of "getting in touch with yourself," and Dylan would seem, with this album, and even with the off-beat and unprepossessing parts of *Self Portrait*, to show that he had "found himself" as a person who truly "has nothin' to live up to," and can, as the saying goes, "let it all hang out."

Deep in the grooves of what would be the last album of original Dylan songs for some time is a casual funkiness that Dylan had yet to explore, touched on by his backup singers who have more soul on this album than on *Self Portrait*. This is Dylan's album for the early seventies, which became known as a mellow, laid-back era up through mid-decade—indeed, two of the most popular soft-rock albums of the next year, James Taylor's *Sweet Baby James* and Carole King's *Tapestry*, capitalize on a demand for mellow tunes and gentle funk well beyond Dylan's ability to supply. In context and in retrospect, there is a nagging sense that Dylan, in not demanding more of himself, was failing himself as an artist.

"A FRIEND OF US ALL . . ."

"We've got Dylan back again!" Ralph Gleason proclaimed a bit prematurely in his review of *New Morning* for *Rolling Stone*. There were real fears of "losing" Dylan during his period as a housebound country squire. Meanwhile, during the spring and summer of 1970, dramatic events were occurring for the counterculture he had distanced himself from. While Dylan and George Harrison were recording together in early May, President Nixon's invasion of Cambodia caused a great public outcry and major protests, leading to the killing of four students at a demonstration at Kent State University on May 4, 1970. Neil Young, together with the band he had recently joined, Crosby, Stills & Nash, recorded an angry, powerful song, "Ohio," which hit the airwaves almost immediately. Dylan and Harrison could not have seemed more removed from such agitations—which continued with a march in Washington, DC, on May 9, of 100,000 against the war. The march took place the day after the final Beatles LP appeared, its title seeming to exhort their fans to turn aside from action and "let it be." Later that month, demonstrations at Jackson State University in Mississippi resulted in two students killed and twelve wounded.

A more indicative return of Dylan occurred the following year with his appearance at the benefit for war-torn and weather-beaten Bangladesh. The show was arranged in August 1971 by Harrison after learning from his friend, Bengali musician Ravi Shankar, of the plight of the country, at that time still fighting for independence from Pakistan. Bangladesh, still known as East Pakistan, had suffered the largest tropical cyclone on record in November 1970, and the government, situated in West Pakistan, responded inadequately. A declaration of independence—as Bangladesh—by the largely Bengal-speaking population of East Pakistan resulted in attempts at violent suppression by West Pakistan on March 26, 1971. Harrison hosted the concert to raise money for the country, making the concert the first rock benefit for a humanitarian cause.

Dylan's performance at the benefit at Madison Square Garden is featured on an entire side of the three LP records of the concert. Dylan took part for the first time in a "super group" collaboration, consisting of Harrison on guitar, former Beatle Ringo Starr on percussion, and Leon Russell on bass. The participation of Russell, a notable figure from his work with "the Wrecking Crew" (an assembly of musicians known for their excellent session work on numerous hits, to say nothing of his contribution as "band master" on Joe Cocker's grand "Mad Dogs and Englishmen" tour), ensured the quality of the performance, unlike the ramshackle show at the Isle of Wight.

"I'd like bring out a friend of us all, Mr. Bob Dylan," Harrison says by way of introduction and Dylan enters to thunderous applause. Positioned as the capstone of the concert, Dylan and company deliver as fine a performance as could be hoped for, with a set list resolutely in the sixties. Opening with a careful, slightly nervous version of "A Hard Rain's A-Gonna Fall," Dylan sets the tone of respectful revisiting. He does not reinvent the songs, but certainly shows himself fully in command of them. "It Takes a Lot to Laugh, It Takes a Train to Cry," from

Highway 61 Revisited follows, in a laidback version with Harrison's guitar highlighting the song's honky-tonk qualities. Then comes a rather upbeat, countrified "Blowin' in the Wind," with Dylan altering the sequence of verses, as was generally the case in live performance, to end with "too many people have died"—certainly the line most apropos for Bangladesh. Next, Dylan offers "Mr. Tambourine Man," with the opening line met by joyous approval from the audience and an attempt to clap along, as though the concert had become a hootenanny. Dylan clearly has his listeners in the palm of his hand. "Just Like a Woman," the final song of the set, is full of warm regard in comparison to the original recording, and the country overtones of the entire set show themselves to be compatible with every phase of Dylan's career. For Dylan fans, it was an encouraging performance, showing a mastery of the repertoire that might bode well for a return to live appearances.

The poor quality of much of *Self Portrait* must have undermined Dylan's belief in producer Bob Johnston. On *New Morning*, Dylan wisely brought in Al Kooper to help out and, in March 1971, made some recordings with Leon Russell as producer, yielding a single, "Watching the River Flow," that just missed the Top Forty in the United States. The song was used as the kick-off for Dylan's *Greatest Hits Vol. 2*, released in November 1971. That same month, Dylan returned to topical songwriting with "George Jackson," a song he composed quickly in response to the killing of Jackson, August 21, 1971, in Soledad prison during an attempted jailbreak. Jackson saw himself as a revolutionary, and his letters from prison, 1964 to 1970, were published as *Soledad Brother*. Some saw Dylan's newfound topicality to be insincere, but it should be noted that the news events that most often inspire his songwriting involve the killings of blacks (as in "Only a Pawn in Their Game") or injustice toward blacks (as in "Hurricane" in 1976) or both (as in "The Lonesome Death of Hattie Carroll").

Dylan's song creates a positive myth about Jackson, in the vein of "John Wesley Harding." "George Jackson" makes no mention of the violence that Jackson himself perpetrated, preferring to speak only of "his love" and the unfair circumstances of his death. While not detailed about Jackson, the song ends with a moral: "some of us are prisoners and some of us guards." The comment points to the dichotomy assumed among the song's listeners: either you side with the guards and choose to keep prisoners under lock and key, or you side with the prisoners and understand why they might choose violence and death to win their liberty.

The second *Greatest Hits* album, a double disc, is more interesting than the first as it includes songs not previously released, such as "When I Paint My Masterpiece" (a song recorded with Russell and covered successfully by The Band on their 1971 album *Cahoots*); "Tomorrow is a Long Time" in a very compelling live performance from 1963 (the song was covered by Rod Stewart on his great album *Every Picture Tells a Story*, released in May); and new recordings of three songs from the Woodstock demos: "I Shall Be Released" (covered by The Band on *Music from Big Pink*, sung by co-author Richard Manuel); "You Ain't Goin' Nowhere" (covered by The Byrds on *Sweetheart of the Rodeo*); and "Down in the Flood," recorded by Sandy Denny, a British folksinger and former lead vocalist of Fairport Convention, for her solo album released in September. The selection, compiled by Dylan himself, ignores his first and third LPs, with two tracks each from the second, fourth, fifth, eighth, and ninth LPs and one track each from the sixth, seventh, tenth, and eleventh. The selection from the tenth (*Self Portrait*) is the Isle of Wight version of "Quinn the Eskimo" which was a hit as "The Mighty Quinn" for Manfred Mann. The selections show an awareness of songs others made popular, such as "All I Really Want to Do," a hit for Cher, "Don't Think Twice, It's Alright," a hit for Peter, Paul, and Mary, and "All Along the Watchtower" which was the highest charting single in the United States for The Jimi Hendrix Experience. "If Not For You," included here, besides being featured on Harrison's successful *All Things Must Pass*, was also a hit for Olivia Newton-John in 1971 and the title of her debut LP. *Volume 2* is also notable for including reworkings of three songs from the Woodstock period, accompanied by Happy Traum, that take advantage of Dylan's strong vocal style in this period.

The two songs with Leon Russell are notable for their funky looseness, making one wish Dylan had recorded more songs in this lively style, complemented by Russell's trademark piano. Both songs cleverly investigate the notion that Dylan doesn't "have much to say" and is striving to produce "that masterpiece." "Watching the River Flow" looks askance at the contentment of the *New Morning* album, suggesting that Dylan is itching to find inspiration back in the city (Dylan moved back to Greenwich Village around the time), while "Masterpiece" takes us on a kind of picaresque journey reminiscent of "115th Dream" or, even more so, John Lennon's "Ballad of John and Yoko," to give us a cartoonish world where "newspapermen eating candy had to be held down by big police" and the singer is haunted by "train wheels rolling through the back of my memory." With a comic evocation of artistic struggles, Dylan, his voice hoarse and down-home, suggests he does not take criticism of his less-than-masterpiece-quality recordings too seriously. "Yup, someday ev'rything is gonna be diff'rint."

AUTHOR AND ALIAS

In 1964 Dylan, or more likely his agent Albert Grossman, accepted an offer from Macmillan for a book of original writings. The book was not expected to be a novel or collection of stories or even an autobiography. The assumption seemed to be that Dylan, recognized as "a poet" in some quarters, would produce a work of poetry. Dylan worked on the book between 1964 and 1966, writing in the disjunctive, associative method found on his liner notes for *Highway 61 Revisited* but, after his accident, chose not to complete or publish the work. As with much of his unreleased material, versions of the text were bootlegged and Dylan felt pressured to bring out an official copy, which appeared as *Tarantula* in 1971. With this somewhat fraught book, Bob Dylan became a published author of an artifact.

The text of *Tarantula* consists of short narratives or expositions at times reminiscent of the oddly oracular phrase making of Rimbaud's *Illuminations* or the stream-of-consciousness poetics favored by Lawrence Ferlinghetti and Allen Ginsberg. To such literary antecedents, Dylan brings a unique sense of verbal rhythm and improvised word play, based on spoken diction. The "prose poems," if they can be so called, are interspersed with brief missives from characters with names even more colorful than those used in Dylan's songs of the period. The song closest in tone to the book is "Tombstone Blues" with its jabs at popular culture, societal demands, fleeting references to people in an amorphous milieu and to literary figures and figures from the blues traditions, as well as asides on the alienated state of poetic logic in its freeform idiom. Occasionally, lines stand out with the force of commentary: "i have never taken my singing—let alone my other habits—very seriously—ever since then—i have just accepted it—exactly as i would any other crime" (108). Using idiosyncratic punctuation, capitalization, and spellings, the language of the book creates a texture that is recognizably Dylan's and the voice is at times funny, though mostly in the manner of a freakish carnival burlesque. Dylan's ear for phrases is the enlivening presence in the text, but literary coherence does not seem a desiderata of the project. In fact, the book is viewed best as an express experiment in how to use language to avoid making any kind of literal sense while remaining intelligible, much as specialized jargon and slang does.

The year ended with no album of new Dylan material, and none emerged in the following year. Dylan earned his first Grammy in 1973 for his participation in the *Concert for Bangladesh* album; in March the film of the concert put Dylan on movie screens around the world, and by November of that year he was on location with his family in Mexico, playing a small part in a film by maverick film director Sam Peckinpah. Dylan, who had not met with much success recording the songs of others and who seemed not eager—or able—to compose an album of new songs, turned his hand to a different kind of album. The soundtrack for the film, *Pat Garrett & Billy the Kid*, would be Dylan's only album of all-new material between 1970 and 1974.

Sam Peckinpah established himself as a major film director with *The Wild Bunch* (1969) and took on the directing duties of *Pat Garrett & Billy the Kid*, written by Rudolph Wurlitzer, to return to the genre that had made his name. Peckinpah was drawn into the film because James Coburn, a colleague/friend, had taken the part of Pat Garrett and wanted Peckinpah to direct. Peckinpah chose Kris Kristofferson, a singer-songwriter turned actor, as Billy the Kid. In addition to casting Kristofferson's wife, the singer Rita Coolidge, as Billy's woman, he accepted Hollywood novice Bob Dylan to write the film score. Dylan was also given a minor role in the film.

The film was fraught with problems endemic to the period. MGM's chief, James T. Aubrey, was hired to make the famed company, now an ailing remnant of the Hollywood studio system, solvent. Aubrey and Peckinpah clashed over the budget, the shooting schedule, and the release date of the film. The version of the film released to theaters in July 1973 was not the film Peckinpah made. Aubrey, as he had on other films, performed a hatchet job, cutting almost twenty minutes of screen time.

It is fair to say that the film's most enduring aspect, as originally screened, was Dylan's soundtrack. Recorded with his friends Bruce Langhorne and Roger McGuinn, the music Dylan creates has a dusty, jangling spurs feel to it and complements perfectly Peckinpah's elegiac film. The "End Theme," with flute and recorder played by Gary Foster, is particularly lovely—sinuous, moody, evoking the kind of twilight world that, in Peckinpah's vision, the life of the outlaw had become. The director creates a stark sense that the greatest is behind. Pat and Billy could once raise hell as they pleased, now the corporations are coming in—land grabbers, investors, men of commerce and vision. The outlaws gotta go. And so "they've hired Mr. Garrett to force you to slow down / Billy, don't it make you feel so low down / To be hunted by the man who was your friend?" That, in the nutshell of one of Dylan's lyrics, is the plot. Everything else on the screen is Peckinpah's slow dawdle to the inevitable showdown, following a circuitous path that allows him to capture lots of scenery, odd and interesting parts by great character actors, and quirky scenes such as Bob Dylan, wearing wire specs, reading aloud the labels of soup cans. Asked his name, Dylan's character delivers his best line: "Alias." "Alias what?" "Alias anything you please."

The soundtrack contains two songs with lyrics: the main song "Billy" (in three different versions on the LP) is in the form of direct address to Billy, now at the end of his rope, playing out his role as outlaw without much hope for any better outcome than that "gypsy queens will play your grand finale." The most telling perception the singer shares with Billy is that "they don't like you to be so free." The line certainly resonates with the career of its author: Dylan's changes in musical styles and in implied audience created a "they"—whether professional critics, fans (both current and former), or interested commentators—who at times feel affronted by his freedom to alter as he sees fit.

The other vocal song is "Knockin' on Heaven's Door," Dylan's first Top 40 hit since "Lay Lady Lay." No doubt the record-buying public was drawn to the moodiness of the song, with female backup singers adding a dirge-like sound. Though not delivered in "the voice of Dylan" per se, the song, when separated from the scenes of a dying sheriff, portrayed by Slim Pickens in the film, conveys a sense of looking back at the already retrospectively understood "sixties": "mama, take this badge offa me, I can't wear it any more / It's getting dark, too dark to see / I feel I'm knockin' on heaven's door." It sounds as though the singer is divesting himself of a persona. And perhaps it is not too much of a stretch to find in the words—"put my guns in the ground, I can't shoot them any more"—a statement of the mood of the United States as it withdrew, defeated, from military involvement in the Vietnam War in August 1973.

The previous November, Richard M. Nixon won a landslide victory in his bid for reelection as president, riding a wave of popularity and demonstrating that his sense of what he called "the Silent Majority" was far more powerful in American politics than the fragmented issues of the counterculture, New Left, and special interest groups—each a minority voice lacking in consensus and political clout. If a final knell for the sixties, as an ideal and as a political hope, were needed, the rout of well-meaning South Dakota liberal George McGovern should do. The defeated elegy for outlaw Billy the Kid matched the chastened mood of the period for those whose hopes for the sixties had been crushed.

Dylan appeared on movie screens in 1972 and 1973 in two very different guises. In *Concert for Bangladesh*, he appeared as himself, a popular, almost legendary performer of a handful of songs; in *Pat Garrett & Billy the Kid*, he appeared as a minor character in a story about a legend of the Old West. Perhaps both roles were fictive, each in its own way. With his two-record summary of his recording career, publication of a sixties artifact like *Tarantula*, and in 1973 his collected lyrics in *Writings & Drawings of Bob Dylan*, there were suddenly a lot of Dylans to take in, some more enduring than others but ultimately none who Dylan really was at the moment. In music, there was a tendency to look for "new Dylans": younger songwriters who would be all too happy to stand in the shoes that he once wore. The most significant was a songwriter from New Jersey named Bruce Springsteen, signed to Columbia by John Hammond. Springsteen, who released his first album and its follow-up in 1973, had no claims to being Dylan "the folk conscience," but he did write "skipping reels of rhyme" on his first LP. Springsteen soon showed enough gifts of his own—including a better sense of radio rock and roll than Dylan ever demonstrated and a feel for the "strut-your-stuff" aspects of rock—to be more than a derivative. While Dylan seemed eager to shed whatever duties "the old Dylan" might be supposed to meet, there were artists coming up who were indebted to him for creating a context in which rock wordsmiths could thrive, and who were capable of surpassing, if not his former greatness, than at least his current status.

That status was both impaired and improved at this time. Dissatisfied with Columbia now that Clive Davis had retired as president, Dylan signed with up-and-coming impresario David Geffen at Asylum Records—conceived as an "asylum" for significant musical artists where they would be nurtured rather than exploited. The publicity for Dylan's first LP for Asylum included the announcement of his first U.S. tour since 1965. In retaliation at Dylan's defection, Columbia immediately released, in November 1973, an album simply called *Dylan*. Often considered the worst LP in Dylan's catalog, the album consists of outtakes from the sessions for *Self Portrait* and *New Morning* and could be said to be an "official bootleg": releasing, without Dylan's participation, material not intended for release. The album is nonetheless notable for the odd assortment of songs it collects and because Dylan's performance of songs like "Mr. Bojangles," a hit for the Nitty Gritty Dirt Band, and "The Ballad of Ira Hayes," a long-time favorite of Johnny Cash's, better his attempt at "The Boxer" on *Self Portrait*.

The move to Asylum indicated Dylan was not simply existing in a twilight world as an "oldie." With the reelection of Nixon and the end of the Vietnam War, it was clear that "the sixties" were truly over. Returning at such time to a more public, viable presence, Dylan, as a forthcoming song would phrase it, was "back in the rain."

NOTES

1. Heylin makes the case that Dylan expected the duets with Cash to comprise more of the album, but the results of their session on February 18, with at least fifteen songs recorded, were all less acceptable than "Girl" (1995, 76).

2. The sessionographies published in Clinton Heylin's *The Recording Sessions (1960–1994)* make clear the extent to which Dylan's next two projects were exploratory, searching for material suitable to his new voice, persona, and approach.

5

BACK IN THE RAIN
(1974–1978)

Even the President of the United States sometimes must have to stand naked.
—"It's Alright, Ma (I'm Only Bleeding)," *Before the Flood* (1974)

The above line—from a song first performed live in 1964 and then released on Dylan's fifth album—does not refer to any particular president. The line simply reminds the listener that even "the most powerful man on earth," as the U.S. president has been called, is at times naked like any other person. The idea is not so different from the old adage that everyone puts on pants one leg at a time. The statement is a homey truth, a deflating of power and reputation and influence, those things that make some people seem like gods to others. In that regard, the phrase "President of the United States" could be changed to "Ruler of the British Empire," without changing the meaning. And yet the line singles out the president of the United States as perhaps the person whose nakedness, for United States citizens, might be most surprising or most humbling.

For Dylan's audiences on his tour from January into February 1974, when the song was performed as part of the solo acoustic set, the idea of the nakedness of the president was construed as a direct reference to Richard M. Nixon. Since the previous summer, the Senate investigation into the president's part in the cover-up of wrongful acts of political sabotage, known as "the Watergate scandal," had gotten closer to making charges against Nixon. Much contention at the time was over "the White House tapes," covert recordings of conversations between Nixon and his closest advisors. On February 6 (the night Dylan and The Band played Denver), the House of Representatives voted to proceed with the investigation of possible impeachment proceedings against Nixon. Transcripts of some of the tapes were released in March, and the charges for Nixon's impeachment were named in July. Nixon resigned in August, 21 months after winning election by the fourth largest popular vote margin in U.S. history.

In 1974, Dylan's words seemed to express the political nakedness of one particular president, who resigned—at risk of being stripped of—his title, his office, and his duties. The line's meaning might have been better written at the time, as "And finally the President of the United States has to stand naked." Taken in that sense, the line received much applause and hooting when sung on tour.

There is another facet to the line: not only are all persons sometimes naked, but stripping away what cloaks us reveals something more essential, more vulnerable. In the period 1974–1978, Dylan himself became more "naked"—in this sense—than ever before.

BOB DYLAN AND THE BAND

Looking back on 1974 and his first tour in eight years, Dylan, speaking twelve years later, admitted to Toby Creswell of *Rolling Stone* (Australia) that he felt he "had to step into Bob Dylan's shoes for that tour" (241). The statement suggests how much Dylan, in the seventies, was still considered something of "a symbol" who, it might be supposed, would not mount a tour unless he had something particular to convey. In that year when the tide turned against Nixon, a politician who seemed to represent everything the leftist counterculture reviled, a tour by a "firebrand" of the sixties might seem a celebration for those who had been organizing against and protesting Nixon's policies since he took office in 1969, to say nothing of the Old Left who had suffered under him as Vice President. Perhaps it was time for retrospect on the political passions of the fifties and sixties.

For others, Dylan was not a seer or a political figure but rather a once influential songwriter who had been taking it easy, not demanding much from himself or his listeners. As a recording artist, Dylan commanded an impressive career of eleven studio albums, two compilations comprising three LPs, and most recently a major motion picture soundtrack that featured his highest charting single since 1969. Yet the "Bob Dylan myth" was such that fans must wonder what Dylan might accomplish next. The fact that the world—particularly the reach and influence of the music industry—had changed since 1966 should also be factored into how the "myth" was viewed in 1974. There was a shortage of heroes of any type at the time, and in America artistic heroes are always in short supply. As a recording artist, Dylan might still have great work ahead of him. Then again, it might be enough simply to remind his old listeners and convince new listeners that he had command of a repertoire still able to express the hopes and fears, joys and tears of their collective condition. The tour was a test of whether or not songs written and recorded over the previous dozen years still held up.

The Band, the collective name for the musicians—Robbie Robertson, Levon Helm, Rick Danko, Richard Manuel, and Garth Hudson—who (except for Helm) had backed Dylan on his tours in 1966, had become quite successful in their own right and not simply as Dylan's sidemen. *Rock of Ages*, a double album recorded at their show on New Year's Eve 1971 at the Academy of Music in New York, was released in 1972 and established them on record as an impressive live act. Touring with The Band was no longer simply a case of Dylan hitting the road with a backing band. The Band had command of a sound and repertoire uniquely their own, which might or might not be the best possible sound for Dylan's return to the stage. Certainly, neither Dylan nor the musicians were the same as they were in 1966. This time, The Band offered sets of their own material in addition to backing Dylan on his. Dylan also continued his practice of a solo acoustic set, received as one of the more riveting aspects of the show.

The tour of Bob Dylan and The Band kicked off on the third day of 1974, and ran to the middle of February, with thirty shows in twenty-one cities. Released a few weeks after the tour began, *Planet Waves* was Dylan's first album of all original material, apart from the film soundtrack, since 1970's *New Morning*. The cover drawing by Dylan depicts a trio of heads, done in the characteristic blocky lines of the drawings in *Writings & Drawings*, with symbols—an anchor, a heart, a peace sign on the lower right, and a trapezoidal shape above it—and inscriptions:

"moonglow" on the left, "torch songs & cast-iron ballads" on the right. The album also features Dylan's handwritten prose on an inside sleeve. The album cover, with the use of Dylan's art printed on textured paper to appear handmade, suggested a continuity with *Music from Big Pink*, The Band's first album, which featured a Dylan painting on the cover, and Dylan's own *Self Portrait*, which also featured a Dylan painting, ostensibly a self-portrait. The implication was that the new album, in reuniting Dylan and The Band, was a return to the version of Americana that both had been engaging in from 1967–1970.

Indeed, the main strength of the album is provided by the textures The Band brings to Dylan's songs that never let the proceedings turn mawkish (always a danger for Dylan's albums of domestic content- ment). The up-tempo numbers swing, the slow songs bristle, and the album's best-known track, "Forever Young," is presented in two ver- sions, both slow and stately and fast and loose, highlighting The Band as accompanists. Though they provide no tunes, no co-writing, and minor backing vocals, The Band is anything but session men. Their instrumen- tation lends Dylan's new songs the group's characteristic blend of coun- try, rockabilly, R&B, rock and roll, and their own elusive brand of musical folklore. The album feels like survivors' music, created to ac- knowledge a new lease on life.

"On a Night Like This," the single, would not have been out of place on *New Morning*, except that the theme of return is unmistakable: "we have much to talk about and much to reminisce," Dylan sings with fresh vitality, kicking off the album. Ostensibly a song of a man revisiting a lover, "to heat up some coffee grounds" and cuddle and coo on a snow- swept night, the song aims to sweep Dylan's audience off its feet as well, to catch them up in the excitement of a collaboration between Dylan and The Band, after all these years.

The next song, "Going, Going, Gone," takes the mood in a very different direction; full of dark foreboding, the song reflects on a life on the edge, lived in restless strife—Robertson's guitar, in its needling jabs, conveys an unsettling sting. "Gone," with its threat of a wished-for disappearance, announces the duality of the album: on the one hand, a warm invitation to share in Dylan's revitalized presence; on the other, a warding off of his fans' intrusions and attachments that have long been an aspect of Dylan's public life.

"Tough Mama" is a standout example of both strains combined: the song addresses a "sweet goddess," "tough mama," and "dark beauty" with a litany of observations including dismissive phrases like "I ain't hauling any of my lambs to the marketplace any more," and "I gained some recognition but I lost my appetite." The lyrics recall the imaginative tributes to women found in "Love Minus Zero" or "She Belongs to Me" though Dylan's new maturity of address admits the thrill of the contemporary female. The rockabilly flavor is funkier than anything Dylan has previously committed to record, extending the riff-rock common to the first three electric albums via the virtuoso interplay of The Band, with Robertson's jaunty guitar work complemented by the swirling, at times regal, organ playing of Garth Hudson, matched by Dylan's expressive harmonica before the final coda.

Four of the songs on the album are love songs that depart from the more formulaic odes to contentment or loss that dominated *Nashville Skyline* and *New Morning*, though there are some similarities. "You Angel You" is similar to "If Not For You" in its tone of affectionate tribute, but here there is a more casual humor: "the way you walk and the way you talk—I feel I could almost sing," Dylan deadpans, while the most ringing line—"I just want to watch you talk with your memory of my mind"—might aim at those who would like to believe they understand Dylan's motives better than he does himself. "Something There Is About You" celebrates a woman with its exuberant delivery, while its more involved lyric contains references to the past, with Dylan speaking of "the phantoms of my youth," and recalling the Great Lakes region of "Old Duluth." As with *New Morning*, which references "that little Minnesota town" on "Went to See the Gypsy," *Planet Waves* seems to revisit the North Country Dylan hails from. The lovely opening line of "Never Say Goodbye" evokes the beauty of a wintery landscape: "Twilight on the frozen lake / A new dawn about to break / On footprints in the snow / The silence down below." More a sketch than anything, "Goodbye" probably made the cut because of the passion in Dylan's vocals which, here and throughout the album, attain a bracing expressivity. "Hazel" is another track without standout lyrics that manages to be strong due to Dylan's tense and vulnerable delivery. Now in his thirties, Dylan sings like a man who might find dismay in being smitten by a younger woman. As with "Tough Mama," the women referenced on *Planet Waves* extend beyond the generic types addressed on *Nash-*

ville Skyline and the more settled version of romance on *New Morning*. Dylan has aged, and desire for women now takes on a more furtive and plaintive dimension.

Two songs on *Planet Waves* further convey Dylan's maturation: "Forever Young," addressed to his children, shows a father's concern. The song's implications are notable: Dylan, who had been associated with the youth movements of the previous decade, here speaks as an elder, seemingly from the heart: "may God bless and keep you always / May your wishes all come true." The sentiments may be banal, but for that very reason they seem unusually heartfelt, and, characteristic of Dylan, there is a tendency to include wishes not so confident: "may you have a strong foundation when the winds of changes shift." The wish for a strong foundation might indicate a certain conservatism, but the acknowledgment of change shows an awareness that whatever might seem certain in 1974 may not be so for long. There is also a certain irony to the notion of remaining "forever young"—as if an entire generation might be frozen in place, unable to grow up. The song receives two performances: closing the album's first side, the song is almost melancholy in tone, with the phrase "forever young" drawn out and repeated twice and the full refrain "may you stay forever young" taking on a somewhat wounded lyricism. With so much repetition, the song begins to seem an elegiac incantation of eternal youth. Opening the second side, the song is transformed into a light and youthful rockabilly version with no refrain, a casual, off-the-cuff benediction.

The other revealing song for Dylan's current state of mind is the closer, "Wedding Song," which captures a sense of married life with an unusually personal intonation. "You gave me babies, one two three, what's more you saved my life," Dylan sings, and there can be no doubt that he is addressing his own wife, Sara, and attesting to the centrality of their love in his life. But the song is not simply a tribute; rather, it lays out the complexity of enduring commitment: "eye for eye and tooth for tooth / Your love cuts like a knife." The yoking of the language of biblical justice with the notion that love can be a weapon is certainly striking, as is Dylan's claim that they were born to be together, and that he can never let her go. Such passionate declarations make the song seem a different kind of protest song. What Dylan seems to be protesting is the fact that married love changes, and that the relationship may no longer be as strong and faultless as it was nearly a decade before when it began. Statements such as "it's never been my duty to remake the world at large / Nor is it my intention to sound the battle charge," and the final line, "I love you more than ever now that the past is gone," reiterate his commitment to the life they have together, but, in gesturing at his public self, well remembered by fans ready to embrace him anew, Dylan at least partly undercuts his contentment. The song was performed several times in concert during the solo acoustic set where its strident claims sounded all the more wishful in the midst of a public appearance.

The standout song on the album may be unknown to casual Dylan listeners: "Dirge" is a stark and riveting performance as Dylan bangs out his characteristic rhythmic piano and Robbie Robertson provides incisive acoustic guitar lines. The lyrics are some of Dylan's most surprisingly dismissive, without the humor that marks the address to Mr. Jones in "Ballad of a Thin Man," or the sympathy in "Like a Rolling Stone." In "Dirge" the person addressed is more shadowy—a figure the singer hates himself for loving, "and the weakness that it showed"; the love is something to be repudiated, though the entire song tries to spell out the hard course that this form of love takes. "Can't recall a useful thing you ever did for me / 'Cept pat me on the back one time when I was on my knees"—such lines at times indicate, as with "Dear Landlord," that the addressee is someone whose power over the singer is resented, even as the singer fights to state his case: "I've paid the price of solitude but at least I'm out of debt." The final verse shows Dylan has not lost his tendency to shift into summation: "So sing your praise of progress and of the doom machine / The naked truth is still taboo whenever it can be seen." The cynicism of the lyrics is unusual for Dylan, almost a pose, one might say, but if so the delivery, as if through gritted teeth, indicates real pain in the position the song expresses. In its vague if forceful denunciations, "Dirge" does not spare either the addresser or the addressee—a tactic that will be noticeable in some of Dylan's most fully realized songs of the seventies.

Planet Waves' main demerit is that it fails to be as cohesive as *New Morning*. But for "Dirge" and "Wedding Song," the second side is slight. The album's main strength is that Dylan has not sounded so vital nor so engaged by the darker edges of his persona since 1966–1967. Because it would be superseded by his subsequent studio album, recorded at the end of 1974, it is easy to overlook *Planet Waves*, but it should be stressed that the album, on its release, attested to a resurrected power in Dylan's singing, while his writing gave reminders of former greatness.

In the interim since Dylan's last tour, rock music had sustained some significant losses, most notably Jimi Hendrix and Janis Joplin in 1970 and The Doors' volatile lead singer Jim Morrison in 1971. With the disbanding of The Beatles, the mantle of British Invasion–era rock was shared by The Rolling Stones, who generated much press with a major U.S. tour in 1972, and The Who, who played extensive tours of the United States regularly in the early seventies. Rock by 1974 was still dominated by a few bands who had begun their recording careers in the sixties: hard rock bands such as Led Zeppelin, who, along with British bands known for "prog-rock"—a type of rock music fused with classical mannerisms to produce long, sprawling works—such as Yes, Emerson, Lake & Palmer, and Jethro Tull were at the height of their popularity with younger listeners. Pink Floyd released *Dark Side of the Moon* in March of 1973, one of the albums most readily identifiable with the period. With its mellow arrangements, prolonged guitar and sax solos, and dreamy ambience, the album created a textured "soft rock" sound while its lyrics looked askance at the world of the high-profile rock star as well as at a larger cultural malaise of meaningless activity in the name of "Money" (an FM radio staple from the LP) and of slogans masquerading as ideas. The album was also to some extent an elegy for the period of creative ferment in rock that was the late sixties.

During Dylan's hiatus from recording, in the period 1971–1973, a new crop of singer-songwriters had risen to prominence: Jackson Browne, Elton John, Carole King, Joni Mitchell, Van Morrison, Carly Simon, Paul Simon, Cat Stevens, James Taylor, and Neil Young had all released albums that established them as songwriters able to articulate the subjective states of their listeners. In that same period, a new style of music was enjoying a vogue. Generally called "glam-rock," its most notable practitioner was the British songwriter and charismatic performer David Bowie, who had created a distinct musical persona with chortling vocals, cranked-up guitar riffs, and flamboyant costumes. Bowie included a "Song to Bob Dylan" on his 1971 LP *Hunky Dory*, much as Dylan had composed a "Song to Woody" on his debut LP. Bowie addresses "Robert Zimmerman" to tell him about a "strange, young man called Dylan" who has seemingly lost his way. "Give us back our family / Give us back our unity," the song rather stridently cries, as though the "we" of the song were Dylan's dependents. The song articulates the feeling that an early hero, a leader who "taught them how they saw," had stepped aside. By 1974, Bowie had become a media sensation in his own right, inspiring rock shows to become more theatrical.

Upon its release, *Planet Waves* ranked number 1 on *Billboard*'s rock music charts for four weeks, the first album by Dylan to achieve that spot in the United States and indicative of David Geffen's effort to promote Dylan as a contemporary rather than a throwback. The four weeks the LP stayed at number 1 were the four weeks during which the tour brought Dylan, dutifully supporting his new album like any other mid-seventies rock act, to various major U.S. cities. The tour was a tremendous commercial success in its own right, and most of the response from fans and critics was laudatory. On *Before the Flood*, the double album recorded mostly at the final concerts in Los Angeles, the enthusiasm of the crowd is audible, and there is a strong sense of presence and a range of associations called up by each song.

On tour, Dylan the "protest singer" is least in evidence—"Blowin' in the Wind" and "The Times, They Are A-Changin'" were the main songs covered from his earliest period, and on *Flood*, the former, accompanied by The Band, sounds more uplifting than when done solo but also more caustic, with the "how many years" before a man becomes free now including, one assumes, the decade plus one since the song became popular. A previously acoustic song like "It Ain't Me Babe" becomes a rave-up, filled with a new exuberance also found in other "put-down songs" such as the jubilant encore "Like a Rolling Stone," and the song that opens the album, "Most Likely You'll Go Your Way (and I'll Go Mine)," with Dylan throwing out "I just can't do what I done before" as a challenge.

Most of the performances ring various changes on the "old Dylan." The calliope tones of "Ballad of a Thin Man" have been exchanged for synthesizer bleats (the instrument of choice for every arena rock band of the era), while Dylan drags out the name of his nemesis "Mr. Johones" as if the character has long since become a joke. "Lay Lady Lay," far from being mellow and seductive, reveals a plaintive urgency, with a country yodel on "when he's standing in front of you-who-who." The easy-going, throwaway vocals on "Rainy Day Women #12 & 35" feel ad-libbed and the chorus of "everybody must get stoned" more celebratory than ever, as it was a given that a veil of marijuana smoke hung in the rafters by concert's end. "Knockin' on Heaven's Door" gains an extra verse and is one of the newer songs that can hold its own with certified classics—Dylan closed the first set with it throughout the tour.

The least successful aspect of the live album is that Dylan's mannered vocals, in their various swoops, hollers, and cartoonish overemphasis, are not easy to like. Certainly these are not reverential deliveries. Though one misses the elastic whine of mid-sixties Dylan, one is spared the capricious gargle of the Isle of Wight shows. The tour has been discussed retrospectively as little more than packaged performances to meet contractual demands. That may have been the case to some extent, but the sound Dylan and The Band created together, if not as innovative as the 1966 tour, can't be confused with any other version of rock practiced at the time, and no songwriter could compress so much of such a varied career into one concert, with songs that, as with "It's Alright, Ma," could step undimmed from the time they were first sung into the present. The best thing about *Before the Flood* is that it shows Dylan enduring and evolving as a performer. And The Band's skill at creating musical textures in large theaters and sports arenas gives the songs a rollicking power that shows how well rockabilly and rock can fuse.

"SINGING THROUGH THESE TEARS"

Bob and Sara Dylan divorced in 1977, a biographical detail that draws attention to the fact that Dylan's songwriting from 1974 to 1978 engages with emotional upheavals in the volatile marriages of the period. The relevance of songs of romantic disruption would not be lost on Dylan's audience, many of whom found their personal relationships in jeopardy and undergoing change. Divorce among those born in the 1940s increased significantly over its incidence in the previous generation. One figure states that 50 percent of white women who married in the late sixties and early seventies eventually divorced, as opposed to 14 percent of white women who married in the 1940s. Divorce increased 40 percent from 1970 to 1975, with peaks in 1979 and 1981. By focusing on the theme of male-female relations, Dylan becomes a different sort of spokesperson for his generation. The notes of conservation sounded on *Planet Waves* ("may you stay forever young") and of commitment ("and if there is eternity I'll love you there again") become more poignant in light of the "flood" of songs that followed, amounting to a sweeping away of the contentment of 1970's *New Morning*. The contemporary view of the thirty-something man toward a woman able to start again on her own is perhaps best encapsulated in the resentful lines on *Blood on the Tracks*: "And I'm back in the rain / And you are on dry land / You made it there somehow / You're a big girl now."

It would be a mistake to see *Blood on the Tracks*, recorded in New York in mid-September and, in part, re-recorded in Minneapolis in late December 1974, as concerned primarily with the Dylans' marital relations. The lines quoted above, directly addressing "you," as is often the case with Dylan songs about women, can be extrapolated to many situations. Featuring Dylan's best lyrics since *John Wesley Harding*—often surpassing the latter with surprising imagery closer to his peak in the mid-sixties—*Blood on the Tracks*, released in January 1975, is one of Dylan's best albums. In many ways, it revisits the terrain of *Blonde on Blonde*, with each song addressed to a woman, or concerned with a woman, or telling a story in which a woman or women feature prominently. As with *Blonde on Blonde*, the focus should not be on whether or not Dylan is charting his own personal relationships, but rather on how its ten songs, like *John Wesley Harding*'s dozen, amount to a single statement.

Blood on the Tracks, we might say, is an album that only someone concerned with the nuances of passionate love would write, and that anyone fascinated by the many ways that eros is manifested in song would appreciate. *Planet Waves* was the "welcome back" album, establishing Dylan's new perspective on the time: wary, more mature, able to express contentment and unease, able to be glib and expansive as well as full of dark foreboding, able to address his children and his wife, and even his past, to some extent. *Blood on the Tracks* shows us an artist truly worth coming back for: to hear the stabs at clarity and confusion, myth and misery, that Dylan confronts so memorably in these songs. Dylan had matured greatly since creating *John Wesley Harding*, and *Blood on the Tracks* shows an ability to tell stories with a prose writer's detachment. Dylan has said he was reading a good deal of Chekhov and Conrad in this period, and a grasp of detail as part of a story, not simply as background, is telling in almost every song on the album.

The album begins with "Tangled Up in Blue." Released as a single, it remains one of Dylan's most certain crowd-pleasers in concert. It's easy to understand why: the song provides a fairly straightforward though somewhat elliptical narrative—with both retrospective and current perspectives—of a love affair that still has hopes for the future. More than almost any previous song of Dylan's, "Tangled Up in Blue" has the feel of a convincing story. Of course, few of the details in the song have anything to do with Dylan's own biography, but the song creates a sense of someone "like" Dylan in his attitudes and responses. When he sits silently while a waitress in a "topless place" "bends down to tie the laces of my shoe," we can easily imagine Dylan in the scene—perhaps even more so when she "opened up a book of poems and handed it to me." Can we imagine Dylan "working for a while on a fishingboat right outside of Delacroix"? Perhaps not, but that's not the point. The point is that Dylan manages to take on the persona of a Kerouackian knockabout, a man who lives to be "on the road, heading for another joint," and who can't understand what the people he used to know have done with their lives (a jab at the settled accomplishments of those who, in one way or another, failed to live up to their earlier ambitions). The song encapsulates not only distinct phases in the love affair between the singer and a red-haired woman, but recreates with feeling the times they lived through.

The song plays with the sense that, for many who came of age in the sixties, life had taken on a tenaciously retrospective nature. Some of the phrases—"music in the cafes at night and revolution in the air"—jump with a sense of the cultural moment that many of Dylan's listeners lived through and, by the mid-seventies, had processed into a personal myth. "Tangled Up in Blue" speaks of the still-unsettled searcher, at the song's opening, "lying in bed, wondering if she'd changed at all," and at the close "going back again," trying to "get to her somehow." The "her" is a woman he loved in those fabled times, back when "her folks" predicted their "life together sure was gonna be rough." After helping her out of an ill-fated marriage, he splits up with her, since they "drove that car as far as they could," and then pursues a series of odd jobs, trying to forget her but unable to do so. Next, we have a flashback to his first meeting with her, while she was working as a waitress and married. The singer "lived with them on Montague Street in a basement down the stairs." The ménage à trois, if that's what it was, fell apart when "he started in to dealin' with slaves," and "she had to sell everything she owned and froze up inside." Our hero can only "keep on keepin' on" and, bringing us up to date, tells us he is going to find her again. The final lines: "we always did feel the same, we just saw it from a different point of view, tangled up in blue" resonate beyond the story we've been told and seem to include us in the feelings and the points of view it expresses so elliptically. The "one who got away," in the past, becomes a figure for the ideals that disappeared or for unfulfilled hopes for love or accomplishment. The singer reaffirms what he felt in the past, but we can't know what possible rapprochement he can have now with the girl he split up with, while she asserted "we'll meet again someday on the avenue."

The next song, "Simple Twist of Fate," is another concert staple, and, like "Tangled Up in Blue," has been performed with significant changes in lyrics, including alterations in the person of the song—sometimes first person, sometimes third. As it appears on the album, the song is in the third person—"they sat together in the park," it begins—until the final verse when the singer speaks in the first person: "People tell me it's a sin to know and feel too much within / I still believe she was my twin. . . ." The shift is striking; like the temporal changes in "Tangled Up in Blue," the change in person brings us into a statement of the singer's present position. We can consider the story of the man and woman in the park, then in the old hotel, and finally separate, as "he hunts her down by the waterfront docks," as moments from the singer's past. The change in person lets us feel, existentially we might say, the distance between the narrated events and the current perspective: "I was born too late." We might recall the parable-like quality of "The Ballad of Frankie Lee and Judas Priest," except that until the last verse the story in "Simple Twist" seems straightforward. We start with a scene somewhat like the end of Michelangelo Antonioni's L'Avventura: a scene of a man and woman unable to communicate. Though having passion for one another, they face a gulf that can't be bridged. They go to a hotel and the woman leaves while the man sleeps—we assume after sex, with Dylan employing the old movie technique of a cutaway from the preamble of lovemaking to the aftermath. But certain images draw attention to themselves, breaking the fabric of the story's realism. The heat of the night hits the man "like a freight / Train moving with a simple twist of fate." It's a complicated notion, not only that heat is somehow like a train but also that the train/heat moves like fate.

"Simple Twist" is haunting because its story feels like a movie we may have seen, and yet we also wonder if we've ever experienced a story in this way. The most telling example of the complex concision of the song is in the scene when the woman walks alone through the streets (having left the man in the room) and hears a saxophone "somewhere far off," then drops "a coin into the cup / Of another blindman at the gate." Between these two details, which may be continuous if the blind man is also the saxophonist, meaning that she has walked all the way to where the saxophone is being played, is the line: "while the light burst through a beat-up shade where he was waking up." It's a brilliantly compressed staggering of four cuts, as in a film: the saxophone playing; the woman walking; the man waking; the coin falling into the cup. But Dylan goes further: "another blindman at the gate" refers to the recipient of the woman's actual charity on the street, but the sense extends to the "coin" of sexual charity she had dropped into the "cup" of the man in the room. Or, to sexualize the image the other way, her gesture mirrors the "coin" he dropped into her "cup"—and not only as sexual figures, for the "coin" may be her payment, if, as seems possible by the fact that he later seeks her by the waterfront "where the sailors all come in," she is a prostitute. In any case, the "blindman" is also a figure for the man in the song who can't quite see how fate is playing with him in the guise of a woman he feels drawn to and even related to, at least in a spiritual sense.

As with "Tangled Up in Blue," which returns to the title phrase to end each verse, "Simple Twist" keeps returning to its title. The two songs share then a recurring invocation somewhat abstract or metaphysical: "blue," "fate." What does it mean to be "tangled up in blue"? We might assume that the eyes of the woman in the song are blue and so the man in the song is entangled in blue as her emblem, but her eyes are never mentioned directly. And even if her eyes are the inspiration for the blue in the song, blue takes on a dimension of its own, as having almost the ability to act. In "Simple Twist," "fate" becomes even more active. And so the two songs present us with lovers at the mercy of "blue" and "fate," qualities they can feel or experience, but not control.

"You're a Big Girl Now" is not as lyrically complex as the first two songs, but is made distinctive by one of the album's best vocals. Dylan milks every line for maximum feeling, demonstrating that the years between his youth and his mid-thirties has added to his ability to express the hurt and distress of real emotion. For all the power of an early song like "House of the Rising Sun" or the searching delivery of "Tomorrow Is a Long Time," Dylan here shows off his voice as a unique instrument. Listen to the verse about the bird sitting on a fence, "singing a song for me at his own expense." His delivery of the lines, "I'm just like that bird, singing just for you . . . through these tears," captures the emotional cost of the song. The "blood" on these "tracks" flows from a wounded heart. The singer is "back in the rain"—recalling "tonight as I stand inside the rain" in "Just Like a Woman"—indicating a state of psychic discomfort, of emotional flux, while the woman is "on dry land," "a big girl" "in somebody's room." The feeling of outrage is muted by a strong suggestion that the situation was inevitable—fated.

The major song on side 1, in terms of length and complexity, is "Idiot Wind," a revelatory account of blame and praise, of self-assertion and self-deprecation, its stringent asides filtered through a whirlwind of emotion, cataloguing an affair where "I kiss goodbye to howling beasts on the borderline which separated you from me." Dylan's pen is inspired on this song, calling up phrases that ring with invective—"you're an idiot, babe, it's a wonder that you still know how to breathe"—and outraged claims—"I haven't known peace and quiet for so long I can't remember what it's like." The song may be the ultimate put-down song, with the refrain referring to a woman as "an idiot" and pointing out how an "idiot wind" blows through all aspects of their life together, and even from "the Grand Coulee Dam to the Capitol," referencing the idiotic political culture of the United States, and recalling one of the Guthrie songs Dylan sang at the tribute concert after his mentor's death.

As a passionate self-defense, "Idiot Wind" is at times overblown: "you'll never know the hurt I've suffered nor the pain I rise above." Along the way, the song throws out odd bits of imagery, eschewing a coherent narrative or system of symbols, with a "lone soldier on a cross," a priest in black "who sat stone-faced as the building burned," "visions of your chestnut mare," and perhaps one of the best lines: "one day you'll be in the ditch, flies buzzing around your eyes, blood on your saddle." The stridency of the vocal provides much of the guts of *Blood on the Tracks*; no previous Dylan song is so wound up with remorse and recrimination. It's a tour de force performance. The version from the

New York sessions included on *The Bootleg Series Vol. 1–3* is remarkably different: sad, chastened, ruminative.[1] When *Blood on the Tracks* is regarded as the "end of a marriage" album, it's because of "Idiot Wind." Most of the other songs on the album take less recriminatory stances, but "Idiot Wind" should satisfy anyone's taste for wounded pride, sexual and intellectual dissatisfaction, and the nervy, anxious struggle between lovers at the end of their rope. The opening lines—in which Dylan casts himself as the inheritor of "a million bucks" when the woman he stole away from "a man named Gray" dies—claim, "I can't help it if I'm lucky." Delivered by a character, the line strikes many listeners as one of Dylan's most honest statements *in propria persona*.

The side concludes with "You're Gonna Make Me Lonesome When You Go," a jaunty tune, mellow in its delivery and in most of its images. "I'll see you in the sky above, in the tall grass, and in the ones I love," the closing lines, strike an expansive, almost pantheistic pose as the singer suggests how his love for the crimson-haired woman will unite with his love of existence itself. Elsewhere, things are a bit more dodgy, as the singer calls up the vexed love affair between nineteenth-century French poets Arthur Rimbaud and Paul Verlaine while insisting it doesn't compare "to this affair." The good humor of the vocal delivery—rhyming Honolulu and Ashtabula—is seconded by lively harmonica sounding as if played by a boy free-footing the open road. The song expresses a come-what-may attitude toward love and being lonesome: if you fall in love, you have to expect to be lonesome as you can't always be with the object of your affection. In its buoyant mood, the song offers a significant ascendancy over the misery most songs associate with loneliness.

Side 2 begins with Dylan delivering a stellar blues vocal. "Meet Me in the Morning," like "Big Girl," is primarily of interest because of how Dylan interacts with the instrumentation. Listen to how the delivery on lines like "I struggle through barbed wire, let the hail fall from above" shows a piercing command of the musical idiom of the song, which takes its place with some of Dylan's other contemplative blues numbers—like "Black Crow Blues" and "Sign on a Window." Dylan's singing can often, as here, become more important than the words sung. "Look at the sun sinking like a ship" may not be a very striking image, but in the vocal modulations on the second iteration each vowel is kept open to create a sense of paused time. The sun and the ship are sinking, but not too fast—both visibly hang on the horizon to evoke the state of the singer's heart.

The most complicated song on the album is "Lily, Rosemary, and the Jack of Hearts," a cinematic tour de force. The narrative of the song takes certain liberties with the story, so that the point of view makes a fascinating contribution in itself. Formerly, Dylan's story songs tended to be reportorial (as in "Who Killed Davey Moore" or "The Lonesome Death of Hattie Carroll") or subjective (as in "Motorpsycho Nitemare" or "Bob Dylan's 115th Dream"), but "Jack of Hearts" tells the story in a more novelistic way, with characterization playing a large part in how we understand what we are being shown. Each character in the song is given a novelistic introduction: "With his bodyguard and silver cane and every hair in place / He took whatever he wanted to, and he laid it all to waste"; "Lily was a princess, she was fair-skinned and precious as a child / She did whatever she had to do, she had that certain flash everytime she smiled." There are also significant cuts in the action as the storyteller distracts us by telling us something seemingly irrelevant to the main action, as when "the leading actor hurried by in the costume of a monk." The next line is almost a non sequitur—"there was no actor anywhere better than the Jack of Hearts"—unless there is an implied relation: the "leading actor" here may be the Jack of Hearts himself, now dressed up as a monk. Though the Jack of Hearts character in the song is not an actor—he's not in the show that is being held in the cabaret—he is an actor for the purposes of the story. The "leading actor" line is a key moment because it's after this that a revolver is pulled on Big Jim. The implication in the song is that the man known as the Jack of Hearts was going to kill Big Jim over Lily, but that Rosemary, Jim's unhappy wife, who is suicidal, decides to kill him and let the hanging judge hang her.

The song's ending is wryly morose, containing the odd, self-negating line: "the only person on the scene missing was the Jack of Hearts." The playfulness of the language in the song is entertaining, but the situations would be little more than an old B-movie Western plot were it not for the device of the Jack of Hearts. The narrator uses the phrase to name the proverbial mysterious stranger who comes to town; to designate the card as well (some of the characters are playing five-card stud) because the stranger looks like the Jack of Hearts; and to imply the phrase's metaphorical meaning: a "Jack of Hearts" is able to play upon the emotions of others, particularly women, to seduce them or to make them aid his intentions. The "future riding on the Jack of Hearts" that Rosemary looks toward indicates the stranger's influence, but the "Jack of Hearts" is also a quality, much like "blue" or "fate" or the "idiot wind," that has effects on people, particularly lovers. In the end, the entire story is told simply to illustrate this principle: one could say that a certain quality of romantic illusion and implication is alluded to by the phrase "the Jack of Hearts," and that the song creates an arena—a cabaret in a town of the Old West—to let those implications play out. The Jack of Hearts, a rogue, escapes with his gang of bank robbers; Big Jim is dead; Rosemary is hanged for killing him; Lily sits "thinking about her father who she very rarely saw / Thinking about Rosemary and thinking about the law / But most of all she was thinking about the Jack of Hearts." More than someone who has loved her and left her, the "Jack of Hearts" is a principle she must come to terms with.

The next two tracks on the album are two of the most striking songs of this period of Dylan's songwriting. "If You See Her, Say Hello" surpasses any previous Dylan song as a retrospect on lost love. The amount of longing, hurt, rueful wisdom, and finally, self-abnegating desire packed into the song is impressive. The singer recounts a story of a love that suffered a "falling out," addressing someone who might see the loved woman, perhaps casually, perhaps romantically: "if you get close to her, kiss her once for me." The perspective is of a lover who lost her but who still feels connected to her ("she's always been inside of me, we've never been apart"). This might seem pathetic, but the very fact that the singer is willing to go to such extremes creates a sympathy with his wounded position. "Or whatever makes her happy, I won't stand in the way / For the bitter taste still lingers on from the night I tried to make her stay." The apposition of "make her happy" and "make her stay" speaks volumes. He wants to make her happy and wants being with him to make her happy, but it doesn't, so making her stay can only make her unhappy. But the delivery of "I won't stand in the way" is full of a heartsick surrender to a will he would change. It's how she wants it to be, and he's going along with it, at considerable cost to himself. The song's close is one of Dylan's best, expressing a bitterness striving to be nonchalant. The singer voices a humiliating need to see her again that goes beyond all the reasons to avoid her: "If she's passing back this way, I'm not that hard to find / Tell her she can look me up—if she's got the time." As with the "you just wasted my precious time" line in "Don't Think Twice," we know she doesn't have time for him now, much as the idea of wasted time says he no longer has time for her, in the earlier song. My time means more to me than she does (in "Don't Think Twice") and her time means more to her than I do (in "If You See Her"); in the first case the statement is a put-down (she wasted my time), in the second, a letdown (she won't have time for me). Such economy of expression with so much at stake—as any sign-off in romantic relations is either a kiss-off or an invitation—is truly masterful.

"Shelter from the Storm," more than any song Dylan recorded in the seventies, harkens to the imagistic songs circa 1965–1966. Like "Gates of Eden," "Shelter" returns to its title phrase, but unlike the earlier song or "Desolation Row," the refrain is each time the same: "'Come in,' she said, 'I'll give you shelter from the storm.'" The ten verses don't tell a story so much as describe moments in an ongoing relation between the singer and the woman who offers him shelter. The shelter can be interpreted as a supportive, sustaining relationship, perhaps, but given the kind of statements made about her—"she walked up to me so gracefully and took my crown of thorns"—and about the singer—"in a little hilltop village they gambled for my clothes"—we are in a world of biblical associations, where the singer is, metaphorically at least, a Christ figure and the "shelter" has a spiritual dimension. Indeed, the song's metaphors gesture toward spiritual quests—"I came in from the wilderness, a creature void of form"—and toward mythic implications—"If I could only turn back the clock to when God and her were born." Throughout the song then, there is a shifting sense of both the kind of shelter offered and what requiring such shelter means.

Unlike the earlier songs to which it bears comparison, "Shelter" does not seek to anatomize a complex world, as in "Desolation Row," or to express koans (paradoxes to be meditated on), as in "Gates of Eden," but rather creates mythic images for a consoling love. Romance in Dylan's hands can have many shades, from funky lust to a poetic interplay with the inspiring power of feminine influence. At a time when the "battle" or "equality" of the sexes was being engaged in earnest—in the workplace, with more formerly male-only preserves opening to women—it might be easy to write off such mythifying as retrograde, a harkening to Romantic poetry's tendency to look to women as erotic Madonnas, their sexuality a form of manna in the desert of arid social relations, or a mantra for spiritual exploration of the Eden within. Dylan's lyric is nimbler than a simple deification of woman, but it does seem to establish the sheltering woman as a muse figure.

The album's final song is wry and quizzical, sung with warm regard. The "Buckets of Rain" "coming out of my ears" matched with "buckets of moonbeams in my hand" might belong in a song for children, yet the song has a distinctly bawdy feel: "Little red wagon, little red bike, I ain't no monkey but I know what I like / I like the way you love me strong and slow." Much like "I'll Be Your Baby Tonight," the closing track of the magisterial *John Wesley Harding*, "Buckets" is an easy send-off, a celebration of the "misery" of love as a strong physical attraction, an agony of the beloved's presence.

The changing of relations between the sexes in the seventies is a timely aspect that made *Blood on the Tracks* such an emotionally relevant album. The year of its release, 1975, was declared the International Women's Year by the United Nations, an act intended to raise consciousness of the unique social challenges faced by, and gradually being overcome by, women throughout the world. The increased divorce rate, while having many causes, can be related to the fact that women in the seventies had more choices and more opportunities to make their way in the world outside of marriage and that so-called broken homes—later called "single-parent families"—were no longer as stigmatized as formerly. The questioning of social conventions and commitments was characteristic of the generation that came of age in the sixties. In the same way that many men refused to serve in the armed forces from compunctions about the government and the military, women refused to remain in marriages they found unsatisfying or demeaning. The generalized ethos of experimentation and adventure, a rallying point of the sixties, extended into home life and efforts to "expand" sexual relationships beyond the traditional marital configuration of a male breadwinner matched with a loyal female helpmate and caregiver to children.

This is not to say that the Dylans' divorce came about because Sara Dylan sought out her own career. Celebrity marriages are always different from those of average people, but the fact of divorce is what the Dylans and many of their contemporaries shared. And divorce was not yet a foregone conclusion for the Dylans in 1975. To complement "Wedding Song," the earnest paean to married love that closes *Planet Waves*, Dylan ends *Desire*, his album of 1976, with "Sara," a nakedly plaintive tribute to his wife that strives to mend—with shared memories—the ruptures in the marriage. While the happy home life of the late sixties and early seventies might have been personally fulfilling for Dylan, it did not give impetus to his best work; the tensions and rancor of marital alienation, on the other hand, provoked him to create *Blood on the Tracks*, generally considered his best work since the mid-sixties and for some time to come.

REPLAYING THE PAST

The decision by Columbia records to release *The Basement Tapes* as a collaboration between Bob Dylan and The Band seems a direct response to the label missing out on the profits from the pairing on Dylan's releases in 1974. In any case, the release in June 1975 of an official version of the demos, recorded in 1967 in and around Woodstock during Dylan's recuperation from his accident, was long overdue. With Dylan enjoying a comeback, and the mystique surrounding the recordings made by Dylan and the proto-Band still persistent, *The Basement Tapes* album sold quite well for an album consisting of tracks never meant to be released commercially.

In fact, the aura surrounding the recordings is furthered by the album. Though *The Basement Tapes* is not an accurate document of those unpolished sessions in 1967, the album is full of charm and atmosphere. The songs from the period are supplemented by unreleased recordings from The Band's early years, together with a few songs that may have been recorded nearer the time of release. With Rob Fraboni and Robbie Robertson working together at The Band's new recording studio, in January 1975, all songs received overdubs and sufficient remastering to make the recording acceptable to professional standards.

A strength of the album is that it better matches the time of its release than the time of the demos. *The Basement Tapes* takes its place among strong albums of the early seventies, such as The Rolling Stones' *Exile on Main Street*, a seminal rock album from 1972 that benefited from a less polished approach to recording (in Keith Richards' basement in France), The Kinks' *Muswell Hillbillies*, from 1971, an album that creates a unique country-rock sound, and Neil Young's edgy and unpolished *Tonight's the Night*, recorded in 1973 but not released until 1975. In that year, *The Basement Tapes* sounded right at home among recordings that strove to avoid formulaic arrangements and slick production values. In later years, the album, which met with high praise upon its release, has been criticized for including songs entirely by The Band that had no part in the Woodstock sessions. That decision very much continues the experience of the tour, with Dylan and The Band as equal collaborators. While that may be misleading as an account of 1967, it has a certain historical validity as the early identity of The Band, leading to their best album, *Music from Big Pink*, emerged from the sessions with Dylan. The Band's status by the time of the release of *The Basement Tapes* justified a supplement to show what the musicians on the Dylan demos, largely unknown in 1967, were able to achieve in their own right.

Some of Dylan's songs are among his most compelling, full of memorable phrases but avoiding the more portentous aspects of his sixties songwriting and pre-dating the more autobiographically motivated songs of the seventies. The variety of themes and moods is striking: "Tears of Rage" is a haunting and indelible cry of wounded pride and betrayal, while "Apple Suckling Tree" is good-natured and ribald. "Please Mrs. Henry" is a comic address to a barmaid from a man who desperately needs to use the pay toilet but who "ain't got a dime." "Clothesline Saga" is generally acknowledged as a takeoff on the 1967 radio hit, "Ode to Billie Joe" by Bobbie Jo Gentry, a laconic Top 40 soap opera that here becomes a gently comic slice of everyday life. Perhaps the most typical songs on the album are full of inspired absurdist free association, such as "Lo! And Behold," "Million Dollar Bash," and "Yea! Heavy and a Bottle of Bread." Other songs, like "This Wheel's on Fire" (co-written with Rick Danko and recorded by The Band for their debut album) and "You Ain't Goin' Nowhere" conjure up a backwoods fatalism that feels as if it has oozed out of the woods of Woodstock. "Going to Acapulco," a song of humorous bathos—"It's a wicked life, but what the hell / Uh, everybody's got to eat"—is sung like a drunken elegy, as if the prospective trip to Acapulco has to provide a form of redemption. "Nothing Was Delivered," like "Quinn the Eskimo" (recorded at the sessions but not included here), spoke to many listeners as recounting the rigors of waiting for a delivery of hard drugs. Many of the songs on

The Basement Tapes walk a fine line between visionary gestures and down-home truths, with lyrics tossed off with stunning insouciance.

The Basement Tapes has the authentic ring of unadorned "roots" music. The added songs by The Band complement the Dylan tracks well—in fact, they are as strong as any on The Band's own records. Gems like "Ain't No More Cane," "Don't Ya Tell Henry," "Yazoo Street Scandal," and "Orange Juice Blues" seem to have been set aside to one day grace the only album that does full justice to the collaboration of Dylan and The Band. In that view, the album marks a late hurrah for The Band, who performed and recorded their farewell concert the following year, on Thanksgiving 1976; the album also arrives as an opportunity to end the tendency to "replay the past" when discussing Dylan's career. With the release of *The Basement Tapes*, the decade from Dylan's breakthrough electric albums to his "return to form" with *Blood on the Tracks* comes to a close—at least until the *Bootleg Series* begins in 1991.

"IT WAS THEN THAT I KNEW WHAT HE HAD ON HIS MIND"

In June 1975, on the same day that *The Basement Tapes* was released, marking, as it were, the release of a ghost of the old Dylan held hostage to this point, Bob Dylan visited The Other End in New York's Greenwich Village to hear songstress Patti Smith perform. Later that year, Smith's *Horses*, produced by ex–Velvet Underground maverick John Cale, would cause quite a stir. The album not only announced a female rock artist who was one of the more interesting new performers and writers, but also presented a style—art rock or punk rock—that would become an influential contrast to the "classic" forms of rock music. Rock, by 1975, had become increasingly reliant on state-of-the-art recording to appeal to a sophisticated audience that found in rock eclectic affiliations with country, jazz, show tunes, and even classical music. In concert, rock bands regularly commanded venues built for sports contests rather than for music. To fill such spaces with sound, rock concerts tended to cut down on improvisation in favor of showmanship. Art-rock sought to strip rock of some of its bombast as well as its slickness, returning to the meaning of effects, of gesture, of minimal productions, and of arrangements that happily retained a garage-band sound and energy. Punk, going further, would deliberately court noise, chaos, and amateurism and exploit a confrontational attitude toward the commercial aspects of rock music with an aesthetic of kitsch, trash bins, and spiked and multi-colored hair. We might say that Dylan's status, in 1974–1975, partook of rock's last period of unchallenged influence as the dominant arbiter of youth culture, but at the same time, Dylan's restlessness in this period signaled an interest in learning from and collaborating with those a bit younger than himself, now hitting his mid-thirties. Younger musicians were more attuned to music that was edgier, less polished, and rather contemptuous of the mellowness that had become a hallmark of mid-seventies' giants, such as the Eagles and Fleetwood Mac.

Seeing Smith's show at The Other End inspired Dylan to begin thinking of a different way to perform, namely with his own band. The evidence of the 1974 tour was that The Band was no longer Dylan's backing band, but recording and performing artists in their own right. What Dylan needed was a collection of musicians able to adapt to the spontaneity of his own inspirations. His uncertainty about what his new sound should be can be seen in the two different versions of *Blood on the Tracks*. In beginning his next album, Dylan, hanging out in the Village as in the old days, began to find collaborators. One was Jacques Levy, a writer for stage shows who had collaborated with Roger McGuinn on the hit "Chestnut Mare." Dylan and Levy began to write together narrative songs very much like mini-movies. Meanwhile, Dylan was also acquiring young musicians: Rob Stoner, a bass player who brought in his friend Howie Wyeth, a drummer; Scarlett Rivera, a violinist of gypsy music; and as back-up vocalist, Emmylou Harris, the gifted singer who had been the late Gram Parson's partner subsequent to the Flying Burrito Brothers. There was much serendipity in all this, as Dylan began to invite more and more musicians to large jam sessions, many arriving through the auspices of Bob Neuwirth, Dylan's crony from the mid-sixties, who had a way of inspiring Dylan to more manic occasions as seen in *Don't Look Back*. Dylan seemed to be searching for a more communal approach to making music. Eventually, the overload of collaborators was pared down to the basic unit—Stoner, Wyeth, Rivera—that would be the bedrock of the new album's sound as well as the basis for the road show Dylan mounted after *Desire* was recorded.

Like the new art rock and punk rock, Dylan's approach was not guided by marketability and the demands of the radio, but by a search for the rapport of performance. The emphasis on the concert experience was very timely. During the summer of 1975, while Dylan was at work on recording his new songs, Bruce Springsteen gave a series of performances in support of his landmark Columbia LP, *Born to Run* (released in August), including a five-night stand at New York's The Bottom Line and four nights at The Roxy in Los Angeles. The shows created a highly publicized renewal of the concert experience. Springsteen, of course, would eventually become an arena-rocker in his own right, but for the moment the up-and-coming artist and the established artist were alike in finding the small venue preferable for rock that was vital, intimate, and at times visionary.

The result of Dylan's search for companions to take on the road was the formation of a kind of impromptu super group—dubbed by Dylan "The Rolling Thunder Revue"—including McGuinn, Joan Baez, Rambling Jack Elliott, Joni Mitchell, Ronee Blakely, Mick Ronson (formerly David Bowie's guitarist on the Spiders from Mars tour), T-Bone Burnett, and even famed Beat poet Allen Ginsberg and soon-to-be-celebrated playwright Sam Shepard. Shepard was along because Dylan intended to film not only the concert performances, but backstage performances as well—featuring scripted interactions as well as the spontaneous scenes common to rock and roll documentaries. On October 30, 1975, three days after Springsteen appeared on the cover of *Time* and *Newsweek* as the celebrated "future of rock," Dylan and his Rolling Thunder Revue sought the past of rock in the traveling road show, playing their inaugural concert in Plymouth, Massachusetts, the founding place of the thirteen original British colonies, soon to be celebrated anew in 1976, the Bicentennial of the founding of the United States of America. Michael Denning has referred to the Revue's "peculiar history-writing by concert touring" to indicate how Dylan and company sought not only to convey their songs to the "North Country" but to capture on film the "North Country's ethnic and racial histories . . . as picaresque adventure" (33–34).

"YOU SHOULD NOT TREAT ME LIKE A STRANGER"

The Rolling Thunder Revue marks an interesting interlude in Dylan's performing career. No longer burdened with the "comeback" aura of the tour with The Band, Dylan had found collaborators willing to improvise with him, both onstage and on film, and to play in out-of-the-way locations and venues. The itinerary of the initial tour was not the usual huge arena affair, and the feeling, look, and sound of the show epitomized a looseness, a celebratory and relaxed panache only available in the seventies. This was rock akin to the life of the traveling minstrel, the troubadour with no direction home. Dylan wasn't only "back in the rain," he was back in the public eye very much on his own terms. Typically wearing a vest and a hat adorned with a flower and often performing with his face in greasepaint, Dylan walked a fine line between clown and poet, a space in which other performers and writers before him had dwelt. The shows owed something to Whitman, to Rimbaud, to the Beats, to carnival sideshows and vaudeville, and to roadhouse blues bands and rockabilly pickers from the heartland. In the midst of this somewhat chaotic atmosphere, Dylan reinvented some of his best known songs and put songs of his various romantic explorations—"Tangled Up in Blue," "Just Like a Woman," "O Sister," "Sara"—in dialogue with one another. It was fitting, inasmuch as he was also making a tour film that was also an exploration of the myths of identity and the twin romances of The Road and The Woman.

The tour also gave stage time to his friends and accomplices, reintroducing a gallery of figures familiar from his heyday: Joan Baez—Dylan finally returned the favor of hosting his sometime lover, muse, and colleague as she had done for him in 1963–1964; Ramblin' Jack Elliott, who could still evoke the influence of Guthrie so important to Dylan's formative years; Roger McGuinn of The Byrds, who had helped popularize the folk-rock crossover that had been so important to Dylan's breakthrough on pop radio; Joni Mitchell and Gordon Lightfoot, Canadians who added songwriting credentials almost as illustrious as Dylan's. Mitchell's "Dreamland," which McGuinn recorded on his album *Cardiff Rose*, is a wonderfully Dylanesque evocation of the tour.

The playing on the live recordings of the shows is at times sloppy, but the enthusiasm is obvious. Dylan attacks signature songs with a variety of effects: "It Ain't Me Babe" veers between cool and warily mocking; "A Hard Rain's A-Gonna Fall" is declaimed with a carnivalesque air; "Hattie Carroll" goes for the throat; "Just Like a Woman" is nakedly raw. The new songs, led by Scarlett Rivera's lyrical and expressive violin, sit easily with the classics, and for nostalgia there's Bob and Joan, the King and Queen of folk, after more than a decade, still cranking out "Blowin' in the Wind," though where they really connect are on covers of standards like "Never Let Me Go" and "The Water is Wide." On recordings, what comes across best is the band's responsiveness to its leader's fitful inspirations. The performances are more theatrical than on earlier tours, and the tour, lasting a little over a month, did not become stale or formulaic. There would be better nights and worse nights, but at each show the audience was treated to a glimpse of Dylan and company trying to master and harness the power of his songs. On any given night, a song could be delivered in all its definitive glory, while another song might feel like a tossed-off afterthought. More than the sum of its parts, each show was worth recording, and there are numerous bootlegs, as well as an official release as *The Bootleg Series Vol. 5*.

On December 8, the first leg of the Rolling Thunder Revue concluded at Madison Square Garden. The show was billed as "the Night of the Hurricane," in honor of Ruben "Hurricane" Carter, a middleweight boxer incarcerated for allegedly murdering two men in a bar in New Jersey in 1968. Dylan had read Carter's autobiography, which pleads his innocence. The adoption of this particular cause—a retrial for Carter—was a subplot of the concerts and the film based on the tour that Dylan released in 1978. Between the two legs of the tour, on January 5, 1976, *Desire* was released, containing several story songs, three of them about actual people. The album stayed at number 1 for five weeks on *Billboard*'s chart, and all but two of its songs—"Joey" and "Black Diamond Bay"—were at one point or another incorporated into the Revue's live shows.

Desire finds Dylan enjoying a refreshed approach to recording, giving the album, produced by Don DeVito, a ramshackle quality very much in the spirit of the live shows. Scarlett Rivera's violin has replaced the organ as the complement to Dylan's harmonica and the change adds a distinct mood to the album, which has a stronger sustained sound than *Blood on the Tracks*. *Desire* also builds on the exploration of narrative on the previous album, as Dylan's collaboration with Jacques Levy produced songs of cinematic compression.

"Hurricane," the opening song, swiftly immerses the listener in a fast-paced tale of murder and police intimidation, using actual names and presenting Carter as a hapless victim of racism. Bigotry—whites exercising power with the racist assumption that blacks are most likely guilty of something—is a driving force in the song, which isn't stinting in its pointing out that the jury in Carter's trial was all white, nor from using the expression "crazy nigger" to express condemnation of Carter by blacks who assumed him guilty. Blunt, direct, the song's verbal attack pulls no punches—Dylan can't help but "feel ashamed to live in a land where justice is a game." A dig at "criminals in their suits and their ties" struck a chord after the light sentences meted out to many of the Watergate defendants. Dylan forcefully denounces a system that could condemn a man like Carter, who is presented as a free spirit simply trying to be "the champion of the world." Regardless of the truth of the story as told, the singer is committed to his version of the events, and the story unfolds with the fast-paced rhythm of television cop shows, a genre that was becoming increasingly lurid.

The commitment to innocence in "Hurricane" becomes somewhat tainted by the evocative elegy that opens side 2. "Joey" purports to tell the story of mobster Joey Gallo from the perspective of those who loved him and saw him as a latter-day Robin Hood, a figure more sinned against than sinning. Whether or not the portrayal is objectively accurate to Gallo—and the song inspired criticism on that score—the mix of cleverness, bathos, and folk-hero colorings in the depiction of Gallo creates a melodramatic storytelling in song. Dylan and Levy show how easy it is to twist history with emotion, using a big crescendo chorus and Emmylou Harris's keening background vocals to create a sense of almost universal mourning for a man who, in the song, recalls Don Corleone in Francis Ford Coppola's magisterial *Godfather* films of 1972 and 1974, a stand-up guy for his family and friends and a scourge only to his enemies. In other words, the sympathetic portraits of both Carter and Gallo inspire certain rhetorical strategies, making both akin to "biopics" or "movies of the week," employing distortions for the sake of dramatic effect.

Along with a gritty crime drama with racist themes and a mobster soap opera, *Desire* also boasts a Hollywood B-Western. "Romance in

Durango" takes its inspiration from the town in which much of *Pat Garrett & Billy the Kid* was filmed, and the phrase "look up in the hills that flash of light" recalls the ending of *The Appaloosa*, starring Marlon Brando, where a gleam from a gun gives away the position of the enemy stalking Brando. Unlike "Lily, Rosemary, and the Jack of Hearts," the western on the previous album, "Durango" is fairly straightforward Hollywood pulp, complete with Mexican trumpets, the sound of jangling spurs, and a chorus with Spanish phrases. Dylan's "acting" in the song— as a renegade on the run with Magdalena—is much more stirring than his performance in Peckinpah's film. One of the strangest and most memorable lines—whether Dylan's or Levy's—is: "the face of God will appear / With the serpent eyes of obsidian." The fun Dylan and Levy are having in composing these pastiches is palpable, as in the rhyming of "a clam bar in New York" with "lifted up his fork" in "Joey."

Two other narratives are even more interesting because they are harder to pin down in terms of their antecedents. "Black Diamond Bay" tells a tale more elusive than "Lily, Rosemary, and the Jack of Hearts" as there is little overt symbolism. The setting, an island gambling casino with international clientele, "forbidden love," and suicide, is the stuff of cheap melodrama, enlivened by telling details—"a Panama hat and a pair of old Greek shoes," an insouciant French desk clerk, and a lock-step sense of intrigue on a picturesque set with flying cranes and storms and, finally, an earthquake that sinks the island. We "pull back," as they say, to find the singer "sitting at home alone one night / in L.A. watching old Cronkite on the 11 O'clock News." The song's tale becomes "just another hard luck story that you're gonna hear"—a sweeping dismissal that could also encompass "the story of the Hurricane," the saga of Joey Gallo, the dying renegade in "Durango," as well as the album's final song about a marriage on the rocks.

"Isis" continues in the vein of the picaresque tale familiar from earlier Dylan albums but is unique in also characterizing, somewhat indirectly, a relation to a woman who shares the name of an Egyptian deity. An inspired mix of genres, the tale also involves "pyramids all embedded in ice" and a search for a rich tomb. The quest—mystical, religious, erotic, and mercenary—is the dominant motif, and it is seconded by such devices as the friendly stranger and, most importantly, rebirth as romantic reconciliation where the singer returns to Isis for a remarriage on the anniversary of their first marriage. The circular romantic tale is matched by the story of the stranger, who dies before excavating the tomb supposed to hold "a body [he's] trying to find." Instead, the tomb is empty, so the singer entombs the corpse of the stranger there. The song's Book of the Dead associations encompass the stranger's quest for his own death and the singer's quest for new life, signaled by reconciliation with Isis. Reminiscent of songs on *Blood on the Tracks* like "Shelter from the Storm" and "Simple Twist of Fate" in its sense of mysticism and quest, "Isis" also partakes of the tongue-in-cheek portentousness of a song like "The Ballad of Frankie Lee and Judas Priest." Performances of the song with the Rolling Thunder Revue, with Dylan taking a cue from Patti Smith and singing sans guitar, were high points of the show.

Three songs on *Desire* continue *Blood*'s theme of romance under duress. "One More Cup of Coffee" is a moody and dark song, with a keening vocal and atmospheric violin; it characterizes a woman in a vein similar to "Idiot Wind," while its refrain, about going "to the valley below," lends the song a fatalistic and even apocalyptic air. "Oh Sister" openly treats romance as a metaphysical relation, rebuking a woman's indifference with "Our Father would not like the way that you act." As a song of its moment, "Oh Sister" can be seen as a mournful riposte to the status of women in search of rights and freedom equal to men. Like "Cup of Coffee," "O Sister" feels rather "Old World," a revisiting of sexual relations as handed down from the fathers. And yet "Oh Sister" is poignant in its evocation of a love running "from the cradle to the grave." The threat contained in a demand for love adds a brooding weight to the song: whether "the danger" of the father's punishment or the eventual loss of the lover in "time is an ocean but it ends at the shore / you may not see me tomorrow."

The third song of romantic relations is "Sara," addressed to Sara Dylan by a husband-lover who tries to make amends in song. The lyrics dwell on glimpses of their life together—"you in a marketplace in Savannah, Lamarr". . . "and on Lilypond Lane when the weather was warm"—and offer a series of imagistic evocations, "Scorpio sphinx in a calico dress" perhaps the most memorable. The nakedness of the song is surprising, since Dylan has rarely made references to actual places and scenes in his life, and could even be construed as a desperate rhetorical strategy. Veiled tributes, such as contained in "Sad-Eyed Lady of the Lowlands," are not enough; the time has come for direct revelations of their life together. Added to "Cup of Coffee," "Oh Sister," and "Isis," "Sara" continues the theme of desire as fraught with heartache and dark forebodings, while the mystical union of opposites comprised in male-female relations offers the possibility of reconciliation and rebirth. Dylan seems to believe he has patriarchal law—and possibly pagan mother deities—on his side, in making his uneasy demand: "don't ever leave me, don't ever go."

As the third song about a real person, "Sara" takes its place with "Hurricane" and "Joey" as tales that raise questions about truth and fiction, even guilt and innocence. Is it true that "Ruben Carter was falsely tried?" Is it true that "in his later years" Gallo never carried a gun? Is it true that Dylan wrote "Sad-Eyed Lady of the Lowlands" in the Chelsea Hotel?[2] In other words, the poetic license of these songs is part of their "desire." They choose to tell tales the singer finds inspiring, conjuring a world of sorrow and struggle richly evoked by Scarlett Rivera's wandering gypsy violin. *Desire* is an odd album in many ways, but it is certainly an album that only someone like Dylan, in cahoots with Levy's sense of the dramatic, would have the guts, the nerve, the inspired ease to pull off.

At the time of *Desire*'s release in January, Dylan and company began the second leg of the Rolling Thunder Revue. As shown by artifacts of this phase of the tour, *Hard Rain*, a TV special that aired in September 1976 and its tie-in LP of the same name, the set list favored Dylan's most recent albums, presenting three songs from *Blood on the Tracks* with blistering conviction. Gone is the warmth of the shows in the first leg of the Revue. The TV show is unadorned and quasi-punk—with no quarter given or asked. Taped on a day of heavy rains in Houston, Texas, with Dylan and his band swathed in bandannas, the visuals of the show were likened to a troupe of terrorists using the airwaves to set their sights on the American heartland. With its edgy close-ups and raw vocals, the show did nothing to further Dylan with fans of the mellow pop rock dominating the radio of the times, nor did it give any concessions to those for whom Dylan would always be an old folkie with an acoustic guitar.

Desire and *Hard Rain* bookended the American Bicentennial, a not insignificant fact. That one of America's premier blues/rock/folk bards should be so visible at this of all times, touring the country at its turning from the postwar boom years to the current "stagflation" and the coming oil shortages of the OPEC embargoes, showed how much the musi-

cal legacy of Dylan had acquired new life. Having taken his early inspirations from Guthrie's songs of the Depression to become a songwriter
relevant to the struggles of the sixties, Dylan was now a figure blending
into mythic retrospect on the previous decade. At his acceptance
speech for the Democratic nomination in July, Jimmy Carter, a Baptist
"Dixiecrat" quoted Dylan's line, "he not busy being born is busy dying,"
a line that in context stressed the degree to which American politics
needed to resurrect itself after the debacle of Nixon.

   Hard Rain presents a Dylan estranged from his wife and thus from
the secure certainties that had helped him transition from the tensions
of his youth into his maturity, now a troubadour willing to risk it all to
get it across. Take "Lay Lady Lay" as an example: from a song of suave
seduction in 1969, to a whooping, cajoling come-on in 1974, it becomes
a brusque dare—"why run any longer, when you're running in place,
you can have the truth but you got to choose it"—and seems to define
the era's possibilities for romance quite well: "Forget this dance, let's go
upstairs / Let's take a chance—who really cares?"

"EVERYBODY'S WEARING A DISGUISE"

As with the tours in 1965 and 1966 that became the basis for *Don't
Look Back* and *Eat the Document* respectively, once again performances and backstage life were filmed on a Dylan tour, but in *Renaldo
and Clara* Dylan was the filmmaker, though joined by Howard Alk, who
worked with him on *Document*. The film concerns a character named
Renaldo (played by Dylan), torn between Clara (played by Sara Dylan)
and The Woman in White (Joan Baez) from his past. Meanwhile, Ronnie Hawkins (the rockabilly singer from whom The Band derived the
name they were formerly known by: The Hawks) was on hand in a few
scenes to be identified as "Bob Dylan." The conception of the film, as
Dylan developed it in conversations and in subsequent comments, was
to investigate the masquerades of identity by using his own imago—the
very recognizable figure we all know as "Bob Dylan"—as the means to
both tell a story and comment upon it from the vantage point of his own
songs in performance. Indeed, performance becomes a major factor in
the film because none of the people involved are quite themselves, and
yet the audience is really in no place to judge. Often, while watching,

we might feel we are seeing typical behind-the-scenes footage, though nothing is quite as it seems. For instance, when Hawkins tries to woo a young girl to a life of rock and roll, we have the sense that the lines he's speaking are off the cuff and that some version of Ronnie Hawkins has used lines similar to those before. Elsewhere he encounters Mick Ronson, in his role as a backstage guard, and the exchange feels largely ad-libbed. Even if we know that it's unlikely that Ronson and Hawkins would have such a confrontation, as themselves, we are more entertained by the distortion of their personalities than intrigued by the scene as drama. The nonprofessionalism of most of the filming keeps us guessing about what is "intended" and what isn't, and that's most of the fun.

One strength of cinema verité is that it allows the viewer to see unvarnished truth. Any viewers expecting something more artificially achieved will be disappointed. The handheld camera and the lack of lighting setups provide visuals that are often little more than home-movie quality. While Dylan has thousands of fans who would be quite content to watch his unedited home movies, the larger film-going public found little reason to accept such a meandering film as a professional product. Whatever hopes Dylan had of recouping the money he sank into the film were quickly dashed by the scathing reviews. Some of the negative criticism was due to the animosity that often greets any artist who tries, unschooled and possibly unskilled, to conquer a new medium; certainly, Dylan had not put the effort into telling a story in film that he put into learning how to tell stories in song. The slapdash aspects of the film might be, for some viewers, a compelling aspect of its authenticity, but the patience of professional critics was severely tested. Dylan's pretensions to "nouvelle vague" techniques are in any case old hat.

Even if one approaches the film with an open mind, led by an interest in the oddities of Dylan as a legendary—possibly mythic—figure, *Renaldo and Clara* is often disappointing. So little effort was put into the continuities of story that it tries the attention even of a viewer versed in nonlinear developments. With no compelling sense of "characters" in any traditional sense, the film becomes almost entirely a succession of skits. Interest is furnished by such oddities as Joan Baez speaking with an outrageous accent, by a face-off between Zen and bop mantras, featuring Allen Ginsberg, or by seeing Dylan at the wheel of a

huge travel bus. The music on the soundtrack is compelling and captures not only some great performances—"Tangled Up in Blue" sung in
intense close-up is a standout—but provides interesting subtext to some
of the action. Dylan also incorporates footage that provides idiosyncratic context to the film: a Thanksgiving celebration with a Tuscora tribe
(Native Americans who aligned themselves with the revolutionaries in
the War of Independence in 1776), street preachers in New York, a
cabaret singer entertaining middle-aged women before turning the
floor over to a poetry reading by Ginsberg, public comments about the
Ruben Carter case, and Dylan's friend David Blue recounting Village
lore while smoking and playing pinball.

As a director, Dylan's approach is not wholly out of keeping with
other sprawling, loosely associative films, such as Robert Altman's celebrated *Nashville*, a movie that brings together country music and the
libertarian views of independent politics. Ronee Blakely, one of the
singing stars of *Nashville*, appears in Dylan's film, where her main contribution is a *Nashville*-like scene that boasts the most sustained acting
in the film. Elsewhere Sara Dylan, still Dylan's wife at the time of
filming, is presented as wistful and vague, a truly Dylanesque muse.
The scene in which she, as Clara, and her husband, as Renaldo, couple
in a room, only to be interrupted by the Woman in White, gives viewers
a strangely voyeuristic glimpse of the Dylans. Such moments, while not
the stuff of cinematic drama, do create interest. One watches the film in
a state not unlike channel surfing: never sure when something will turn
up that has a certain appeal, if only as an unexplained slice of the
seventies.

Renaldo and Clara is an anticlimactic end to one of Dylan's stronger
periods. In another sense it marks a transition to a more surprising
stage. The film depicts the musical life of the late seventies as rather
adrift, with Beat trappings and folk activism well on the way to being
clichés. Sagas of on-the-road hedonism and self-discovery were already
familiar, and, while it's true that every working band experiences some
version of such things, the hope that Dylan would offer some particularly meaningful account of that world was not satisfied. Dylan, always
fascinating to watch, can only carry such a film so far, and is at his best
on stage. Yet, though the film fails on many levels, it is also one of the
more quizzical and unusual rock movies ever made, an epic-length dis-

aster in some ways, but also a sprawling memento of the chaotic charm of the period.

NOTES

1. Heylin and others prefer the version on the original acetate that Dylan suppressed, which is superior to the *Bootleg Series* track but, to my mind, is still too much in the spirit of a demo. On the official release and in performance on *Hard Rain*—which is perhaps the definitive version—Dylan finds the teeth of the song. Those who prefer the New York acetate of *Blood* tend to argue for its autobiographical authenticity—as, for instance, in the change from "Call Letter Blues" to "Meet Me in the Morning" (Heylin 1995, 106–7).

2. Lester Bangs, with his usual pugnacious pose, dismisses *Desire* because Dylan is not "being straight" with him (213), as if the purpose of a song must be to tell the truth, the whole truth and nothing but the truth. *Desire*, to my mind, is about the process of fictionalizing and hero-icizing that is part of all our narrative media—even rock journalism.

6

THE CHANGING OF THE GUARD
(1978–1981)

HOW THE SEVENTIES ENDED

> The Seventies I see as a period of reconstruction after the Sixties,
> that's all. That's why people say: well, it's boring, nothing's really
> happening, and that's because wounds are healing. By the Eighties,
> anyone who's going to be doing anything will have his or her cards
> showing. You won't be able to get back in the game in the Eighties.
> —Bob Dylan to Jonathan Cott (1978, 186)

"Wounds were healing," Dylan says, an apropos comment on how
the battles of the sixties changed in the seventies, but also suggesting his
own personal growth. From the early period when his artistic development had become a point of reference for many, he moved into a
period when he tried to become more private, only to have his private
life become the catalyst for a return to more vital songwriting. Had the
wounds healed as Dylan came to the end of the decade?

Many struggles for political recognition were fought in the streets in
the sixties; the battle for a more liberal state had its victories, but with
the onset of the seventies, the United States began to face an economic
crisis and a growing conservative backlash against the policies of President Johnson's "Great Society." The years of the Carter administration,
1977–1981, were years in which the difference between the sixties and
seventies was becoming evident enough for those who had placed their
hopes in the cultural collectivism of the earlier period. The U.S. with-

drawal from Vietnam in 1975, though a "victory" for peace, presented a setback for the U.S. military; many believed the United States and the USSR would find other grounds upon which to stage a more direct confrontation between the forces of communism and capitalism. Alarmist concern extended beyond the proliferation of nuclear arsenals—and the increasing number of countries with nuclear capabilities—to the "no nukes" movement which was against nuclear energy in all its guises.

The boredom Dylan speaks of has to do with the lack of direction in the arts and in rock music. The period of "revolutionary energies" was no longer influencing the mainstream of either politics or music. While not yet as bad as things would get—as Dylan's glance ahead to the eighties suggests—the corporatism of U.S. culture was a dominant feature of commercial undertakings like films and popular music, creating hard realities for independent productions like *Renaldo and Clara* as the "art house cinema" was on its way to becoming a thing of the past in all but the largest cities. The late seventies could still claim holdovers and throwbacks in most media, with the only real provocations coming from the fringes. Otherwise, a peppy populism was the dominant note.

In England, the late seventies was the period of the transition from punk—at its most livid in 1976—to what was generally called "New Wave Music," a style that expressed the bleaker, edgier, more mechanistic feel of the coming decade. Computer technology and digital technology, the cutting-edge tools of all media-based arts, led the way into the eighties. This constituted a major change in how "state of the art" recordings would be made, thus altering the expectations of the listening audience, so that Dylan's fast and loose approach became even more outdated as studio engineers dismissed his preferred "live in the studio" method.

Rock is rather unforgiving of its aging practitioners, as there are always younger artists to set the tone and direction of the genre. Thanks to the baby boom at the end of World War II, the late seventies found a large number of persons hitting the transition from youth into the early stage of middle age. Certain figures who had long represented "the sixties"—and Dylan was preeminent among them—would become touchstones for the transition. Would they still appeal to the young? Would they keep their aging fans' attention as the latter drifted into the cares of their maturity, in many cases distancing themselves—as the coming decade would show all too well—from the beliefs and passions of their youth? As the most visible figures for a generation moving toward its forties, artists like Dylan would face the challenge of "speaking to" and "speaking for" a generation loathe to surrender its youth. The viability of rock itself would come increasingly into question as the eighties progressed.

And what of Dylan? He had mythified certain aspects of his private life and was now a divorced father faced with the prospect of not only reimagining his erotic life, but also reinventing his creative life. What should be the guiding principles of the next phase of his career?

TOUR '78

In February 1978, Dylan undertook a series of concerts in Japan. The markets of thriving Japan were eager for entertainment from the West, with Budokan arena in Tokyo becoming a popular venue where rock acts met with appreciative welcomes. There, Dylan debuted a new road show that traveled to Australia and back to Japan. Gone were the impromptu performances so valued in the Rolling Thunder Revue, replaced by very precise arrangements with an eight-piece band and backup singers. The new incarnation of Dylan was closer to the kind of "showman" one associated with the musical acts of his elders—most notably Elvis Presley, who had died in August 1977. In the decade after his 1969 "comeback," Elvis had developed a Las Vegas show with a repertoire to appeal to his middle-aged fan base. Dylan, now in his late thirties, could be said to be reaching a moment that tests the career of many artists in a youth-based medium. With his influential earlier albums still available for those passing through the phase when Dylan's idiosyncratic poetry stimulates the search for an authentic grasp of self and community, the current Dylan might become a self-parody or a nostalgia show. It is a credit to Dylan's instincts and abilities as a performer that he became neither. The "big band" shows were both a respectful retrospective, as might be expected from an artist after more than a decade and a half of recording, and a reinvention of his sound and persona.

Dylan at Budokan, at first only a double LP tie-in for the audiences in Japan, recorded at shows early in the tour, was eventually released in the States in April 1979. Neither before nor since has Dylan shown himself in such glib command of all phases of his output. Dylan's voice was strong and versatile in this period, enabling him to find surprisingly varied approaches to songs from all phases of his career. To do so, without revisiting again the hallowed folk movement, retreading the rockabilly shadings of The Band, or attempting an unlikely revisiting of the stoned ferocity of his youth, required considerable presence of mind. The innovation Dylan developed was the introduction of black backup singers who brought a soul inflection to the concerts and kept his vocals on point, as well as the use—for the first time in his career—of that most ubiquitous instrument of the late seventies, the saxophone.

The sax had long since lost its cultural associations with be-bop and jazz experimentation to become the preeminent instrument for mellow arrangements, aligning rock with the cooler and more sensual aspects of soul, R&B, and light jazz. The adoption of the saxophone as the lead instrument—accompanied by guitar, keyboards, violin, and Dylan's trademark harmonica—breathed contemporary life into the Bob Dylan songbook. If this was "middle-of-the-road" rock, it was also a renovated approach to one of the great song catalogs of our times. "I Shall Be Released" on the Budokan album showcases the strengths of the new approach, which makes its case for seeing the song as a gospel-flavored show tune, complete with wailing sax and a big crescendo in each chorus. Other distinctive touches were the African-influenced drum patterns in "Oh Sister" and "One More Cup of Coffee," and the use of flute to evoke the youthful detachment of songs like "Mr. Tambourine Man" and "Love Minus Zero." "It's Alright, Ma" became a rocker along the lines of "Ballad of a Thin Man," and "Don't Think Twice" an easy-going reggae strut. On the 1978 tour, Dylan explored a range of musical settings for his best-known songs, and then, for most of the next decade, proceeded to apply those lessons in writing new material.

The tour made a great impression on fans and critics in Europe and England in the spring of 1978, though the concerts in the States in the summer and fall of 1978 did not meet with praise in the press. U.S. critics seemed eager to distance themselves from the taint of the sixties still associated with Dylan; others, to some extent proprietary about Dylan and ready to dismiss any wrinkle of his career that did not satisfy either a prescriptive sense of what rock "should be" or what Dylan's historical position must be, tended to write off any contemporary version of Dylan's music as posturing. While certainly professional and successful musical entertainments, the concerts were in no way confrontational or spontaneous. For the first time in his career, Dylan's command of his material showed that his music could become an easily accessible version of contemporary rock. It was a sign of the times; one would be hard-pressed to find major rock acts—*pace* The Grateful Dead—courting spontaneity and "jamming" over carefully rehearsed solos and arrangements. Even Bruce Springsteen, new to playing in arenas, was performing shows that were more or less choreographed and thrilling audiences.

"I WON'T, BUT THEN AGAIN, I MIGHT"

Eschewing the pickup bands on his last few records, Dylan recorded *Street-Legal* with a band that had already proven itself on the road, and the textured sound of Dylan's live shows should have made for a musically satisfying album. Unfortunately, the recording process, at Dylan's own rehearsal/recording space, Rundown Studios, overseen by Don DeVito, did not translate the stage polish of the band to the finished record. Rather than accept the methods of multitrack recording, which uses overdubs and individual tracking to make each instrument as pristine as possible, Dylan chose his characteristic live-in-the-studio method (Heylin 1995, 124–25). *Street-Legal*, released in June 1978, is certainly not all that it could be aurally. And yet in terms of its material, it is one of the strongest of Dylan's albums from the seventies (as was perceived by critics and fans alike in Britain). U.S. rock fans and folk fans were perhaps put off by the backup singers, the saxophone, the sense of a "big production" poorly recorded, but for all that, the album gains a certain "cred" by not being a slick product. This is no Steely Dan album nor was it meant to be. The term "street-legal" designates an automobile passing the minimum level of drivability for an old clunker to be driven in public. The album is not pretty or state-of-the-art, but it gets where it needs to go.

Most of the songs continue *Blood on the Track*'s interrogation of romantic relations, though four songs develop the more imagery-driven style of a song like "Shelter from the Storm": "Changing of the Guards," "No Time to Think," "Señor (Tales of Yankee Power)," and "O Where Are You Tonight (Journey Through Dark Heat)." These songs develop

Dylan's tendency to make big statements that transcend individual concerns with a more mythic perspective. "Guards" is a meditation on a world out of joint, with lyrical references toward the occult, the Tarot, and other mystical figures. Dylan's vocals have not sounded this feverish in some time. The effort to simply get all the words out gives the song a propulsive urgency aided by backup singers offering choral "ooohs" for the first two lines of each verse and reciting the fourth after Dylan. The melody is given a sonorous treatment by Steven Douglas's sax, creating a graceful counterpoint to the song's chugging rhythm. While perhaps a bit too reedy and thin in its sound, this opening stream-of-consciousness track features many remarkable lines and shows that Dylan, in abandoning the narrative story songs featured on *Desire*, has found an imagistic style even less grounded in place or action than his older visionary songs. The constant refrain, "changing of the guards," comes to seem a circumstance devoutly to be wished, as the song calls for a change well beyond those broached in "The Times, They Are A-Changin'." Dylan, if not invoking an outright apocalypse—in the sense of revealed truth—is at least suggesting that the days of the powers that be are numbered: "'Gentlemen,' he said, 'I don't need your organization / I've moved your mountains and marked your cards / But Eden is burning. Either get ready for elimination / Or your hearts must have the courage for the changing of the guards.'" The song ends with one of Dylan's most sweeping gestures toward revelation: "And cruel Death surrenders with its pale ghost retreating between the King and the Queen of Swords." Death and the King and Queen of Swords are figures in the Tarot deck, and the line sounds like the outcome of a reading as well as suggesting a symbolic achievement that conquers death.

"No Time to Think" is even less focused, running through a lockstep lyric that nonetheless features entertaining rhymes and some brilliant throwaway lines. The cool delivery gives the song a tongue-in-cheek tone in the style of Dylan's earlier comic songs. The quickness of the rhymes and the oddity of the associations—"betrayed by a kiss on a cool night of bliss in the valley of the missing link"—along with refrains consisting of four abstractions—"Socialism, hypnotism, patriotism, materialism" is a particularly memorable string—create an antic mood, as if the perspective of the song is that of a figure much like The Fool in the Tarot deck: a view that sees the world as "decoys / Through a set of

deep turquoise / Eyes." While insisting on the urgency of time—
"there's no time to think" is the line constantly repeated—the song
manages to convey a sense of ring-around-the-rosy stasis, of circling
through a barrage of images without any forward progress.

"Señor (Tales of Yankee Power)" is one of the standout songs on the
album, a darkly conceived first person address to a Yankee overlord.
The voice seems to speak for an underclass abused by big business and
the invasive, self-serving policies of the United States with regard to
Latin American countries. The sound is chilling and sinister with lines
that imply a need for change, violent if need be: "can you tell me where
we're headin' / Lincoln County Road or Armageddon?" The perspective
of the singer is bemused, perhaps even desperate—"this place don't
make sense to me no more"—with occasional segues into evocative if
cryptic imagery: "a marching band still playing in that vacant lot"; "a
gypsy with a broken flag and a flashing ring." In the vein of a song like
"All Along the Watchtower" or "One More Cup of Coffee," "Señor"
creates a mood of anticipation, tinged with dread, partaking of a foreboding fairly familiar in Dylan's songs that here attains one of its most
superlative instances.

The album's final song is a rare vocal tour de force. "O Where Are
You Tonight" builds to a frenzy as Dylan fires off verses extraordinary in
their heroic claims: "I've bitten to the root / Of forbidden fruit / With
the juice running down my leg"; "If you don't believe there's a price /
For this sweet paradise / Just remind me to show you the scars." The
song has rarely been given its due among Dylan's critics, though one
senses that, if he were to sing the identical song in his characteristic
mid-sixties' *Blonde on Blonde* drawl, the song would be hailed as a
masterpiece. As it is, the song's instrumentation never quite achieves
the recklessness of the lyrics, feeling, especially in the rather polite
guitar solo at the end, more friendly than frenzied. Yet Dylan's vocals
offer much stabbing conviction, as in the delivery of the line "I won't,
but then again I might—O if I could just find you tonight!" The song
seems addressed to a current muse, and the figure behind the invective
of the song is a woman who, like "Absolutely Sweet Marie," is not able
to be pinned down. The song presents a dark night of the soul—or, as
the subtitle would have it, a "journey through dark heat"—and ends the
album with a resounding sense of Dylan as one who has been tested but

who has come through. "If I'm there in the morning, baby, you'll know I've survived."

What test? The other songs on the album add up to a consideration of the psychic disturbances of romantic love, from the sympathetic direct address of "Baby Stop Crying" to the quizzing of intentions in "Is Your Love in Vain"; to a rueful, if upbeat, sense of inevitable breakup in "True Love Tends to Forget"; to a straightforward consideration of going separate ways in "We Better Talk This Over"; to a sense of new erotic possibility in "New Pony." "Baby Stop Crying," a hit in Europe, finds Dylan offering a fairly conventional lyric about proving his love for a woman who has "been down to the bottom with a bad man." The chorus, in its trio of repetition, is primarily a showcase for the backup singers who add a very savvy sense of emotional investment. "Love in Vain" spins out a form of questionnaire in which the singer makes demands of his lover, while also allowing for the difficulty of making love matter: "I've been burned before and I know the score, so you won't hear me complain." The overriding question is delivered twice, after sketching—in the voice of an eligibility quiz—the domestic comforts a woman can provide: "are you willing to risk it all?"

"True Love Tends to Forget" boasts some characteristic Dylan wit in its final couplet: "Don't keep me knockin' about from Mexico to Tibet" to rhyme with the title phrase. Elsewhere "this weekend in Hell is making me sweat." The song doesn't take its situation seriously—like "Don't Think Twice," "I Don't Believe You," and "Most Likely You Go Your Way," the song shrugs at the inevitable sundering and refuses to pull its punches. "We Better Talk This Over" is even more canny in its appraisal of the impasse of lost passion: "You don't have to be afraid of looking into my face / We've done nothing to each other time will not erase." The position of the song makes it kin to some of the great broken romance songs on *Blonde on Blonde*—such as "One of Us Must Know"—or *Blood on the Tracks*' "You're Gonna Make Me Lonesome." There's a rueful sense of no longer wanting to indulge a love that has gone wrong—"two-faced and double-dealing"—while at the same time maintaining a testy independence—"I'm exiled and you can't convert me." The song includes one of the most clear-eyed couplets for the value of a concluded romance: "Don't think of me and fantasize on what we've never had / Be grateful for what we've shared together and be glad." Later in his career Dylan would team up with The Grateful Dead and even compose songs with Robert Hunter, Jerry Garcia's lyricist; the feel of "Better Talk This Over" has the kind of positive spin The Dead are known for, while the shuffling groove of the song would not be out of place on the band's 1979 album *Shakedown Street*.

The mention of conversion above is interesting in the light of Dylan's subsequent conversion to Christianity during the 1978 tour; even more interesting is the line in "New Pony": "baby, but that god that you been prayin' to gonna give you back what you wishin' on someone else." The line takes the song's image for a new lover—as a pony to "climb up on top of"—toward a statement of principles. The previous line mentions voodoo, and a will to wish ill on someone else through prayers to a pagan god. But regardless of what god is prayed to, the un-Christian idea of praying *against* someone brings a rebuke of such ill will. In the midst of a bawdy song of sexual ascendancy, suggesting the costs of having to shoot one pony (named "Lucifer") only to find a better one, Dylan testifies to a sense of vocation. With a funky blues delivery, the line rings with the kind of "touch me not" sentiment found in lines like "don't ask me nothin' about nothin' I just might tell you the truth."

Despite its at times uninspired recording, *Street-Legal*, with its songs full of the need to arrive at a personal vision of truth, is the last great Dylan album for some time. Songs like "New Pony" and "O Where Are You Tonight?" go furthest to show the extent of the estrangement Dylan might be feeling at this point—not only from his family, friends, and fans but even from his earlier personae. The songs about romance are deft and economical and the visionary songs show Dylan to be awash in cryptic images and language he is struggling to master. One might expect a turn from such complexity to songs more simple and straightforward. *Slow Train Coming*, the album released fifteen months later, would find Dylan ditching his more tangled self-conceptions in pursuit of the simplicity of soul that befits a true Christian. This unprecedented change in direction had mixed results.

"A PROPHET IS NOT WITHOUT HONOUR, BUT IN HIS OWN COUNTRY . . ." (MARK 6:4)

> I follow God, so if my followers are following me, indirectly they're
> gonna be following God too, because I don't sing any song which
> hasn't been given to me by the Lord to sing.
> —Bob Dylan to Bruce Heiman, KMEX (Tucson, Arizona) (273)

The extremity of the position stated above, in an interview Dylan gave on the radio while on tour in 1979, nearly four months after the release of *Slow Train Coming*, illustrates why Dylan at this time perplexed his fans anew, and more so than ever before. While the switch from the folk song to rock and surreal poetry had been jarring, making his listeners question whatever they believed they already knew about Bob Dylan, the change to singing only songs that carried a message of belief in Jesus Christ was even more astonishing. Dylan presented his new music as not only an artistic departure but also as having a different relation both to himself and his listeners. To "follow" him now, as a fan or as a casual listener, was to "follow God." While other artists Dylan admired—notably Elvis Presley and Johnny Cash—had often sung devotional songs and made statements about their efforts to be followers of Christ, Dylan took the sense of devotion to a further extreme, as if any former purposes as an artist/entertainer or as a writer/performer were irrelevant. The absolutism of the change drew critical flak even as it impressed some with its commitment.

Those who caught Dylan's shows in 1979 and 1980, besides hearing new songs played with great conviction by a crack touring band, encountered a new Bob Dylan: a proselytizing preacher, a man with a message he was no longer content to let his songs enunciate, rapping between songs with his audience about faith in Christ. The need for Christ, in Dylan's mini-sermons, had to do not only with one's personal salvation but with the ultimate fate of the world. Dylan often offered doomsday pronouncements, indicating that whoever did not discover Christ soon, for real, risked losing everything "when He returns." Dylan's conversion was not simply a decision to "get religion" for the sake of "a closer walk with Thee," but was couched in terms of eschatological prophecy, of ideas about "end times" and "the last days." Rather than a believer spreading the joyful news, Dylan sounded like an Old Testament prophet, calling down God's wrath on an atheistic, materialistic, immoral world—in the name of Jesus.

For a writer who had, in his youth, presented listeners with songs like "A Hard Rain's A-Gonna Fall," "With God on Our Side," and "When the Ship Comes In," the tone of these pronouncements was not unfamiliar. Dylan's early work at times alluded to planetary destruction, to World War III, and described the world as a modern Babylon without values or peace of mind. With *John Wesley Harding*, Dylan had shown his ability to construct modern fables, to brood upon the state of his own soul, and to find the message of love. The vision of love that concluded that landmark album—the love of a man and a woman—was not enough to sustain the mature search for meaning that came in the wake of his own failed marriage and, it seems, a loss of conviction about his own ability as a writer to discover truth in his own "message." In other words, Dylan's crisis at the end of the seventies was fueled both by his personal needs and by a more general feeling of crisis in the world at large. According to his biographer, Howard Sounes, women close to him at the time, such as Mary Alice Artes and Carolyn Dennis, who was also a member of Dylan's band and eventually his second wife, were instrumental in his move toward Christ, but other musicians in his circle had converted as well (324–25). Dylan tells the story of a conversion moment or "born-again experience" while on tour in 1978 (Hilburn, 279, 281).

For all its turmoil, the sixties represented only the early stages of the Cold War, with less developed nuclear capabilities and, in the West, unprecedented prosperity. By the end of the seventies, the bite of economic crisis had become a concept: "stagflation," with low growth, low wages, high prices. And, with the oil crisis, the costs of the gas-guzzling lifestyle of the modern world became evident, causing anxieties about the parts of the world—particularly the Arab world—whose oil supplies the "first world" relied on to a great extent. For some, the sense of global crisis was very much in the air as the eighties dawned, with the USSR's invasion of Afghanistan in December 1979 inspiring prophets of doom to foresee an imminent Armageddon. What's more, this was the period of such events as the Three Mile Island accident at a nuclear power plant in Pennsylvania, so that the sense of a world imperiled by nuclear power set off more doomsayers. For some, such events bring to mind biblical prophecies, in the belief that any major catastrophe or cataclysm must be in keeping with God's plan for mankind. Such associations were by no means rare or obscure, with books like Hal Lindsay's *The Late Great Planet Earth* trumpeting how biblical prophecies could be interpreted to identify the 1980s as the time of Christ's second coming. First published in 1970, the book played to fundamentalist fears, and the film version was one of the top-grossing movies of 1979. Christianity, both in its millennial variety and in its populist reach through televangelists, had become a viable platform from which to condemn everything from abortion to homosexuality, calling for a strict interpretation of the Bible to determine civil policies. Such self-righteous judgments on the modern world in the name of Christ would be with us well into our current century.

Dylan's new direction capitalized on this spirit. *Slow Train Coming*, released in August 1979, was much better received than *Street-Legal* (the first Dylan album since *Another Side* not to crack the Top 10). *Slow Train* reached number 3 in the United States and earned Dylan a Grammy for Rock Vocal Performance, Male, for the lead song "Gotta Serve Somebody." One reason for the album's success was that Dylan found in Jerry Wexler and Barry Beckett producers able to record with both slickness and muscle. The record meets the AOR requirements of a smooth radio sound, abetted by the sinuous guitar of Mark Knopfler. Knopfler, the lead guitar, voice, and songwriter for Dire Straits, had not yet attained the mega-stardom that would come in the mid-eighties, but he had already created a radio-friendly sound with the hit "Sultans of Swing." That said, *Slow Train* can best be described as having a great side 1 and a rather spotty side 2, with only "When He Returns," the closer, offering a song of sufficient quality to match the album's first side. Still, the combination of production and musicians on *Slow Train* proved effective, and Dylan's Christ-centered message reached a wide audience.

And yet there was considerable resistance to the message when it dominated Dylan's shows. Such was the typical disjunction between Dylan's albums and the expectations surrounding his performances. For some, Dylan should be a greatest hits machine, forever recreating a long-gone heyday. Those better informed might avoid the concerts altogether, preferring some more secular version of rock and roll salvation. Those who wanted to hear Dylan's new music played with maximum conviction were ecstatic at his shows.

The album's hit, "Gotta Serve Somebody," achieves a better mix of female singers with the overall sound than anything on the previous album (with the possible exception of "New Pony"), giving the song a richer texture, its bass and drums creating a percolating groove, as if ready to bubble over into outright funk at any moment. The song feels at times quite lighthearted—with the aside "You can call me Bobby, you can call me Zimmy"—and also slyly taunting, offering a litany of situations that might occur before one finds the Lord, much like the possibilities in which "they'll stone ya" in "Rainy Day Women #12 & 35." Here, the exhortation is that one will have to "serve somebody": the devil or the Lord. The urgency of the singing at times lifts the song from the fanciful into a register that makes the promise of a coming revelation convincing. Dylan cannily announces his conversion with a song that plays with his listeners, tossing off rhymes and affecting the stance of a glib preacher reaching his audience through his savoir faire rather than his humility.

"Precious Angel" is an example of how a great sound—with horns, Knopfler's liquid guitar fills, and girl-group backing vocals embellishing lines like, "you either got faith or you got unbelief and there ain't no neutral ground"—tempers the message of Dylan's new music. The swankiness of the track emphasizes that God's mercy may be best found embodied in a woman who can "torch up the night." There are some truly odd lines—"but there's violence in the eyes, girl, because our forefathers were slaves / Let us hope they've found mercy in their bone-filled graves"—and a new version of Dylan's characteristic whine in "I just couldn't make it by myself, I'm a little too blind to seeee-heeee." The song, not wholly successful, shows Dylan's verbal imagination struggling to find images to embody his new convictions. As might be expected, a Christian message, in Dylan's terms, might take some odd turns: "On the way out of Egypt, through Ethiopia, to the judgment hall of Christ." Dylan may well be identifying with the Hebrew exodus from Egypt, here coming to Christianity due to the influence of "Ethiopia," standing perhaps for his black girlfriends, all of whom may have influenced his move to gospel, though it seems Mary Alice Artes was the main catalyst (Sounes 317–26).

The third track is where *Slow Train Coming* really arrives. Here Knopfler's fills are more supportive than distracting and the vocal from Dylan, while edging toward a kind of lovesick bleat at times, achieves a restrained dignity in most of the verses. The song lays out a reworking of an old blues conceit: being persecuted for one's beliefs or for one's love, here one and the same. Dylan's singer is a man whose friends will forsake him, but who begs to be "set apart from all the plans they do pursue." It might seem an oddly separatist credo—rather than uniting all in the true faith—as the singer insists that, though shunned and misunderstood, his belief in "You" will not be swayed. The song demonstrates an effective yoking together of the belief in God's love and the belief that a lover finds in his beloved. The success of the song is in Dylan's skill at evoking "the blues" of both kinds of love.

"Slow Train," more or less the title track, is a rare lyrical tour de force in this period of Dylan's writing. The attitude of the song is rather prickly for a Christian, with Dylan, in the era of the oil crisis, railing against OPEC—"shieks walking around like kings, wearing fancy jewels and nose rings, deciding America's future from Amsterdam and Paris." If Dylan seems an unlikely patriot—think only of his "115th Dream"— the sentiment is much in keeping with the Christian U.S. view of "the infidels" of the Muslim nations. The "with God on our side" ideal that Dylan had held up for sharp scrutiny in his song of that title seems to underwrite the idea that the United States, in its status as a self-defining "Christian nation," is morally superior to the nations of unbelievers. In the name of this rather reactionary God, the song is generally cranky toward the singer's contemporaries, or "companions"—"all their earthly principles they're gonna have to abandon." But when has a holier-than-thou attitude been delivered with such a strong groove? And Dylan, enlightened by his conviction of true belief, effectively distances himself from the high-priced charlatans professing Jesus on the airwaves of the United States, taking aim at "nonbelievers and men stealers talkin' in the name of religion," while throwing down a gauntlet for the godly: "they talk about a life of brotherly love—show me someone who knows how to live it." Knopfler's guitar helps create the barbed vibe of the song, a coiled rant by someone feeling "lowdown and disgusted."

Side 2 starts with "Gonna Change My Way of Thinking," which speaks of a woman who can "do the Georgia Crawl" and "walk in the spirit of the Lord," while telling us that heaven and earth were made about the same time. With a little more work, the song might have said something interesting about the change in Dylan's thinking, but as it is, the singer simply spouts homilies. "When You Gonna Wake Up" runs further afield, yoking together Marx and Henry Kissinger and offers: "There's a man named Christ and He been crucified for you / Believe in His power, that's about all you gotta do." As fulfilling as that thought might be for the faithful, it offers little as a claim for belief in Christ or even as a statement about what his belief in Christ means for Dylan. Elsewhere there are pat put-downs that sound like the views of any armchair curmudgeon: "Adulterers in churches and pornography in the schools / Gangsters in power and lawbreakers making rules." Certainly, Dylan, like a Mr. Jones surveying the current world, might be moved to say "Oh my God, am I here all alone?" The song deserves better verses as its chorus, in a gospel-inflected blues, asks the rhetorical question: "when you gonna wake up, strengthen the things that remain"—a phrase cribbed from the Bible that Dylan puts to good effect.

Two other songs on the side are essentially good musical grooves that have little to say. "Do Right to Me Baby (Do Unto Others)," as the catchiest song on the album, is brighter than "Serve Somebody," reciting a host of "don't wannas" that might strike Dylan's listeners as reminiscent of "All I Really Want to Do"; in both cases the pronouncements are good natured, and the refrain, "Do right to me baby and I'll do right to you too / You got to do onto others like you'd have them do unto you," takes a tenet of scripture and makes it singable and danceable. "Man Gave Names to All the Animals" provides a shuffling dance with a hypnotic repetitive rhythm as it reels off "just so stories" about how Adam, as the Bible tells it, named all the creatures of the earth. The rhymes are simplistic, aiming at the whimsy of a children's nursery song without quite achieving it. The lyrics of the song were eventually made into a children's book.

Finally, Dylan saves the best for last. "When He Returns" shows that, in the hands of a fertile writer such as Dylan, even a topic as hoary as the imminent Second Coming can find a striking presentation. Set against stark piano, the song could be seen as the antidote to the shattered values of "Dirge" (from *Planet Waves*). There, Dylan voiced a darkly jaded feeling that saw through love as merely prideful and self-serving. Here, trust in Christ has the power to redeem such a fallen world, offering a vision of Christ as—using a metaphor Christ applied to himself—"a thief in the night." The song also effectively cites Christ's line "he who has ears to hear, let him hear" to suggest that, like Christ, Dylan's songs are aimed only for ears that can grasp their spiritual

value. "It is only He who can reduce me to tears," Dylan sings, capturing the change in his outlook much more effectively than the ranting
elsewhere on the album. Delivered in a stringent vocal that caterwauls
into oddly drawn-out phrases on each fourth line, "When He Returns,"
is a tour de force, presenting Dylan as a seeker grappling with the
power of his own faith: "How long can you falsify and deny what is real /
How long can you hate yourself for the weakness you conceal?" Recalling "you have no secrets to conceal" in "Like a Rolling Stone," the line
aims to unmask the vanity of living without God, as if we are all "Miss
Lonely" and rock and roll is no longer the answer, if it ever was.

Sharp in his condemnations of the modern world, Dylan makes his
faith on *Slow Train Coming* sound judgmental and opportunistic, a way
of setting himself apart from and above others while also enjoying hot
times with church-going ladies. But in the final song on the album—
while still threatening the end of the world upon Christ's return—
Dylan's grasp of how identification with Christ drives the chariot of
Christianity in both its power and its humility begins to come through.
One begins to believe he really means what he's singing about, that the
return of Christ is imminent and necessary. And yet there is still much
doubt as to whether the message of Christ is best for Dylan's songs, and
even more, whether Dylan's songs are the best settings for Christ's
message. It is clear, however, that Dylan has found a belief in something beyond human history and beyond the present: heaven, as the
realm of God and of the eternal, matters to him as an answer to dark
doubts about his fellow man. Christ is still primarily a prophet to Dylan,
as he is in the Jewish tradition. Crucial to Dylan's Christ is his status as
the prophet who fulfilled his own prophecy—in dying and being raised
from the dead—and who will yet fulfill the prophecy about coming in
judgment at the end of human time. Ron Rosenbaum's reaction to the
album was maybe best: "Perhaps we're lucky he's only claimed he's
found Jesus; it wouldn't be totally surprising if he claimed he *was* Jesus"
(Thompson, 236).

"BORN AGAIN" BOBBY

Saved, the follow-up "Born Again" album, was released in the brutal
summer of 1980, when a heat wave in the central and southern United

States caused over a thousand deaths, joined by a drought of almost biblical proportions. Such "hell on earth" conditions might inspire more credence for an imminent heavenly intervention. The album, however, did not garner nearly the attention, sales, or critical approval of its predecessor. In general, *Saved* feels as if Dylan has become the celebrant of a rock-gospel cult of Christ. The music is infectious and, much more than on the previous LP, imparts the sense that belief in Christ is an upbeat and joyous affair. Four of the songs, "Saved," "Solid Rock," "Pressing On," and "Are You Ready," have the enthusiasm of a prayer meeting, making the album a genuine gospel effort. The performances, delivered with Dylan's usual live-in-the-studio recording technique, are not as fully successful as they might be, partly because one feels that this music, perhaps more than any other album in Dylan's career, would benefit from a live audience. But Tim Drummond's melodic bass guitar in "Solid Rock" is a distinct pleasure, while "Pressing On" rocks with a full head of steam provided by the impassioned backup singers. The songs attest the joy at being "saved" by Christ's sacrifice, stating confidence in the "solid rock" of faith, finding a duty to be "pressing on" against doubts, and finally, giving an exhortation to be "ready" for Armageddon. Obviously, only those with God on their side will be overjoyed at the ultimate destruction of this fallen world. Dylan's lyrics stop short of calling for "the Rapture"—the actual bodily lifting of the faithful up into heaven—but the implication is that being saved means not only release from punishment for sins committed on earth but from the earth's inevitable destruction.

The other four original compositions include a love song to a woman ("Covenant Woman"), a love song to Christ ("What Can I Do for You"), a song of personal testimony ("Saving Grace"), and a narrative testimony ("In the Garden"). "Covenant Woman" repeats some of the sentiments of "Precious Angel," though without the more abrasive flights of imagery; the song is heartfelt and humble, with the singer thanking God for a woman to whom he feels "closer than any friend." The song's uplift depends upon seeing a romantic relationship in terms of God's plan—"he must've loved me oh so much to send me someone as fine as you." When "profane" or sexual love must first be understood in Christian terms, we might say the conversion is complete. More interesting is "What Can I Do for You" which, like "I Believe in You," addresses what feels like a secular love song to Christ, but unlike the earlier song, here the emphasis is not on the persecutions the speaker endures for his faith, but rather on Christ's unrepayable sacrifice. "You've done it all and there's nothing anyone else can pretend to do" sums up the singer's sense of debt to Christ, but also his sense that Christ has achieved all that matters. It's a strong testament of faith and, as with other songs of Dylan's that feature rhetorical questions, makes its strongest case as a questioning of one's own pride.

"In the Garden" is one of the more successful Christian songs, again using rhetorical questions, this time to recount scenes from the life of Christ. The song presents stark but effective sketches of Christ as a teacher, healer, and savior and articulates the outlook of the faithful toward the unbelievers: did they know, did they see, did they hear, did they dare speak out against him? Each time asking whether "they" grasped the meaning of Christ's presence and concluding with the question, "when He rose from the dead, did they believe?" The last question, one of the key doctrines in belief in Christ as God, arrives with considerable force as the question that puts all the others into perspective. The song is an effective reworking of events from the Gospels to ask the central questions of the Christian faith and to voice its status in a world of unbelievers. Of all the Christian songs Dylan wrote in this period, "In the Garden" remained in his return to secular concerts in the eighties.

On *Saved*, the heartfelt piano tune is "Saving Grace," and unlike *Slow Train's* "When He Returns" and its disquisition on the Second Coming, the subject is a personal testament to Christ's power. Dylan opens with a line of humility: "If You find it in Your heart can I be forgiven"—we might think he's addressing a lover, or possibly even his fans, only to find that he's speaking to his Savior. The song has the kind of ready defiance of nonbelievers that Dylan once reserved for the Mr. Joneses of this world. Dylan's model might be a well-known hymn like "Amazing Grace" in asserting that "grace" is what saves the sinner from perdition. Much less a "wretch" than the singer of "Amazing Grace," Dylan seems to take pride in his ability to endure.

The quest for Christ's grace inspires these two albums, but Dylan's attempts to describe his faith tend to come off heavy-handed. Granted, the position of the singer in any of Dylan's songs can be quite mercurial. His love songs run a wide gamut from hurt and reproachful to expansive and jovial, from mystical to bawdy, from romantic to callous. There seems no reason his attempts to register the effect of Christ's love in his heart should be any different. What is off-putting to listeners who have sought their own individual, at times highly creative, meanings in Dylan's songs is that the songs on *Slow Train Coming* and *Saved* do not admit the same degree of interpretive latitude. And if that is also true of some of his love songs, the difference is that the love songs speak from a truly universal position of a lover addressing or describing a beloved. When the "loved one" becomes the Lord, the emotions must circumscribe an individual relation to a higher power. Whether or not we feel called to share in Dylan's faith before God, we must also decide whether Dylan's claims about his faith and his version of Christ resonate. Many of the songs do, and in that sense they succeed, but Dylan's phrases seem at times deliberately antagonistic, at times clumsy, and often indulge a contemptuous, un-Christ-like dismissal of those who haven't accepted Christ.

Saved is the last Dylan album, to date, with an entirely Christian theme.[1] The next album, *Shot of Love*, released in August 1981, is more eclectic and for that reason more satisfying. As a transitional document, *Shot of Love* is interesting and even more so when one considers that the album exists in two different versions: a potential and an actual. "The Groom's Still Waiting at the Altar," a track recorded for the LP and released as a B-side to the single "Heart of Mine," was subsequently, in CD versions, added to the album. There were other songs written for the album and suppressed as well, most notably "Caribbean Wind" and "Angelina," two songs with the kind of vibrant stream of consciousness Dylan had not indulged in since *Street-Legal*.[2]

A SHOT IN THE ARM

On *Shot of Love*, Dylan's position toward the Christian faith is most in evidence in the song "Property of Jesus." Written in the tone of Dylan's put-down songs, "Property" takes aim as critics who denigrated Dylan's conversion, suggesting they are jealous of his righteousness, "because he can't be bribed or bought by the things that you adore." The jibe that his critics "resent him to the bone" for being "the property of Jesus," would act as the proverbial "red rag" to many critics' bull. Other songs express a relation to Christ that is more subtle, delivered in the title track with a funky R&B vibe due in part to Bumps Blackwell sitting in as producer and, in "Dead Man, Dead Man," a loose shuffle, complete with sax and wailing background vocals. Dylan's religious fervor, we might say, is moving away from gospel toward something with more "street cred." Add to the mix the straight-ahead blues tune "Trouble"— a song that simply describes the fallen world without making any gestures about its end or salvation—to see that Dylan is arriving at a unique gospel-blues sound.

Love songs on *Shot of Love* move toward the secular, but with a more high-minded sense of love's benefits than in songs typically addressed to a beloved. In fact, "Heart of Mine" addresses the singer's own heart, exhorting it to not pursue an unworthy, perhaps adulterous, affair—"If you can't do the time, don't do the crime." The version released on the album enlists Ron Wood, of The Rolling Stones, and Ringo Starr, the former Beatle, and for that reason might be considered a notable track, if only to find these three friends together in the studio. The song is loose, off-the-cuff, sounding more like a rehearsal than a finished track. Such would be the nature of most of Dylan's albums in the eighties. Sessions, often with some famous sidemen sitting in, would yield a few tracks that might never be given a definitive treatment, with neither overdubs nor better takes. Likewise, "Watered Down Love" sounds a bit lopsided; the recording aims for a pop buoyancy, with horns playing the hook, whereas on tour the song had a leaner, hard-rock sound. In other words, even apart from decisions about which tracks to finish and include, the decision about how a song should sound on a record starts to seem increasingly arbitrary, with this album in particular receiving many reworkings with different participants. The problem is less a lack of commitment to the material and more an uncertainty about how to make an album in which all the songs fit and contribute to the whole.

Even so, *Shot of Love* features three standout songs and a fourth so peculiar it merits some comment. The title song is a blast of soul and an indication of how far Dylan is able to go from the kind of music that made his reputation. With the emphatic background vocals at times almost dominating the song, and with the aggressive R&B sound of the rhythm section and Steve Douglas's sax, the song seems to blast out in an entirely new direction for Dylan. And in its lyrics, the sanctimony of some of the previous Christ-beholden songs has been tempered by the sense of humor that had been lacking in recent work. The litany of atrocities committed against the singer—"you only murdered my father, raped his wife, tattooed my babies with a poison pen, mocked my God, humiliated my friends"—mounts with a sense of the absurd, even as it gives voice to some of Dylan's concerns: the mocking of "his god" by those who don't accept his conversion, as well as, figuratively, murdering "The Father," a glance at the atheistic stance of those for whom "God is dead." The song is appealing in its ability to convey the themes of a fallen, godless world that Dylan, in a kind of pilgrim's progress, feels called upon to explore, but the terms are more in keeping with the stance of anyone who is looking for truth in a false world. Jesus gets mentioned but in such a way as to make his presence in the song a source of tension: "like the men who followed Jesus when they put a price upon His head." In other words, a reference to the moment at which one either stays the course or cuts and runs. Even the possible Rapture gets deflated: "Called home, everybody seems to have moved away / My conscience is beginning to bother me today." The "shot of love," then could be both profane and spiritual. We could say that Dylan is looking for something new again.

"In the Summertime" is a mature love song, able to look back on a remarkable affair and speak of it with respect rather than regret. What could be a mournful song of lost youth—the "summertime" of young love and regard—becomes instead a reflection on how the lessons of the past build mansions in the future: "and I'm still carrying the gift you gave, it's a part of me now, it's been cherished and saved, it'll be with me unto the grave and then into eternity." Without overstating the possible "life after death" that his Christian faith makes available, Dylan suggests the possibility of an endless love, the kind that might be shareable, ultimately, only with one's Creator. The song begins: "I was in your presence for an hour or so, or was it a day, I truly don't know," a statement that could more easily address the fleeting feeling of God's presence in one's life than a lover's absence, but at the same time, the lyric lets us see how the moment of recognized love, whenever it occurs and of whatever duration, is the point. The virtue of feeling creates the moment that shall not pass away. Learning the language of Christ's love, as both sacrifice and promise of life everlasting, has deepened Dylan's vocabulary in singing about earthly love.

And a new humility that comes with the realization that there is something beyond the artist's own self-conceptions is present in two other songs on the album. In "Lenny Bruce," Dylan attempts to sum up his feelings for a more or less contemporary figure greater than himself. The occasion for the song, we might suppose, is that Dylan, having written about his sense of persecution for his newfound faith, conjures up another figure who "showed the wise men of his day to be nothing more than fools." In other words, there's still something of a soapbox in this tribute to the taboo-breaking comedian, but at the same time there is sincere awe that finds in someone who "just had the insight to rip off the lid before its time" a source of inspiration: "he was the brother that you never had." Dylan seems unable to pay tribute in song to any but a fallen hero, but here the terms of the tribute suggest the accomplishment: "he fought a war on a battlefield where every victory hurt."

The final song on the album is even more remarkable as Dylan takes stock of the period of strong personal belief which, if not ending, is at least changing. "Every Grain of Sand" shows Dylan trying to assess the wisdom and humility that comes with belief in something greater— whether we call that God's love or a divine plan or simply "meaning." The song opens with the soul-searching sense of coming to terms with events—"In the time of my confession, in the hour of my deepest need." The lyrics abound in genitive abstractions: "the morals of despair," "the flowers of indulgence," "the weeds of yesteryear," "the memory of decay," "the mirror of loneliness." Because Dylan is not prone to such phrases, we can assume that there is a particular reason for such constructions, which are generally regarded as lacking in specificity. In this case, the effect is deliberate—we hear nothing of the actual confession or of what provokes the "deepest need"; instead, the song uses abstractions to support its sense of "sub specie aeternitatis"— the need for universal application beyond any individual's experience. The reflection "every hair is numbered like every grain of sand," a proverb in itself, epitomizes the sense that all of creation has its place and serves its purpose in the whole. Stripped of any images that would situate the song in a specific time and place, "Every Grain of Sand" makes its claim upon the timeless state of "hanging in the balance of the reality of man"—a phrase that would be rather ponderous if not for the delicate delivery and the solemn tone of the song. Dylan caps off this reflective tune with one of the most lyrical and meditative harmonica solos he has ever recorded.

With this song, positioning his own needs within a divine framework that includes all of mankind and all of the earth, Dylan might well choose to rest from his labors. There would not be a new album for two years and that album would be the start of a time of searching and veering about for a course by which to steer not only his recording career but also the very creativity that sustains it.

NOTES

1. In an interview with Mikal Gilmore in 2012 about *Tempest*, Dylan states that he had "wanted to make something more religious." When finally asked about that remark by Gilmore, he mentions "Newly written songs, but ones that are traditionally motivated . . . like a 'Just a Closer Walk With Thee'" (44, 51). Perhaps further Christian songs will be forthcoming.

2. These two songs seem to be referred to by Dylan in an interview in 1981 with Neil Spencer, though he doesn't name either. "Angelina" seems to be the song he likens to "Visions of Johanna," while "Caribbean Wind" would be the song that "goes way back and then it's brought up to the present" (179–80). The latter was released on *Biograph*, in a live version, and "Angelina" on *The Bootleg Series Vol. 1–3*.

7

ROCK AND ROLL DREAMS
(1983–1990)

ROCK, INC.

In the years between Dylan's Christian albums and his subsequent work, the music industry went through a transformation. In 1981, MTV debuted on cable television. Initially, the numbers of music videos available to the VJs was limited, but with each passing year the notion that a song must have a televisable video to reach maximum saturation gained ground. While this new marketing strategy was fine for many artists who began their careers in the 1980s, creating visuals for songs did not suit aging rockers quite so well. Occasionally a long-lived band like The Rolling Stones might concoct a video that was not a complete embarrassment, and slightly younger artists already given to visual presentations, such as David Bowie and Peter Gabriel, brought a certain artistry to the medium. But for figures like Dylan, Neil Young, or Van Morrison, television seemed a rather suspect forum for the presentation of mature rock music. Such mavericks would find themselves eclipsed by the corporatist rationales, with emphasis on image-conscious acts that became the hallmark of the era—led by the ubiquitous Michael Jackson, ready at any moment to be sponsored by Pepsi, or vice versa.

This was also the period in which compact discs (or CDs) began to replace long-playing vinyl disks as the preferred means to store and sell musical performances. The move to digital recording began in the late seventies, but with the change to digital formats for playback, replacing analog technology, and, with the eventual proliferation of the personal computer, the notion of how to record and market music was beginning to change. Such changes had ill effects on the work of virtually every rock artist born before 1949.

In a radio interview in 1984, Dylan half-jokingly suggests that if he were starting out "in this day, with the kind of people that are running record companies now, they would . . . you know . . . bar the doors I think" (Cott *Essential*, 313). It is not an exaggeration to say that in the eighties Dylan had become something of a has-been. For those who still cherished memories of his former work, the current albums were in some ways a confrontation, but mostly a disappointment. Dylan continued to remake himself, but no new version captured the collective imagination. Worse, the uninformed could do little but trot out the obligatory associations with folk, protest, folk-rock, and the sixties. Dylan's Christian phase had alienated those who preferred their rock and roll hedonistic, as well as those who expected rock to denounce the contemporary world from a leftist, rather than evangelical, perspective. Dylan's gradual move away from the moralizing critique of his religious songs left him without a rationale as coherent or vehement. The period 1983–1990 finds Dylan at his most rudderless and tentative to date. He produced two worthwhile, if not great, albums and a number of partially realized projects that both frustrate and intrigue. The period was also marked by numerous collaborations, some more successful than others.

"THE PAST IS JUST A MEMORY"

Infidels, a challenging and varied album, was released in late October 1983. Its sound is reminiscent of *Slow Train Coming*, though with a looser feel by virtue of the Caribbean where Dylan had been spending time unwinding on his yacht and due to the hot and talented rhythm duo known as Sly and Robbie, stars of reggae. Dylan enlisted Mark Knopfler as producer and the musicianship on the album is of high caliber, including former Rolling Stones lead guitarist Mick Taylor, giving Dylan's songs a muscular, at times brooding, setting. More problematically, Dylan chose to leave off two songs that would have transformed the album, "Blind Willie McTell" and "Foot of Pride." As with *Shot of Love*, the final track list for the album was not quite what it could have been had Dylan been satisfied with the recordings of the songs in question. And yet those who regard the album as incomplete judge by what was left off rather than what is present. *Infidels* is Dylan's most successful LP of the eighties.

As the title suggests, the album is in an antagonistic relation, if not exactly with Dylan's audience, then at least with its context. One meaning of "infidel" is simply "nonbeliever," used of anyone who is antireligion, or who has no faith at all. The more common designation is of someone who holds a religious belief contrary to "the one true faith." For Christians, Jews and Muslims are "infidels." For Muslims, Jews and Christians are. This is worth keeping in mind because Dylan, who had recently presented himself as "the property of Jesus," was perceived as vacillating in his religious convictions at this time.

Dylan's departure from the previous three LPs' Christian viewpoint may have been spurred by renewed curiosity about Judaism, if only because he had attended his third son's bar mitzvah in Israel (Sounes 356). The term "infidels," then, might be aimed specifically at Islam, particularly as "Neighborhood Bully" takes the side of Israel in its struggles with Palestine. Dylan's lyrics mock the views of those who find Israel at fault for the strife in the Middle East, while also referencing the benefits the Jewish homeland has conferred on the area. The Israeli-Palestinian conflict was one of the ongoing, insoluble problems of the twentieth century. At the time of the song, Israel was being severely criticized for the invasion of Lebanon, and was implicated in the massacre of Palestinians at the Sabra and Shatila refugee camps in September 1982. The song is remarkable as the first time Dylan articulates in song a sense of Jewish persecution: "he's wandered the earth, an exiled man . . . he's always on trial for just being born." Taken as a topical song, "Bully" may seem hamstrung by its conviction, but the slings and barbs Dylan aims at those opposed to Jewish sovereignty have a certain schoolyard brashness. Dylan's pro-Israel stance—if it is one—made the album seem "conservative," for many.

Another topical song, "Union Sundown" uses the voice of an American Everyman to deplore the loss of confidence in U.S. manufacturing, due to the weakening of the unions that sustained the working class in the United States since the 1930s. Dylan refers to the cheap wages of workers abroad, kept at barely subsistence levels by global corporations. The point is not so different from 1963's "North Country

Blues," but the political conscience of 1983 found the message retrograde. To mourn the fact that the United States was on the wane as a commercial powerhouse was seen as siding with a jingoistic nationalist position that progressives tended to criticize. And yet Dylan, as with the miner's wife speaking in the earlier song, manages to catch precisely the grief and gripes of a working class that felt betrayed. The fact that in 1981 President Ronald Reagan crushed the air traffic controllers' union, thus creating a kind of "open season" on the staples of U.S. labor that had been in place since FDR, made Dylan's song timely and relevant—the unions "are goin' out just like dinosaurs." The song takes aim at the decline in values of the period, as the eighties are notorious for a "get rich at all costs" mentality: "capitalism is above the law / It says, 'it don't count 'less it sells.'" One would be hard-pressed to state the mantra of the decade more succinctly.

A hectoring attitude is also found on "License to Kill," which decries the hubris of the human condition—"Man thinks because he rules the earth, he can do with it as he please." As with "Masters of War," "License" sees a tendency to violence as deeply inscribed in the American ethos. While not as biting as the earlier song, the tone is elegiac; it looks back to the era of "touching the moon" (i.e., the late sixties) as the period when our doom began to be apparent. The lines with the best jab are certainly "maybe an actor in a plot, that might be all that you got till your error you clearly learn." The reference to President Reagan, a former Hollywood actor, seems unmistakable, and the notion that a great error has been committed in the name of the United States is what troubles the "woman on my block" who frets about man's "license to kill." The title might refer to U.S. foreign policy sacrificing its sons—"they bury him with stars"—as well as to the kinds of laws favored by the NRA (which made great strides under Reagan) to allow gun ownership to flourish as an expression of American freedoms—"his brain has been mis-managed with great skill." Dylan's post-Christian writing barely skirts sermonizing at times, but without a sense of salvation. The line "Who is going to take away his license to kill"—another of those nagging rhetorical questions common in Dylan's songs—doesn't suggest that Christ will do so. The sense of spiritual bankruptcy is strong on the album, and Dylan's viewpoint is more caustic than compassionate: "this world is ruled by violence, but I guess that's better left unsaid."

Sly and Robbie give "Man of Peace" one of the standout grooves on the album, providing an almost laid-back attack that serves well the theme of mercurial appearances. Dylan addresses a theme that surfaced on the Christian albums: the idea that a "Man of God" or "Man of Peace" could in fact be "Satan," emphasizing the notion that "good intentions can be evil." Rather than insisting on the Second Coming of Christ, Dylan seems to be more concerned about the coming of the Antichrist, indicating how Christian imagery can serve the devil's purpose: "following the star / The same one the three wisemen followed from the East." The image is reminiscent of the "rough beast" "slouching toward Bethlehem to be born" with which W. B. Yeats ended his famous poem of apocalypse "The Second Coming."

"Jokerman," *Infidels'* most intriguing song, opens the album and comes closest to the kind of scattershot, cut-up imagery of a song like "Changing of the Guards" on *Street-Legal*. Like the earlier song, "Jokerman" encapsulates situations and actions in a cryptic or notational way: "Well, the books of Leviticus and Deuteronomy / the law of the jungle and the sea are your only teachers." The song's poetic flights deliberately play with well-known images and cultural markers: nightingales, bread upon the waters, Sodom and Gomorrah. Even well-known phrases—"fools rush in where angels fear to tread"—combine with details like being born "with a snake in both of your fists" and sleeping in a field "with a small dog licking your face." The title character—Jokerman—is "a manipulator of crowds," who might serve a higher purpose but is perverting his duty. A kind of herald who arrives shortly before "night comes stepping in," Jokerman has no response to the birth at the end that, as with "Man of Peace," may allude to the Antichrist. What makes the song so rich is what makes it so elusive. Dylan seems to be inventing an archetype as we listen, building on a range of associations and loose poetic conceits. As with a figure like Mr. Jones in "Ballad of a Thin Man," any attempt to make a definite character out of Jokerman risks being too literal. But the comparison also shows progress in Dylan's sense of imagery; more than simply an extended evocation of a carnival and a clueless interlocutor, "Jokerman" is rife with metaphysical implications.

Love songs on *Infidels* also share an evangelical aura: from the notion that his bed companion might have been married in a former life "to some righteous king who wrote psalms beside moonlight streams" (in "I and I") to the statement (addressed to a lover in "Sweetheart Like You") "they say in your father's house there's many mansions, each one of them got a fireproof floor." These two songs have to be among the more unusual expressions of early middle-aged desire (Dylan turned forty-two the year the album was released); on the one hand, the singer of "Sweetheart" sounds like an old-timer trying to seduce a woman with the idea of a settled life where she can be "at home, taking care of someone nice who don't know how to do you wrong." But coupled with this kind of outdated sweet talk are ideas of a woman able to "make a name for yourself"—even if it means crawling across "cut glass to make a deal." The singer takes potshots at the corrupt world—where to be important is to have "done some evil deed" and where patriotism is the refuge of scoundrels. The classic clichéd pickup line—"what's a sweetheart like you doin' in a dump like this?"—gets inflected a variety of ways: ironic, seductive, sweet, and pathetic by turns. Aided by Mick Taylor's sensitive guitar work, the mood of the song is quizzical, looking askance at the rituals of seduction but primarily trying to needle a young woman for her own good. It may be a paternalistic gesture (Dylan got flak from most commentators for seeming to speak for patriarchy), but Dylan's vocal suggests he is winking at the song's stance. In any case, the song is a more benign address to another "Miss Lonely," lightly teasing rather than scathing.

"I and I" is a remarkable song, not quite the caliber of "Dirge" or "Señor," but in that vein of dark soul searching, its refrain containing lines of burning challenge: "I and I, in creation where one's nature neither honors nor forgives." The harshness of this idea aligns the speaker with the God of the Old Testament, as the singer asserts the justice of "an eye for an eye and a tooth for a tooth." We might link this idea to "Neighborhood Bully" and see Dylan quoting the Torah as possibly in favor of Israel's more bellicose intentions. Whether such a geopolitical reading is sanctioned, we can at least see the song as a parting from Christ's valuation of forgiveness and meekness above all, as "I and I" becomes "eye for eye." The juxtaposition creates an interesting sense of duality: of God and the Devil or, in a secular sense, of consciousness and conscience, or the God of Abraham and the God of Jesus. Musically, the song benefits from its moody reggae-inflected sound, while Dylan's delivery sounds at times hoary, at times petulant. "Someone else is speaking with my mouth, but I'm listening only to my heart," he allows. Who is Dylan at this point, and what does he want to say?

"Don't Fall Apart on Me Tonight" ends the LP with a lighter touch. The singer, part of an enduring couple, tries to overcome his woman's dissatisfaction by appealing to memory, flattery, and a wry stab at self-portraiture: "but it's like I'm stuck inside a painting that's hanging in the Louvre / My throat starts to tickle and my nose itches but I know that I can't move." The recording makes the most of Sly and Robbie's precise but shuffling reggae groove, underscoring the song's slippery attitude; the singer seems to be warning the woman and pleading as well, trying to appeal to a complex sense of all they have been through, though with a great caveat: "yesterday's just a memory / tomorrow's never what it's supposed to be / and I need you"—the implication is "right now." A now-or-never request that gives the song an urgency that the mellow harmonica, the sly steel guitar, and the casual, "jossing" delivery down-play. It's one of the more likeable songs of this period of Dylan's work, echoing a song like "I'll Be Your Baby Tonight" and by that comparison showing how much more querulous is the claim to lasting romance in the early eighties.

Infidels, then, is an album that shows Dylan still needled by the times, attempting to communicate his discontent. The biblical imagery and the gestures toward totalizing figures make the album's lyrics more evangelical than his pre-Christian albums but with none of the latter's Christ-centric messages. While not the definitive Dylan album for the period that it might have been, *Infidels* is Dylan's strongest album until, arguably, *Oh Mercy* six years later.

"JUST PUT SOME BLEACHERS OUT IN THE SUN"

In the summer of 1984, Dylan toured Europe in support of *Infidels* (the album only reached number 20 in the United States but cracked the Top 10 in the UK). Doubtless the concerts were quite invigorating as Dylan had a topnotch collection of musicians behind him: Mick Taylor, who had played lead on the best Rolling Stones albums and on their celebrated tours in 1969 and 1972; Ian McLagen, who played keyboards for The Faces, Rod Stewart's old band and a more or less second-string Rolling Stones; and on drums, Colin Allen, who had played with many blues and R&B greats.

Real Live, a selection of songs recorded at shows in England and Ireland was released in November 1984—at the end of the month that saw Ronald Reagan's landslide reelection as president of the United States over Humphrey-era liberal Walter Mondale. If one looked to Dylan for any saving grace in such times, when to be called a "liberal" was to be tainted with the legacy of "unworkable" sixties solutions, the live album, combining songs from his best albums with a few new ones, might fill the bill. Alas, the realities of the forty-something slump are all too apparent on this lackluster album. With such a band, and with Glyn Johns producing, the LP could have gone a long way to show that "rock 'n' roll can never die," as Neil Young says. Johns, if he never did another worthwhile thing, could rest on his laurels for having produced Led Zeppelin's debut album in 1969 and The Who's masterpiece, *Who's Next*, in 1971. With Taylor's attack on "Highway 61 Revisited" giving the song Berryesque brightness, this could have been Dylan's *Get Yer Ya Ya's Out*. Instead, the band sounds pro forma, the production more middling than a bootleg, as if this pickup band of one-time greats (or has-beens, if one wants to be unkind) has no sense of innovation. This is "classic rock" as any bar band would present it. Dylan's vocals are clear and definite, even fun at times—he gets an impromptu sing-along on "It Ain't Me Babe" (which might indicate his audience has heard it all too often), and it's a pleasure to hear him ripping through "Tombstone Blues"—with Carlos Santana, no less, sitting in. "Tangled Up in Blue" has many new lyrics, including some gems: "I could feel the heat and the pulse of her as she bent down to tie the laces of my shoes." But on the new songs—"I and I" and "License to Kill"—Dylan's whiny caterwaul does little to convey the presence the songs have on *Infidels*.

Despite the lackluster recording, one can glimpse a crisp, soul-inflected "Ballad of a Thin Man," a very sensitive "Girl from the North Country," and a powerful "Masters of War." The latter is very timely as, during this period, Reagan was touting his Strategic Defense Initiative to override the Mutually Assured Destruction doctrine on nuclear war; this meant that the official rhetoric, more than ever, was "a World War can be won, you want me to believe." As a record, though, *Real Live* does nothing to make its listeners believe in rock's durability or in Dylan's belief in rock. It's 1984 and Dylan and his band are at best recalling a past heyday. Their version of rock has learned nothing from punk and new wave, and lacks conviction, stifling any real return to form.

Contrast the album with Dylan's appearance, March 22, 1984, on *Late Night with David Letterman*, eight months before the release of *Real Live*. Backed by much younger musicians born around the time Dylan's recording career took off, the performance, with a stripped-down band consisting of bass, drums, and guitar, is generally hailed as Dylan's coming-of-age in the eighties, showing that he could turn punk-influenced rock to his advantage. The performance of "Jokerman" gives the lie to Dylan's comment quoted at the start of this chapter. Some visionary record exec should have signed that act.

MIDDLE OF THE ROAD

In popular entertainment, 1984 is the year of the runaway sales of Michael Jackson's LP, *Thriller*, which made the *Guinness Book of World Records*. One of the great crossover LPs of all time, *Thriller* was released in 1982 and went on to top charts for soul, R&B, and pop, spawning three state-of-the-art videos, a TV special, and seven Top 10 singles. Jackson became the new "King" and a one-man revitalization of the music industry. Along with other big sellers like Madonna and Prince, Jackson showed that a new generation, born in the late fifties, had arrived. What's more, these three frontrunners dispelled the idea that the most influential musical artists in the United States should be white and male. There were a few holdouts though. White Soul got a big boost thanks to George Michaels, and the biggest selling rock act of the year was Bruce Springsteen, a working-class guy from New Jersey who began his career hailed as "a new Dylan" and now, at thirty-five, enjoyed huge sales and saturation airplay with his album *Born in the U.S.A.* Springsteen had made the conversion to pop, synths, and hooks as never before. Such successes epitomize the mainstream, overriding the inheritors of sixties-style R&B, based on 12-bar blues, the guitar-driven sound of seventies-style rock. Alternative music tended to take the form of abrasive and gloomy punk-derived New Wave, as in the British band The Cure that helped spawn the new "Goth" look, and moody new bands like R.E.M., U2, and The Smiths. And yet all factions and forms were only too eager to reach the mass audience that MTV made available.

The world of entertainment is generally liberal in its politics, accepting of and at times influential in social progress. Rock in the eighties tended to be, like its American cousin country music, more conservative and predominantly white and male in its demographics. The shift in tastes of young white boys to rap and hip-hop was making rock largely retrograde. For recording artists who began their careers in the sixties, much in this change of status was perplexing. While youth might sometimes be attracted to an artist who got word-of-mouth attention through the endless "best of all-time" lists that magazines like *Rolling Stone* promulgated year after year, aging rockers found themselves playing to aging fans, their concerts a nostalgia binge. To his credit, Dylan, while continuing to play the landmark songs of his youth, continually revamped himself, trying to change with the ever-changing times.

This effort resulted in three distinct ventures that occurred at mid-decade. The first was the "We Are the World" single, a charity event for starving Ethiopians, organized by Harry Belafonte and Ken Kragen for USA for Africa, with the song written by Lionel Richie and Michael Jackson. The single, released in March 1985, involved the vocal talents of a host of big-name recording artists and was notable for its huge success—even people who didn't think much of the song bought it for its historical significance and because proceeds went to the effort to feed Ethiopia. Dylan, long associated with social causes concerning blacks in America and humanitarian causes, such as the benefit for Bangladesh, was no surprise as a participant and his presence on the song is to his credit. And yet there was something vaguely embarrassing about seeing the likes of Dylan, Paul Simon, or Bruce Springsteen, all known as wordsmiths and unique voices in rock/pop, intoning the anodyne lyrics of the song, its tune an example of radio-friendly Easy Listening. The song had no bite and the video of the song showed a collection of well-meaning musical Fat Cats emoting in front of microphones, with legends like Ray Charles, Stevie Wonder, and Dylan rubbing elbows with insipid contemporary radio darlings like Huey Lewis and Daryl Hall.

At this time, Dylan was involved in what would prove to be a somewhat discursive record-making process. *Empire Burlesque*, released in June 1985, seemed promising but, despite what Dylan himself described as the good intentions and interest of his label, was disappointing. While some were intrigued that Dylan enlisted hot producer Arthur Baker, famed for his dance remixes of new wave tracks, among other things, to finish off the final product, others were dismayed by an attempt to appeal to a youthful taste ill-suited to Dylan's music. The album lacked a consistent sound; the *Shot of Love*–era soul of "Never Gonna Be the Same Again" sat uneasily beside songs that begged for a more streamlined and harder approach. The album's hodgepodge range might recall *Self Portrait*, with eighties synth bleats and electronic rhythms replacing the kitschy strings of the earlier album's nod to pop radio. If *Street-Legal* is an album of great material undermined by its recording technique, *Empire Burlesque* is a decent album let down by a scattershot approach and, as with *Shot of Love* and *Infidels*, too much filler. Granted, even albums as firmly entrenched on "all-time greatest" lists as *Highway 61 Revisited*, *Blonde on Blonde*, and *Blood on the Tracks* have lesser songs that leaven the better ones, but *Burlesque*'s lesser songs tend to devalue the whole. And Dylan's best albums have an overriding character to which all the songs contribute. *Burlesque*, uneven and disparate, gives only glimpses of what a fully successful Dylan album of this time might offer. Given Dylan's tacky "threads" on the cover shot and in photos that look like a bad magazine spread on the inner sleeve—which even includes a lyric sheet!—the design and packaging seem aimed for some as yet untapped audience, offering them a burlesque indeed of "Bob Dylan."

The opening song, "Tight Connection to My Heart (Has Anybody Seen My Love)," borrows lines from Humphrey Bogart movies to suggest a contemporary film noir situation, though with a danceable rhythm line somewhere between reggae and funk. Dylan's delivery is suitably tongue-in-cheek and gets the album off to a relaxed, smirking start. "The Real You at Last" flirts with the idea that there can be any "real you" in a culture of put-ons and put-downs. "I'll Remember You" and "Emotionally Yours" both provide glimpses of Dylan's current way with a heartfelt love song. The former song's gesture to a failure to live up to the past—"though I could never say / That I done it the way / That you'd have liked me to"—resonates with anyone trying to take stock of Dylan at this point. "Emotionally Yours," which the O'Jays turned into a soul hit, boasts a lovely melody, something Dylan's detractors tend to overlook as among his lasting talents, but the song, for perhaps the first time in Dylan's career, sounds like "product." "Clean Cut Kid," a pica-resque denouncing of the treatment of veterans, is both comical and angry—"Everyone's asking why he couldn't adjust / Adjust to what, a dream that bust?" With a few flashes of wit in this tale of general abuse by the "They" that run the kid's life, the verses are a bit too unstruc-tured for classic Dylan; the song ends on an anticlimax rather than its strongest statement. "When the Night Comes Falling from the Sky" takes up the kind of pithy sketching of emotional blackmail and psychic distress that Dylan has long been a master of. "This time I'm asking for freedom / Freedom from a world which you deny." The song can be seen as a return to the kind of territory covered by the likes of "Idiot Wind" and "O Where Are You Tonight?" expressing the limit situation of a relationship that spills beyond whatever two people might mean to each other to arrive at an indictment of the times they live in: "I've seen thousands who could have overcome the darkness / For the love of a lousy buck, I've watched them die." The initial recording of the song, with Steve Van Zandt of Springsteen's band, is fiercer and more dynam-ic than the track on the LP, and the final product was treated with the reverb drum sound popular at the time, an effect that makes the song fit as a background track at some middling club.

The last songs on the album, "Something's Burning, Baby" and "Dark Eyes," are two of the more successful. The first offers a labile vocal over a repetitive, martial drum pattern, punctuated with odd sonic touches that give the song an unpredictable feel, suiting well its worried questions to a woman about how her feelings have changed. One of Dylan's skills, since the albums that made both love of Christ and love of a woman patterns for salvation, is to make the end of a love affair seem like an apocalyptic moment, poised on the threshold of complete revelation. "Dark Eyes" takes up the burden of a singer who, as he reflects upon a host of disconnected images, is constantly brought up short by "dark eyes." We might recall the startling line, from "Romance in Durango," that gave to the face of God "serpent eyes of obsidian." Whether the eyes are the eyes of God or of a woman the singer can't forget or of the faces of the dispossessed, the song conveys a stance, somewhat like that of a prophet—"I live in another world where life and death are memorized"—called upon not to denounce the world so much as find a vision of something beyond it.

Musically, Dylan is still working some version of the rock-soul-gos-pel-blues bag he's been in since *Street-Legal*, largely because of his willingness to use backup singers and to marshal sax and synths to fill out his sound, à la Stevie Wonder, an artist able to exploit all tendencies of contemporary music from amazing funk to sappy pap. If one compares *Burlesque* with an album by any of Dylan's contemporaries, one quickly sees how the tastes of the current crop of music engineers and radio execs is deliberate in its betrayal of everything that made sixties-style music vital, but which strikes the youth of the eighties as retrograde. Neil Young, Lou Reed, The Rolling Stones, George Harrison, Ray Davies, David Bowie, Tom Petty—all are more or less adrift in the mid-to-late eighties, their signature sounds suffering as they try to stay afloat in the environment of digital recording, music videos, and rock as glitzy entertainment. As Dylan himself pointed out in an interview from 1986: "you can't compete with a market that's geared for twelve-year-olds" (*Essential*, 317).

The other major event of the mid-eighties for Dylan's listeners was Columbia's release of *Biograph*, a box set of five LPs or three CDs spanning 1961 to 1981, a recording career that, in the mid-eighties, felt like ancient history. The children of the "children of the sixties" were now in their teens, their parents forty-somethings coping with middle age. In such a climate, *Biograph* served several purposes: to create a wave of nostalgia for the youth of aging listeners, so that hearing the songs in their new settings might open the floodgates of memory; to repackage Dylan for younger listeners who, having missed the chance to hear the songs in their initial release, might welcome an encapsulated view of a twenty-year career; to stimulate Dylan fans, critics, and admirers to take stock of where their hero was at present, contrasting his most recent work with famous and not-so-famous tracks from his past. Arguably, *Biograph* did all these things, breaking into the Top 40—significant for a multi-disk release—but was less successful at creating a coherent retrospective of the career. The principle of selection was too spotty, the arrangement rarely creating fully satisfying "sides"—an important failing in the era before CD shuffles and programmed playlists.

The retread aspect is hard to ignore as the songs included on *Bob Dylan's Greatest Hits* are all present again, in the same versions. Some alternate versions of great songs—"Visions of Johanna," "It's All Over Now, Baby Blue"—and demos or live tracks could have been great songs: "Up to Me," "Abandoned Love," "Caribbean Wind" are included to whet the appetite for the vast holdings of unreleased Dylan material. Such material, some of it essential, would begin to find regular, official releases in the next decade.

One of the benefits of the *Biograph* package is rock journalist (later, filmmaker) Cameron Crowe's account of Dylan's career. In very compressed form, it manages to hit all the highlights—with ample commentary from Dylan himself. Dylan is given a lot of space to talk about his own antecedents; stressing how far his own tastes diverge from the rock pantheon he is usually placed in, he mentions that he doesn't much admire anyone under fifty. What's more, he goes into a minor screed about the current state of rock which is all too accurate, claiming more than once that rock music, which once was somewhat dangerous and unacceptable, had become, by 1985, purely a big ticket venture, underwritten by beverage manufacturers and being used to sell the high consumption products of American commerce. Dylan speaks like an irritated renegade, a throwback whose sense of musical possibility remains firmly entrenched in fairly obscure folk, blues, gospel, soul, and other forms of music with no direct purchase on the mass products of rock and pop. Dylan also expresses his reticence at "dissecting" his songs or trying to historicize his achievement. He takes exception with the idea of "the sixties" as a cultural turning point, and voices frustration with the various takes on his work, whether critical or favorable. Sounding a bit cranky and a bit of a crank, Dylan speaks as he pleases, as a unique musical artist who has seen a period of creative flowering become an era of crass endeavor.

"OH, IF THERE'S AN ORIGINAL THOUGHT OUT THERE, I COULD USE IT RIGHT NOW"

As extensive retrospective, *Biograph* invites a critical evaluation of Dylan's career. Why were there so many wrong turns and less than successful albums, why so few landmark songs after the sixties when there is such a wealth before 1968? Even if his initial transformation—from a leading writer of new folksongs to an electric iconoclast—had been unsettling, each transformation thereafter was more questionable. And yet from the point of view of the 1980s, a time when music, films, and any medium with a commercial basis were becoming more meretricious, Dylan's corpus displays a rare capacity for idiosyncratic reinvention. While some changes yielded better results than others, most were undertaken with little regard for market considerations and with little marketing—unlike the kind of media-savvy blitzes that launched *Thriller* or *Born in the U.S.A.* And the fact that *Biograph*'s sales indicated that "old Dylan" could outsell current Dylan was no doubt a rather discouraging prospect for an artist still making music without much concern about what his fans might want to hear. If Dylan's listeners hanker for repeats of his classic songs, why not give them alternate takes and live performances? And if his fans regularly collect even the tracks Dylan deemed unsuitable for release, like warm-ups and outtakes, then why bother to construct a professional product? *Empire Burlesque* showed how a more commercially savvy touch could go awry.

In subsequent albums—*Knocked Out Loaded* (1986) and *Down in the Groove* (1988)—Dylan reached his nadir. These are collections of odds and ends with little attempt to create an album with a distinct purpose, sound, or statement. If they make statements, it is as commentary on the ad hoc nature of Dylan's music-making lifestyle: going into a studio when and where it might suit, laying down tracks with the many musicians he comes into contact with, sometimes capturing a successful cover of someone else's song, sometimes taking the time to do justice to one of his own compositions. The latter were becoming fewer. As he beseeches in "Brownsville Girl" from *Knocked Out*: "Oh, if there's an original thought out there, I could use it right now!"

On side A, "They Killed Him," written by Kris Kristofferson, is given a big treatment, recorded with a children's chorus, Steve Douglas on sax, and the backup singers dominating. A commemoration of self-sacrificing leaders who died prematurely, the song combines Mahatma Gandhi, Martin Luther King Jr., and Jesus Christ, and is given a spirited rendition, as is "Precious Memories," a traditional tune arranged by Dylan, though the two tracks place the singer in somewhat mawkish territory. Perhaps if one were Dylan's age. . . . More biting are the original compositions "Drifting Too Far From Shore" and "Maybe Someday," both of which offer nervy tell-offs of a lover, throwing out odd barbs—"We weren't on the wrong side, sweetness, we were the wrong side"—and offhand comments like "I always liked San Francisco, I was there for a party once." In general, as a collection of "outtakes,"

Knocked Out Loaded is likeable enough because of its shrugging, "whatever we got" attitude.

The only selling point of the album—the song that is "a must"—is "Brownsville Girl," written with award-winning playwright Sam Shepard. The song, which began life in a looser version called "New Danville Girl" in the *Empire Burlesque* sessions, is a singular tour de force that makes the rest of the album mere filler: "Got My Mind Made Up," written with Tom Petty and performed with his band, The Heartbreakers, is a decent up-tempo rocker without much interest, other than the singer's claim that he's "going off to Libya"; "Under Your Spell," written with Carole Bayer Sayer, has a subtle vocal, at times colorful lyrics— "pray that I don't die of thirst, baby, two feet from the well"—and a pleasant melody.

"Brownsville Girl" is a rare example of Dylan actually returning to an earlier song and getting it right for a later album ("Mississippi" is another). The framing story features the narrator trying to recall a particular Western film starring Gregory Peck, a recollection that breaks up as he tends to identify with the actions in the film as well as the vague situation in which he, perhaps, "sat through it twice": "I don't remember who I was or where I was bound." The addressee of the song is the "Brownsville girl" with whom the narrator had an adventure "down in Mexico," by way of the Alamo, that involved her bearing witness for him in a courtroom, and, at the same time that he recalls to her (and us) those events, he also tells the story of traveling across the Rockies with a different woman, who reminds him of the Brownsville Girl. Together the current pair call upon Henry Porter's wrecking lot in Amarillo, Texas, where they encounter Ruby. Thus, situated within these narratives is a past tense narrative of the visit to Ruby, a narrative that mostly consists of quoted dialogue.

The Ruby segment is charmingly odd. It consists of three verses which are ABAB whereas all other verses are ABCB. Ruby is characterized with a kind of generic particularity—red haired, older than the couple, "broken-hearted," yet amused and bemused by their intention to "go all the way till the wheels fall off and burn." The key lines attributed to her say much about her character. "Even the swap meets around here are getting pretty corrupt" indicates her disillusion with where she lives, intruding with a sense of shrinking possibilities into the expansive road trip of the young lovers; her other telling line charac-

terizes them with admiration: "Oh you know some babies never learn."
A sadder but wiser sage, Ruby provides a prosaic reality at the heart of
the trip with the second lover, which is already being measured against
the initial time with the Brownsville Girl: "she don't want to remind me,
she knows this car would go out of control."

The earlier journey—involving perhaps a mistaken identity or an
arrest for an actual crime—exists in the deep background as the narrator's wild oats, a tale that, like the film being recalled, is both defeatist
and heroic. In the film, Gregory Peck, the gunslinger, is shot in the back
but wants the townsfolk to tell the story as if his killer "outdrew me, fair
and square." The intention is to give the killer a reputation as a gunslinger—so that he will face the same fate as Peck's character. The
doubling in the movie extends to the doubling in the song, where the
second woman exists in the space created by the Brownsville Girl, and
where the singer, identifying with Peck in the film, is perhaps ponder-
ing the way in which he was, metaphorically, "shot in the back." In
other words, there's a sense that betrayal at one point or another under-
mines the rapport with the Brownsville Girl: "I ain't in the mood anymore to remember the time when I was your only man."

Irregularity is in the very structure of the song; not only does the
verse form change, but there are initially six verses before the chorus,
then two groups of four verses divided by a chorus and followed by a
chorus, then three verses and a final chorus. Before the penultimate
chorus, the singer brings us to the present where he is standing in line
in the rain to see a new Gregory Peck movie, so that, in a sense, the
entire song is an internal address to the Brownsville Girl, sparked by
fragmentary memories of the initial Peck film and mixed up with the
visit to see Ruby, in the company of the girl with "that dark rhythm in
her soul." The final three verses act as a kind of coda bringing all the
elements back to the present as figments from the past, including the
delightful information that "the only thing we knew for sure about
Henry Porter is that his name wasn't Henry Porter." The past—and this
is the main point of the song—is where heroic acts and romantic events
take place, where the Brownsville Girl does "the best acting I saw
anybody do" and where the singer said "hang onto me baby and let's
hope that the roof stays on." Recalling the film is in a sense reliving the
film, and both the film and the viewing of it happened "a long time ago,
long before the stars were torn down." The placement of the song in the

present makes it an elegy for the singer's youth, for his love affair with the Brownsville Girl, and for the great acting careers of Hollywood icons like Gregory Peck. "The stars" of Hollywood had indeed been eclipsed by 1986.

In that year, several of Dylan's contemporaries and near contemporaries produced works near their best ever—as with Paul Simon's *Graceland*—or their best for the decade, as with Van Morrison's *No Method, No Teacher, No Guru*, while, in the previous year, Tom Waits created one of the most intriguing and satisfying albums of the decade with *Rain Dogs*, and, late in that year, Leonard Cohen's *Various Positions* presented "Hallelujah," an amazing song that would be much covered in the decades ahead, including by Dylan himself in a live performance. Elvis Costello, on *King of America*, showed himself capable of an interesting hybrid "American" sound, developed with T-Bone Burnett, who had been on the Rolling Thunder Revue, and musicians who had played with the real Elvis; newer artists given to memorable ways with song lyrics—Nick Cave and Robyn Hitchcock—were beginning to produce albums that showed much potential. Meanwhile, bands who began their recording careers in the eighties released peak albums—R.E.M. with *Lifes Rich Pageant* and The Smiths with *The Queen Is Dead*. In other words, Dylan's halfhearted mid-to-late eighties albums show a weak hand, matched against other work produced in this period. Had he been willing to go back for other abandoned songs and include "Foot of Pride," "Blind Willie McTell," "Tell Me," and "Angelina," then *Knocked Out Loaded* would indeed have been "loaded." Instead, those gems would have to wait for the first *Bootleg Series* release in 1991.

The next Dylan album, *Down in the Groove*, released in May 1988, shortly after Dylan's forty-seventh birthday, is almost entirely forgettable, except for a few songs that merit release, if not on an official album then on an official bootleg. Indeed, the fact that it was becoming difficult to distinguish "commercial" products from "illegitimate" releases says much about Dylan's production at this time. The decisions that make an album a commercial success—beginning with material and extending to musicians, arrangements, and production and, more and more crucially, to marketing campaigns and music videos—continued to elude Dylan in this period. Given that his material at this time was less than stellar, there seemed little reason to try for success by other means. The new song on *Groove* is "Silvio," a collaboration with Robert Hunter, a lyricist known for his compositions with the Grateful Dead's Jerry Garcia, which offers lines like "Staked my future on a helluva past" and "I've seen better times, but who has not," effective as tongue-in-cheek references to the has-been status dogging Dylan at this point. The chorus—"I gotta go, find out something only dead men know"—seemed a backdoor entry for the idea, proposed on the Christian albums, that something better awaits us after shuffling off this mortal coil. The B side, as it were, to this upbeat track is "Ugliest Girl in the World," a little novelty romp played for laughs that gestures to the kind of whimsy Dylan's collaborative project The Traveling Wilburys achieves. A cover of "90 Miles an Hour Down a Dead-End Street" is stunning in its delivery, boasting the kind of beguiling choices Dylan could occasionally still pull out in live performance. Another song alluding to the idea that Dylan might not only be tired of his own art and of the pressure of being "Bob Dylan" but of life itself is "Death Is Not the End," an outtake from *Infidels* offered here with backing vocals by Full Force, a hip-hop band, that soulfully suggests happiness in the life to come. The list of musicians on *Groove* is impressive, including Eric Clapton, members of The Grateful Dead, and Sly and Robbie, but none of the big names manage to contribute a noteworthy musical effect. The album is rather less than the sum of its parts. A song here and there, lifted out and placed elsewhere, might manage to shine a bit more.

The 1988 album involving Dylan that merits praise is *The Traveling Wilburys Vol. 1*, the production of a fake five-man "band of brothers," devised by George Harrison in collaboration with Jeff Lynne, Roy Orbison, Dylan, and Tom Petty. As such, the lineup offers a great mix of younger and older artists. Orbison's career extends back to the debut period of such greats as, in addition to himself, Elvis Presley and Johnny Cash. Harrison proved himself to be the Beatle, after the group's break-up, most in keeping with its lighthearted attitude, and had collaborated with Dylan in the past; Lynne came to fame through his band, Electric Light Orchestra, which began as a Beatles-meets-prog rock outfit and gradually became a big radio hit maker of the late seventies; Petty began his career in the late seventies and by the late eighties was the bandleader for one of the few remaining "old time rock and roll" bands still commercially successful, having a lot to do with his ability to add his Southern influences to the mix; he had already backed Dylan on tour and composed and recorded with him. *The Traveling Wilburys, Vol. 1* was a great commercial success with an infectious sound, by turns Beatlesque, in its use of hooks and harmonies (arguably, no one recording at this point knew better than Jeff Lynne how to use harmonies like The Beatles did, and he had helped breathe new life into Harrison's recording career on the latter's *Cloud Nine*); Dylanesque, in its odd, verbal sallies, particularly in a memorable Springsteen takeoff called "Tweeter and the Monkey Man"; Golden Oldie, in melodies that smacked of Orbison's heyday; and very much eighties, in its production values and its style-over-substance attitude.

The album, and the five together in music videos, went a long way to showing that the greats of the sixties still had life left in them. Dylan sounds like he is enjoying the camaraderie of making music as he did in the Big Pink period, writing songs simply for the fun of it. Collaboration was becoming the main feature of this period of Dylan's work, with *Traveling Wilburys* the most successful collaboration in terms of wide audience appeal. The follow-up album, *Traveling Wilburys, Vol. 3*, in October 1990, not as successful, was a more standard rock LP in sound. Essentially a comical album, the songs have a tendency toward deliberate parody or humor.

A chief characteristic of Dylan's songwriting in the 1980s is a tendency to be fairly ornate with poetic conceits, often borrowed from sources ranging from the Bible to films, while also generating many throwaway lines, often strikingly odd or laconic or, at times, biting. Rarely does a lyric fully maintain a grasp on its mode potent enough to enter the canon of great Dylan songs. And yet more than a handful make the grade: "Brownsville Girl," "Jokerman," "I and I," "Blind Willie McTell," "Foot of Pride," "Don't Fall Apart on Me Tonight," "Tight Connection to My Heart," and "Something's Burning, Baby." The problem with Dylan's recorded work at this point is largely attributable to failings in follow-through, and of choices about which version to release. Uncertainty about what should be "the Dylan sound" at this point extended as well to live performance.

PLAYIN' IN THE BAND

By 1986, performers like Prince and Madonna were already showing their age. To their credit, they had the talent to continue past the point at which "youth culture" worshipped them. Dylan had passed that point around 1970, and by the mid-eighties his following was fairly static, largely due to live performance rather than albums. Among his contemporaries, The Rolling Stones had also ceased getting much critical incentive for their new releases, but still commanded adulation and huge incomes through live performances. Dylan, a legendary presence in his own right, was not then and never had been a "rock star" in the manner of Mick Jagger, The Rolling Stones' lead singer and showman. By mounting big tours in support of the albums—shows that consisted primarily of songs from earlier eras that people recognized and liked better than the new songs—The Stones could move more units than if they didn't tour. Like The Stones, the audience for Dylan was not clamoring for new work—they wanted to hear and see the songs they already knew and loved played live. By touring, essentially nonstop, Dylan kept his legacy alive, could stir up interest in his considerable back catalog, and perhaps prod a listener or two to seek out his current recordings. The big sellers among Dylan's records would always be the compilations—like *Greatest Hits* and *Biograph*—which brought together the highest number of celebrated songs. The Stones also thrived on such repackagings.

For The Stones, however, performing did not present the same kind of problem as it did for Dylan. As long as Jagger and his primary collaborator Keith Richard were willing to play together onstage, some configuration of "Stones" would accompany them. That necessarily included Charlie Watts, the drummer. But the bass player, Bill Wyman, bowed out for good after the 1989 tour, and by 1986 there had been three different second guitarists. The Stones, as a band of musicians, were a known entity, and people wanted to hear them play. As a solo performer, Dylan always had to face the question of whom he would play with. Hired musicians do not always make a cohesive sound, certainly not a famed one, such as The Stones or Springsteen's E Street Band could boast. Playing with already existing bands who have a practiced way of playing together risked turning Dylan's sound into someone else's—which happened on Tour '74 with The Band—or risked a certain incoherence when the band tried to play "Dylan's way." In the period 1986–1991, Dylan would face some version of all these pitfalls, though he eventually arrived at a concert style that suited his current working conditions.

The True Confessions Tour of 1986 featured Dylan, with his backup singers, playing with Tom Petty & The Heartbreakers. This was a potentially fine choice since one problem with the 1984 tour was the lack of any strong musical direction. On this tour much emphasis fell on Petty as liaison between his band and Dylan, and it generally worked. A film of an early concert in the first leg of the tour, in Australia, directed by Gillian Armstrong, was released on VHS as *Hard to Handle*. The concert shows Dylan benefitting from the strong backing of the band and from his rapport with his singers—The Queens of Rhythm. The version of "Knocking on Heaven's Door" is particularly effective as a duet with Petty, echoing the duets with Roger McGuinn in The Rolling Thunder Revue. With The Heartbreakers, Dylan has a band strong on keyboards—Benmont Tench—and the kind of subtle and lyrical lead guitar—Mike Campbell—that his music requires. And Stan Lynch and Howie Epstein create a steady rhythm section, though, on *Hard to Handle*, it's obvious that some of the finer points of how to end songs are still being worked out. Dylan and The Heartbreakers were also captured, about midway through the tour, when they were broadcast from their concert in Buffalo, New York, to the Farm Aid festival in Texas. Dylan's rendition of Ry Cooder's "Across the Borderline" was stunning, and in general Dylan seemed to have found a groove playing with Petty's band, with Petty's command of the stage adding to the chemistry.

Shortly after the show was broadcast on Farm Aid, Dylan appeared with Petty and The Heartbreakers at RFK Stadium in Washington, DC, with The Grateful Dead as the headliners. Since the late seventies The Dead's Jerry Garcia had been covering Dylan songs, most notably "Knockin' on Heaven's Door," and gradually a number of Dylan songs became part of The Dead's repertoire, with Bob Weir even willing to tackle lengthy songs like "Desolation Row"—songs that had been absent from Dylan's performing repertoire since the sixties. When Dylan joined The Dead on stage for that very song, it was more noteworthy than successful, but it sparked further collaboration.

A teaming of Dylan and The Grateful Dead might seem a natural extension of the place both musical acts had reached by the late eighties, and in some ways it was. The Dead had always been a renowned live act, never able to capture on vinyl or tape the unique experience that attending one of their live shows could be. Their legions of followers knew this, and though they religiously taped the numerous shows The Grateful Dead played from year to year, they flocked to the shows in expectation of something that, simply put, "you had to be there" to experience. Dylan, for his most avid fans, provided similar thrills when heard in person. Together Dylan and The Grateful Dead might have been sublime indeed. Not so. The problem that no one involved seemed able to overcome should have been obvious: The Dead are a uniquely intuitive group of musicians, able to jam endlessly if they so choose, able to meander in a fluid manner or bash through a song with rockin' gusto. With Dylan they seemed hamstrung, tied to the unthinkable position of being a backing band. And though The Dead have delivered at times inspired renditions of Dylan's songs, when they played his songs with Dylan the result was middling at best. Dylan seemed unable to find his songs in the midst of their noodling approach and because Dylan's delivery is so mercurial and shifting, even within one song, there seemed to be no common ground—certainly not melody or harmony—upon which the performance styles could unite. The collaboration lasted for only six concerts in the summer of 1987, spawning an album, *Dylan & The Dead*, that feels even more like a bad bootleg than *Real Live* does. If one wants evidence that the sixties were dead in the eighties, that album would be a good place to start.

Dylan then joined up with Petty and The Heartbreakers again for a European tour that began in Israel and ended in England. In *Chronicles*, Dylan characterizes the first tour with The Heartbreakers ("True Confessions") as grueling. He had lost the thread, no longer able to put across his songs in a meaningful way. "My own songs had become strangers to me, I didn't have the skill to touch their raw nerves, couldn't penetrate the surfaces. It wasn't my moment of history anymore" (148). A new inspiration struck him, Dylan says, when he heard an old jazz singer after meeting with The Dead for their shows, and he found himself able to connect again with his songs, finding a new way to vary his approach and play with The Dead. Thereafter the second tour with Petty and The Heartbreakers ("Temples in Flames") was varied and vital, in his view. It does seem that the experience of playing with The Grateful Dead dynamited Dylan out of his comfort zone and opened him to the requirements of his considerable repertoire.

In 1988, Dylan enlisted guitarist G. E. Smith as bandleader and introduced a wide range of his own compositions into his sets, as well as covers of both obscure folk songs and sometimes well-known songs by other artists—a performance tactic The Grateful Dead used to enliven their shows. While Dylan's set list never veers entirely from its handful of crowd-pleasing greatest hits, there is always some uncertainty about what nearly forgotten song he will pull out of his pocket and whether he will handle a song with reverence or a shrugging indifference or, indeed, with a surprising conviction and insight. The songs become the score of his mood, but it's hit or miss as to whether Dylan is able to captivate all his listeners. In 1988 alone Dylan played seventy-one concerts, earning the new lineup the nickname "The Never-Ending Tour." Simply, the title suggests that Dylan had become a troubadour in the fullest sense of the term, playing night after night, year after year, like some kind of rock incarnation of the Wandering Jew. By the time Smith left the band in October 1990, they had performed 240 shows together. As the 1980s rolled into the 1990s, Dylan was a hardworking musician again, a minstrel boy singing for his supper night after night all over the globe.

8

GOOD ENOUGH FOR NOW
(1989–1997)

For many, 1989 will forever be remembered as the year the Berlin Wall came down. The dismantling of the Soviet Union swept away a political reality that had dominated the decades since 1945 and the end of World War II. Like all his contemporaries, Dylan had come of age in the world of the Cold War between the United States and the USSR. What's more, the beginning of his performing and recording career would be forever associated with significant events in the hostilities between the two super powers: the dispute over missiles in Cuba in 1963 and the U.S. involvement in the war between North and South Vietnam, which lasted from 1962 to 1975. During the transition from the seventies to the eighties, the sense of an impending Armageddon, precipitated by the struggles over natural resources and the volatile conditions in Latin America, Africa, and the Middle East, had influenced Dylan's writing in his Christian phase, as he refashioned himself as a prophet of doom awaiting the Second Coming. By the mid-eighties, the unworkability of the Soviet system began to become evident, particularly after the Chernobyl disaster of 1986 shook the USSR and made some kind of détente with the West almost inevitable. The commercial explosion in the West—abetted by the strident conservatism of U.S. President Reagan and British Prime Minister Thatcher against "the Welfare State" and in favor of big business and banking—created a global hierarchy of haves and have-nots. The slackening productivity of the USSR proved unable to resist efforts for national autonomy, first in

Poland and eventually in many of the countries pressed into the Soviet "union" at the close of World War II. With the collapse of the USSR in the early nineties, the United States emerged as the last man standing—the only nation involved in World War II that had yet to suffer a major political or economic setback. Despite recessions and failed military ventures, the United States remained a powerhouse and a peacekeeper for the foreseeable future. At the same time, the drive to capitalize on the global economy spread even to communist China, and with the opening of Chinese markets came cries for more democracy, leading to peaceful protests in the spring of 1989 and violent repression in Tiananmen Square on June 4. The changes wrought by globalization and multiculturalism produced more insistent demands for political autonomy, rights, and recognition of a wider range of ethnicities.

The fortunes of popular arts like rock music had shared in the general commercial glut of the eighties. Dissent—as in the raucous force of punk in the early part of the decade—had largely dissipated by mid-decade. In the late eighties, alternative bands were emerging that would create the spirit known collectively as "grunge" in the early nineties. Jane's Addiction, The Pixies, Nirvana, Pearl Jam, and others presented a new energy for youth disaffected by the normative strains of the eighties as the Beats and early rockers had been by the stodginess of the fifties. The last decade of the twentieth century was notable as well for musical forms like trip hop, house, electronica, and a resurgence of British pop with bite, by the likes of Pulp, Suede, and the most famous, Oasis. The sonic landscapes inherited from the sixties were also inspiring new permutations in bands such as Smashing Pumpkins and the Flaming Lips, in revitalized LPs by R.E.M. and U2, as well as in a second coming of punk, as teenybopper music, with Green Day. The nineties were much more eclectic than the previous decade, with many kinds of music clamoring for attention.

Dylan's career outlasted the Cold War and the Soviet Union and, with the election of William Jefferson Clinton as forty-second president of the United States in 1992, entered a new era marked by the end of Republican dominance of American politics—a situation that held at least until the year of Clinton's reelection in 1996, when the Democrats lost Congress. The late nineties and the late sixties existed in an interesting historical relation as the sixties generation found itself in middle age with the new youth culture at times looking to its elders as mentors, as seen in events such as Neil Young recording with Pearl Jam or Dylan playing the Woodstock festival on its twenty-fifth anniversary in 1994 (on a program that included holdovers from the original festival), along with veterans of the Lollapalooza Festival of alternative rock, such as Nine Inch Nails and Red Hot Chili Peppers. In many ways, the test of longevity for musical artists whose careers began in the sixties was having survived the late eighties. In 1989, Dylan released *Oh Mercy*, arguably his best album of the decade. The record boasted better production values than any of his albums since *Infidels* and, like his best albums of the past, *Oh Mercy* achieved a notable consistency in tone and approach.

"WHAT WAS IT YOU WANTED"

In *Chronicles*, Dylan writes about the recording of *Oh Mercy* with Grammy Award–winning producer Daniel Lanois at the helm. Lanois was in the process of developing a signature sound that graced U2's *The Joshua Tree* (1987), Peter Gabriel's *So* (1988), and Emmylou Harris's *Wrecking Ball* (1990); the album he made with Dylan remains one of the best-sounding LPs in Dylan's career and is generally regarded as his most satisfying album since *Blood on the Tracks*. The songs on *Oh Mercy* avoid the contentiousness of songs on *Infidels* and *Empire Burlesque*, as well as the imaginative flights of songs like "Blind Willie McTell" or "Brownsville Girl." In many ways, a "safe" album in terms of its material, *Oh Mercy* has a consistency of tone that is darkly musing, gripped by a sense of something momentous emerging between the lines.

"Political World" and "Everything Is Broken" set a tone of general dysfunction. Dylan's take on the banalities of the moment don't give much evidence of an actual engagement with the issues of the day. Rather, the idea is that the world of today is fraught with disappointment and failure, with politics as the name for a kind of game playing that overrides the individual. Lyrically, the songs are slight, but their musical conviction is convincing. In his account of working with Lanois, Dylan mentions that the producer expected Dylan to write songs like those he wrote in his heyday, such as "With God on Our Side" which the Neville Brothers recorded with Lanois (178). "Political World" gestures toward a sweeping comment, but Dylan clearly has no intention of climbing a soapbox for the sake of a cause or to espouse action. "Political World" looks askance at the processes by which the world is shaped, much in a take-it-or-leave-it vein.

Songs like "What Good Am I?" and "What Was It You Wanted" have a meditative quality; the first suggests, humbly, that a lover has an ethical responsibility to be "good" for his beloved ("what good am I if I know and don't do?"), while the other seems at times to be a querulous questioning of a shadowy interlocutor whose intentions are rather baffling: "Why do you want it? Who are you anyway?" Combined with "The Man in the Long Black Coat"—a somewhat satanic figure or at least a figure for fatality—these songs give the album a sense of foreboding and questioning. With "Ring Them Bells," a song in the vein of "Every Grain of Sand" in its effort to take stock of situations beyond the ken of any one man, we have a continuation of the more transcendental, or faith-based, aspects of Dylan's songwriting: "Ring them bells for the chosen few / Who will judge the many when the game is through." A tissue of pious-sounding reflection, "Bells" gains more from its tone than from actual statement. "Disease of Conceit" and "Shooting Star" continue the sense of humility as a fact of existence, where "conceit" is the undoing of the ego in the face of what it can't control, and "Star" is an acknowledgment of how hard it is to live up to one's own ambitions, though neither achieves the grandeur of "Series of Dreams," left off the album. The chastened nature of *Oh Mercy* is reflected in one of Dylan's great romantic songs, "Most of the Time," which adds its tone of regretful forgetting to a long line of Dylan songs about almost getting over someone, such as "Girl from the North Country" and "If You See Her, Say Hello": "I don't compromise and I don't pretend / I don't even care if I ever see her again—most of the time."

The more masterful production of *Oh Mercy* makes it an album able to hold its own with recent and important albums by Dylan's contemporaries, such as Neil Young's *Freedom* (1989) and Lou Reed's *New York* (1989), albums that show a refreshingly prickly attention to the contemporary world. *Under the Red Sky*, Dylan's album of the following year, is something of a disappointment, much as the second Wilburys album, that same year, is not nearly as strong as the initial release. It's as if Dylan, revitalized with *The Traveling Wilburys Vol. 1* and *Oh Mercy*, suffers sophomore slump in both his collaborative and solo efforts. Critics have generally considered *Red Sky* sloppy and uninspired, and it could be said that Dylan returned to his eighties mode of bringing in big-name guests—George Harrison, Elton John, Stevie Ray Vaughn, to name a few—while not finding his best material. In speaking of the recording process with the often second-guessing Dylan, co-producer David Was uttered a telling line: Dylan "fights every minute of his day between the necessity of doing what he does and the contingency of it" (Heylin 2011, 637). The album also suffers from the decision, by Don and David Was presumably (since it never occurred on any other Dylan album), to fade songs out while Dylan is still singing! Since the album has a playing time of only thirty-five minutes (some Dylan albums are closer to fifty minutes), the decision has little to support it. The effect on "God Knows" suggests an indifference to Dylan's words that has never previously been the case, while on "2 x 2," the fade suggests a continuation ad infinitum that is effective.

There are some strong songs here—such as the title track, an elegiac children's rhyme that says much about the mood of the album: "the man in the moon went home and the river ran dry." For the most part, Dylan seems playful and offhand, letting throwaway lines accumulate before occasionally landing something that bites or stabs, as in "Born in Time" with its shrugging "you can have what's left of me," or the great quip in "Talkin' T.V. Song," "sometimes you got to do like Elvis did and shoot the damn thing out." "Wiggle Wiggle," trashed by some critics, is actually a lot of fun ("wiggle till you vomit fire") and suggests, again, a children's rhyme not quite for children ("wiggle till it answers, wiggle till it comes"). "Unbelievable" shows Dylan still able to write a catchy number, one that, like much recent Rolling Stones material, recycles recognizable rock and roll riffs, marrying them to gripes about the state of the world: "it's unbelievable you could get this rich this quick." As with much of Dylan's eighties material, the general mood is irascible, with "2 x 2" working odd changes on a Noah's ark scenario (more flood imagery) in a compelling march and "Cat's in the Well," a high octane rocker, ending with what is perhaps one of Dylan's best album-closing lines: "good night, my love, may the Lord have mercy on us all." One song that captures a new vibe for Dylan, generally unremarked by those who denounce the album, is "Handy Dandy"; Dylan offers a humorous sketch of a feckless roué, mellowing into a genial twilight. Aspects of the portrait suit Dylan himself, perhaps, as a veteran of more scenes than most people will know about, a grandfather, a "living legend," here trying on the guise of an aged player of the game of life: "He finishes his drink, gets up from the table, he says, 'ok boys, I'll see you tomorrow.'" The persona sketched here seems to prefigure the dapper card-shark appearance Dylan would affect early in the next century.

LIFETIME ACHIEVEMENT

Bob Dylan's recording career began in 1961 when, before his twentieth birthday, he signed with Columbia Records. Thirty years later, on February 20, 1991, The National Academy of Recording Arts and Sciences awarded Dylan the Lifetime Achievement Award. As Dylan later told Mikal Gilmore, he was dubious about receiving the Grammy: "Well, we all know that they give those things out when you're old—when you're nothing, a has-been. Everybody knows that, right? So, I wasn't really sure whether it was a compliment or an insult" (417). The night he received this possible insult, Dylan claimed he was "extremely sick" with "a fever—like 104." He performed a raucous electric version of "Masters of War"—a song originally released in 1962 at the time of the Cuban Missile Crisis. This time the song, which Dylan had revived in his live repertoire around 1981, would be interpreted as a commentary on the latest policing conflict the United States had undertaken: The bombing of Iraq following the latter's invasion of Kuwait had begun in January. Questioned by Gilmore, Dylan denied he had intended a comment on the conflict. Other commentators felt that, regardless of its appropriateness, the song fell flat and was to some of them "unintelligible."

Perhaps even more interesting than the song Dylan chose to perform were his comments at the microphone when accepting the award from a nonplussed Jack Nicholson. Dylan said he was reminded of something his late father had told him, then after an extended pause added "well, he said so many things"—to considerable laughter. Then, in a rush: "'Son, it's possible to become so defiled in this world that your own mother and father will abandon you. And if that happens, God will always believe in your own ability to mend your ways.'"[1] Did he mean, some wondered, that the United States had defiled itself by continuing its role as a "master of war"? Or was it a comment on receiving an award that might in some way "defile" its recipient? Or was it a comment on the state of the music industry or even the state of Dylan's own career? Even offhand moments at a televised award program could still spark speculation about Dylan's intentions and motives.

The "Lifetime" Grammy wasn't the only marker of Dylan's status as "grand old man." "Bob-Fest," a gathering of a diverse range of musical artists to perform Dylan songs at Madison Square Garden on October 16, 1992, to mark his thirty years of recording for Columbia, attested not only to the vitality of Dylan's songs but to the great respect and admiration he inspired among his fellow musicians. Granted, Dylan, though touring continuously, had not played Madison Square Garden since 1986 when on tour with Tom Petty, and much of the turnout for the event had to do with the greats who shared the stage: Johnny Cash, George Harrison, Stevie Wonder, Eric Clapton, Neil Young, and Petty, as well as figures from the folk sixties like The Clancey Brothers and Richie Havens, young artists such as Eddie Vedder and Mike McCready of Pearl Jam, and Tracy Chapman. One of the more interesting moments was an all-star rendition of "My Back Pages," with Harrison, Petty, Clapton, Young, and Dylan taking verses in turn. The performances all showed conviction and could be taken as ample evidence that Dylan had left a living legacy. Thirty years of making music, fifty-one years old. What was the point of continuing?

"I'D ALREADY GONE THE DISTANCE"

How easily Dylan's past could overshadow his present was demonstrated again by the release of *The Bootleg Series Vol. 1–3* in 1991. This compendium of outtakes and suppressed gems suggested that great Dylan material in the storerooms of Columbia awaited the light of day. No doubt much of it was of interest only to the completist or the historian, but almost everything included on this three CD set was noteworthy. Included, for instance were a great performance of a traditional standard, "Moonshiner," that's better than most of *Bob Dylan*; little throwaway items from Dylan's live-in-the-studio method such as "Sitting on a Barbed Wire Fence;" a fun unreleased Woodstock recording, "Santa Fe;" outtakes from the New York sessions for *Blood on the Tracks*; and important songs left off *Infidels* and *Shot of Love*.

Had Dylan included the latter songs on *Infidels* or another album at the time, the sense of Dylan in the early to mid-eighties would have been different. Some of the songs, like "Blind Willie McTell," "Foot of Pride," "Angelina," and "Lord Protect My Child" contain arresting verbal flights colored by the craggier aspects of Dylan's post-Christian persona. "Pride" and "Angelina" do not add up to fully coherent songs, but the sense of outrage in "Pride" makes it a strong performance, with vivid moments of description and deft putdowns: "they take all this money from sin, build big universities to study in, sing 'Amazing Grace' all the way to the Swiss banks." "Angelina" is almost hallucinogenic, a tour de force of striking images—"worshipping the body of a woman well-endowed with the head of a hyena"; "up those spiral staircases, past the tree of smoke, past the angel with four faces"—and an elastic delivery suggesting introspection and confrontation. Joined with "Caribbean Wind," from 1981, released on *Biograph*, these songs would have made for a compelling, mystifying album. The songs, in their unfinished or unfinalized versions, have an additional aura by virtue of their relative obscurity.

"Blind Willie McTell," an atmospheric blues number, lets Dylan show off his vocal powers while moving through an impressionistic account of the historical forces of slavery and Southern culture that gave depth of suffering to McTell's blues singing. With its many elegant lines, mounting tension in Dylan's voice, and culminating condemnation, "but power and greed and corruptible seed seems to be all that there is," the song was greeted as a revelation when it appeared on the *Bootleg Series* and has in subsequent years won strong approbation as one of Dylan's middle-period masterpieces.[2] There are two extant versions, each with its advocates, but neither satisfactory to Dylan who began playing the song live in 1997, adding it to his regular playlist in 2012. "Lord Protect My Child," while not as lyrically powerful, also gives ample evidence of the strength of Dylan's blues-derived sense of gospel in this period.

With its swirling drum pattern, "Series of Dreams," from the *Oh Mercy* sessions, sounds like the epitome of the Lanois method and that may be the reason Dylan chose not to include it. The lyric's sense of the fleeting nature of meaning comes across in the various phrases about what dream images cannot be—"nothing that would pass inspection."

With the telling line "I'd already gone the distance," Dylan seems to say, yet again, "I've got nothin', ma, to live up to" and nothing to prove.

UNPLUGGED

The next phase of Dylan's recording career finds him returning to solo performance of songs written by others, many of them in the public domain. The struggle to compose an album's worth of songs had become an ordeal Dylan was less and less willing to engage in. Dylan seemed to be seeking his roots, going back to the sources of his art. *Good as I Been to You* (1991) sounds a bit rushed, the choice of songs giving us a glimpse of Dylan as an interpreter of folk tradition, building on his practice (on the Never-Ending Tour) of including covers among his acoustic numbers. The album is a bit hodgepodge in its selection—some high points are "Jim Jones," "Arthur McBride," and "Hard Times." Dylan takes credit for arrangements that originated with others and the performances sound, at times, like he is singing to himself. The collection ends with the old chestnut "Froggie Gone A-Courtin'": "if you want any more verses, you can sing 'em yourself." It might be Dylan's way of saying to his fans that if they want more songs, they can write them.

By recording the album in his garage studio, Dylan might seem to shrug off any attempt at a commercial release. In fact, though, acoustic recordings were on the rise in popularity, thanks in part to MTV's Unplugged series. Eric Clapton's appearance on the series, playing acoustic versions of his songs, was recorded in January, released in August of 1992, and won multiple Grammys. *Good as I Been to You* was recorded mostly in the summer and released in November, joining the revived reception of acoustic performance and, indeed, critics welcomed Dylan's traditionalist performances more than his previous album of originals. The do-it-yourself aspects of *Good as I Been*'s recording were also factors much in the air at the time, as "lo-fi" and self-produced recordings were a prominent aspect of "alternative" music in the nineties, a backlash against the processed sound and soulless studio methods of much eighties music.

Good as I Been gives us Dylan as a genial old folkie, and indicates that he might at last be content to be the folk singing sensation—

reviving only tried and true material—that his initial fans saw him as thirty years before. But the next album, *World Gone Wrong* (1993), also solo acoustic, recorded at home, and containing no songs written by Dylan, is another matter. Here we can see the seeds of Dylan's reemergence, four years later, with one of his best later albums. The songs on *World* are darker than *Good as I Been*, showcasing a cagey world-weariness that suits the later stage of Dylan's career. Sounding like a grousing, melancholy oldster, Dylan delivers songs of passion and betrayal like "Delia" (with its refrain "all the friends I ever had are gone"), "Love Henry," and "Lone Pilgrim." Each song, like the testy blues whine "Blood in My Eyes," finds Dylan more engaged and deliberate than on the previous album. It's as if the singer had finally reached the age he imagined himself to be when he recorded his first album, "fixin' to die" as a "man of constant sorrow" who "can't be good, baby, / Honey, 'cause the world's gone wrong." The playing is more strident, and Dylan at times almost loses the weight of being Bob Dylan, merging with each song's writer. The CD contains liner notes in which Dylan riffs in prose, conjuring up a world of song able to explore all facets of the human condition with honesty, passion, and an abiding sense of fate and chance. The album won Dylan a Grammy for Best Traditional Folk Album and demonstrated that Dylan's grasp of such material could be bettered by few living interpreters of the folk-blues tradition. Dylan, like the United States after the fall of the USSR, was becoming, perforce, the last man standing.

Dylan himself joined the ranks of those recording "unplugged" shows and albums for MTV—one of the more revelatory shows up to that point had been Nirvana's, recorded mere weeks before the shocking suicide of Kurt Cobain in April 1994. *Bob Dylan: MTV Unplugged*, recorded in November 1994 and released in early May 1995, is a warm performance by Dylan and his band. The set list favors the early years with a lyrical "The Times, They Are A-Changin'" and focused renditions of the antiwar songs "John Brown" and "With God On Our Side"—and the great mid-sixties songs, well represented by three classics from *Highway 61 Revisited*: "Tombstone Blues," "Like a Rolling Stone," and a near perfect "Desolation Row"—graced by Bucky Baxter's pedal steel guitar—and by "Rainy Day Women #12 & 35." More recent work is represented by "Shooting Star" and "Dignity," a song from the *Oh Mercy* sessions released in an electric studio version on Dylan's *Great-*

est Hits Vol. III in 1995. The song boasts lyrics that mark the associative style that would become typical of Dylan's compositions in the coming century, offering a series of observations without any particular context or fixed addressee. The protagonist of a song like "Dignity" is uncertain—at times it might be Dylan himself, though with flashes of hyperbole—"asking the cops everywhere I go: have you seen dignity?"—and acerbic asides: "someone showed me a picture and I just laughed / Dignity never been photographed."

The theme of "Dignity" seems apropos for the late nineties, a time when Dylan found himself dignified by an unprecedented number of awards and celebrations. In 1990, Dylan was made a Commandeur des Arts et des Lettres by the French Minister of Culture, and in 1997 was awarded Kennedy Center honors, his career lauded at the ceremony by Gregory Peck, "star" of Dylan's "Brownsville Girl," who seemed actually to be somewhat in awe of the singer. Dylan looked uncomfortable shaking hands with President and Mrs. Clinton, but the moment signaled the full maturity of the youth of the 1960s, now in their fifties. Even the president of the United States must sometimes get to meet Dylan, we might say. In 1997, Dylan received the Lillian and Dorothy Gish Award, the fourth time it was awarded since its inception, for "an outstanding contribution to the beauty of the world and to mankind's enjoyment and understanding of life." These honors showed the degree to which Dylan's influence had marked persons in all walks of life, not simply other musicians and music fans.

There were at the time few artists of popular music who could command such a diverse range of effort, and fewer whose songs were so regularly rerecorded, performed, studied, and quoted. One might say that Dylan had indeed "gone the distance" and could rest upon his laurels. However, Dylan seemed determined to show that his kind of music was never primarily a young man's form. From the start, he affected a wisdom beyond his years and now, at 56, one might assume he would have something more to say about a lifetime of experience.

"DREAD REALITIES"

Speaking to Jon Pareles in the *New York Times* upon the release of *Time Out of Mind* in September 1997, Dylan characterized its songs as "more all-encompassing." "They were more filled with the dread realities of life" than his albums in the eighties (394). "Dread realities" is a good phrase for what haunts the album. Not every song feels cut from the same mold, but there is a consistency to most of the record that gives it an appeal that goes beyond whatever one normally means by "popular music," which is to say that the temporal focus of the record is very long indeed. Its sights are not trained on the immediate present or on what "the age demanded," to use Ezra Pound's dismissive phrase. "What Was It You Wanted" Dylan asked in a song the last time he worked with producer Daniel Lanois; we might say that *Time Out of Mind* gives us what we might have been wanting without necessarily knowing it.

Part of what makes the album distinctive is the low-key production that, on most songs, puts Dylan's vocals out front, giving the listener access to the crevasses of a voice grown craggier than ever but with silken shadings that can be surprising, gliding over lines with a winsome drawl on "Trying to Get to Heaven," or stretching or swallowing words under the weight of anxiety, as on "Cold Irons Bound," a vocal that won a Grammy, as did the album for Album of the Year. Almost every song can be described as atmospheric, not a word one would generally associate with the production values on many previous Dylan LPs. Within the sonic frame, Dylan delivers songs that build from the blues, often with lyrics that are as direct and darkly fashioned as anything in his corpus. If *Oh Mercy* was humble and chastened, *Time Out of Mind* is rueful, morose, and at times prickly with a sense of impending disaster or removed to a taciturn indifference. There is mature fatalism here, and it should grip anyone for whom music speaks to the soul's trials.

The album displays an evenness of tone that was mostly imposed by Lanois. Left to his own devices—as will be the case on every subsequent Dylan release to date—Dylan might have gone for greater variety. As it is, there is much here that repays repeated listening. A song that seems a throwaway, "Dirt Road Blues" maintains interest for a certain *je ne sais quoi*, its tinny sound reminiscent of an old recording from the days of the gramophone. On a few songs the lyrics seem undeveloped, as if one is listening to a scratch track recorded with temporary lyrics—for instance, "Til I Fell in Love With You" and "Make You Feel My Love"—but there is a certain wisdom in the simple phrasings. Not since *Nashville Skyline* has Dylan seemed so willing to engage with the simplistic sentiments of pop songs. So when Billy Joel and Garth Brooks, both masters of the middle-of-the-road kitsch of their respective genres, recorded hits of "Make You Feel My Love"— "When the wind is in your face / And the whole wide world is on your case"—one can only assume that deathless phrases weren't the test of the song's success. In Dylan's version, the lovely melody and the tender vocal does a lot to make clumsiness augment sincerity—as when Bernie Taupin couldn't remember if those eyes "are green or they're blue."

As a lyricist Dylan has mellowed, but as a vocal presence he has gained stature and variety. "Love Sick," the opening track, sets a stark, eerie tone against which Dylan intones a willful vacillation between attachment and alienation: "Could you ever be true? / I'd do anything to be with you." The song immediately establishes marked nuances in how Dylan bends his phrasing. And almost every song offers a phrase that stands as shorthand for its emotional pitch: "This kind of love, I'm so sick of it"; "You left me standin' in a doorway cryin'"; I'm tryin' to get closer but I'm still a million miles from you"; "I'm tryin' to get to heaven before they close the door"; "I was alright, 'til I fell in love with you"; "It's not dark yet, but it's getting' there"; "I'm twenty miles out of town in cold irons bound"; "there's nothin' that I wouldn't do / To make you feel my love"; "I don't know how much longer I can wait"; "my heart's in the highlands, and that's good enough for now."

The two songs that perhaps best epitomize the album are "Not Dark Yet" and "Highlands." The first has the feel of grim survival, speaking of a "world full of lies," a burden "more than I can bear," and "every nerve in my body feels so vacant and numb." It's not a pretty picture of aging, of feeling disconnected even from one's own inspirations, but a haunting one. "Highlands" continues the theme in a lighter vein, with perhaps the album's most telling couplet: "All the young men with their young women looking so good / Well, I'd change places with any of them in a minute if I could." Elsewhere, the singer would like someone "to turn back the clock for me." The song's centerpiece is a comically offhand dialogue the singer has with a waitress in an empty restaurant in Boston; she asks him to draw her portrait and, apparently judging him, says "you don't read women authors, do ya?" The tension between the kind of flirtation a younger man might direct at her and the more rueful feelings of the aged singer are clearly present, as is also a bemused sense of the woman's aggressiveness. The reference to Erica

Jong, best-selling author of *Fear of Flying* (1973), a talismanic book for women's experience of the sexual revolution, not only dates the singer—it's possible the waitress has never heard of her—but also makes a wry comment on what would, once upon a time, have been a subtle pickup line (for what Jong termed "the zipless fuck"). Instead, the singer ducks out and, on the street again, is accosted by a "mangy dog" and political canvassers, while all the time trying to keep his mind fixed on "the highlands." The latter are suggested not only by the spritely melody of the song but by numerous details culled from Scots ballads. Dylan not only pays tribute to a tradition from which he derived some of his early melodies but also manages to express both debt and desire—the highlands as both a source and a longed-for destination that becomes almost mythic.

Vocally, *Time Out of Mind* creates a new Dylan, one who no longer has to be measured by his previous triumphs. This point can't be made emphatically enough. In the popular press, Dylan's career is a collage of clippings, always referencing his early work. That an artist should constantly be held hostage to his past is as absurd as it is common—in the popular arts as well as the fine arts. Many a significant artistic career is only noted when it first enters the history books, while subsequent developments appear only as footnotes to the initial influence. Dylan, had his fifties continued in the mode of "lifetime achievement" and other honors, would have become, definitively, an artist forever trapped in the sixties to mid-seventies, a contribution to the time capsule. With *Time Out of Mind*, Dylan established a new position: an artist of the nineties, approaching the turn of a century fully empowered, in live shows, by a changing repertoire he at times reinvented effectively and, on record, a fifty-something blues-folk master with a gripping sense of "dread realities"—love and life and joy thwarted by the ills brought about by time. The album's title refers to a deliberate relation to time, suggesting either that time has been forgotten, or that something, such as his musical antecedents, has existed "time out of mind," which is to say longer than anyone can remember.

Dylan suffered a health crisis shortly after recording the album, contracting histoplasmosis, and for a brief time there was fear that perhaps this album might be his last. Had it been, he would've "gone out" on a peak, having established the tonalities of his mid-fifties: no longer a writer of anthems, nor an electric poet of mind-bending imagery, nor a country gentleman nor a singer-songwriter of cinematic narratives, nor a proselytizer for Jesus or a proponent of gospel-blues, but a wary, sharp-eyed bluesman accepting that no one stays "forever young," and attesting to a love that has "taken a long time to die." Dylan's illness was successfully treated and he returned to touring and eventually to recording. The albums he produced in the next decade spell yet another phase, one that truly reinvented what a Dylan song could be and for which, even if everything else he did were erased, he might still be remembered in the decades to come.

NOTES

1. These words were identified as echoing Rabbi Shimshon Rafael Hirsch's commentary on Psalms 27.10. This led to conjecture about whether Dylan's father passed along wisdom from the rabbi to his son or if Dylan deliberately placed the words of the rabbi in his father's mouth (Schreiber). In any case, Dylan spoke the words as received wisdom.

2. For a thorough discussion of this song in context, see Wilentz 2011, 172–206.

9

BOB DYLAN REVISITED
(2000–2012)

THINGS HAVE CHANGED

The soundtrack Bob Dylan wrote for *Pat Garrett & Billy the Kid* in 1973 went unnoticed by the Academy of Motion Pictures Arts and Sciences. "Knockin' on Heaven's Door," a hit, was not nominated for Best Original Song. Twenty-seven years later, "Things Have Changed," a song Dylan wrote for *Wonder Boys*, Curtis Hansen's adaptation of a Michael Chabon novel, was nominated and won. Things had indeed changed. The generation of "New Hollywood" mavericks was fast becoming "Old Hollywood." Dylan, now a grand old man of what used to be "youth music," commanded the respect of those in power in Hollywood, now mostly of his generation and the generation that grew up with his music. The film, an underrated dark comedy with great performances from all its principal actors, focuses on the mentoring relationship of pot-smoking Professor Tripp (Michael Douglas), teacher of "creative writing," and his suicidal, not-quite-out gay student James Leer (Toby Maguire). Getting a new Dylan tune for the film was quite a coup for Hansen, and the song set the tone of the film. Quizzical, wry, haunted, the song, from the man who once stridently declared "The Times, They Are A-Changin'" for his generation, shrugs, "I used to care, but things have changed."

If the song sets the tone of the times, it was because no longer caring could be said to be true of those in Dylan's generation and older who knew with certainty that they had already lived the better part of their lives and seen the best of their times. *Time Out of Mind*, Dylan's last release of the twentieth century, speaks of the grim side of outlasting one's youth. Dylan, while biologically in what might be called his prime, affects the point of view of youth culture in painting himself as a man in decline. "Things Have Changed" feels almost empowered by indifference to the changing world and, released in 2000, pivots in the space between the end of the twentieth century and the beginning of the twenty-first.

The end of the millennium was marked by, among other things, fears that the changeover from the 1900s to the 2000s would cause problems for digital systems that had been programmed with dates represented by only two digits. The "Y2K" fears about how well computer systems would make the transition was perhaps sensible for power stations and nuclear reactors and other plants important for maintaining the business-as-usual aspects of modern life, but some people seized on the uncertainty to add to millennial fears that the end of the thousand years since the year 1000 might well be the end of life as we know it, or even the moment for the Second Coming of Christ. Somewhat different from his position twenty years earlier when, in 1980, Dylan wrote songs that seemed to expect imminent apocalypse, Dylan in 1999 merely gestures to the notion of end times ("standing on the gallows with my head in the noose / Any minute now I'm expecting all hell to break loose"; "if the Bible is right, the whole world could explode"), while remaining insouciant about such tensions: "Lot of water under the bridge, lots of other stuff too / Don't get up, gentlemen, I'm only passing through." "Things Have Changed" is a fabric of non sequiturs, Dylan indulging what soon becomes his characteristic persona— comic, offhand, changeable, able to switch between cliché and sharp aphorism at will.

A major event of the year 2000 in the United States was the most contentious election in U.S. history. Whatever the doubts may have been about Kennedy's victory in 1960, the victory of George W. Bush in 2000 over his opponent Al Gore came down to the vote count in Florida, due to the electoral process. Bush was the first president since 1888 to be elected without winning the popular vote. The Supreme Court's interference in the election, in addition to being unprecedented, demonstrated the extreme partisanship of U.S. politics. Such partisanship had dominated the second term of Bill Clinton, and the show-down between the parties in the 2000 election, with no clear victor, under-mined any consensus in U.S. politics.

Another key element in divining the mood of the times was the great "dot-com bust" of 2000-2001. The growth in Internet-based companies began in earnest around 1997, making a clear divide between older technologies and new. The Internet boom was the creation of new providers of goods and services through home personal computers, building the next great wave of consumer luxuries that became "neces-sities." The gadget era would increase exponentially in the new century with the vast online culture made available by the Internet and, eventu-ally, Wi-Fi (or wireless access).

"Things" had changed to a startling extent in the new century. So much so that children born in the nineties and children born in the 2000s are distinct in terms of their "digital nativism." And anyone born before the nineties lives with the residual memory of the analog world's outmoded technologies such as typewriters, home phones, record players, VHS machines, Polaroid cameras, 35mm film, and broadcast television. The technologies of the twenty-first century swept away much of what came before, inspiring great forms of collectivism—such as the inability to work or "process" words without a personal computer and without Microsoft as the interface between user and computer, and the inability to have a social life without e-mail and online networks such as America Online, Facebook, Twitter, or dating sites such as OKCupid, or to conduct basic research without Google and Wikipedia.

The power and allure of the online world were greater than televi-sion, for many; popular music remained a key reference point, now accessed through computers and personal devices for storing mp3s, such as the iPod by Apple, leading to a decline in sales of prerecorded discs and stereo components, and a new culture of "sharing" that went well beyond the retaping of music that had been common in previous decades. Music, in such formats as the Apple store or amazon.com, became less and less a matter of individual artists offering successive "works" or albums, but an infinite variety of individual tracks storable in the thousands and tens of thousands, more easily pirated than ever before and more ubiquitous. Dominating such a playing field required more than ever the support of the major controllers of such "provid-ers"—so that the conglomerated nature of musical and digital networks made certain artists widely available and remarkably successful, while others sought and found niches in the network as best they could.

For an artist like Dylan, one might imagine that the changed status of the music industry would lead to less recording in favor of live performance. While it's true that Dylan's rate of public appearances did not decline in the new century, his recorded output easily outdistanced his production in the nineties with a succession of successful albums.

"THINGS SHOULD START TO GET INTERESTING RIGHT ABOUT NOW"

In response to the bombing by Japan of the United States naval base at Pearl Harbor, President Franklin D. Roosevelt spoke of the date— December 7, 1941—as one that "will live in infamy." The surprise attack mobilized the United States to join the Allied nations fighting the Axis nations in World War II. Sixty years later, the attack on the United States on September 11, 2001, carried out by suicide pilots trained by Osama Bin Laden's Al Qaeda terrorist organization, using commercial airplanes to attack the World Trade Center, the Pentagon, and other targets, would be likened to Pearl Harbor. The Japanese attack resulted in a grand mobilization of the United States, as well as the internment of Japanese Americans in detention camps. The "war on terror" declared by President George W. Bush resulted in, eventually, the invasion of Afghanistan, then Iraq, and a level of surveillance, scrutiny, and harassment that demonstrated how swiftly terrorism creates terror, justifying for its victims "war" by any means, and almost at any cost.

On the day of the shattering event that wounded New York, shocked and outraged the country, and provoked waves of belligerence and fear as well as heartfelt tribute to the many who lost their lives, including hundreds of brave first responders who tried to help, a much less wrenching event took place. Columbia records released Bob Dylan's first album since his bout with a life-threatening disease and his first album self-produced under the alias Jack Frost: *"Love and Theft."*

The attack, called "9/11" in the press, was deemed so momentous by the media and the general public that its place in contemporary awareness quickly moved from the status of "Pearl Harbor" to the status of a moment dividing "before and after" in U.S. foreign relations, in U.S.

domestic policy, and in the culture of the United States. Released at such a fraught time, Dylan's new album, with its many mellow and light-humored songs—such as "Moonlight," "Po' Boy," "Floater"—might seem out of touch with the mood of the moment. Admirers seized on songs with darker tensions, particularly "High Water (for Charley Patton)," "Lonesome Day Blues," "Sugar Baby," and "Mississippi" for their air of trying to make sense of murky situations. Taken as a whole, the album, in its strong embrace of what has generally been called "roots music," proclaimed Dylan a master of so many distinctly American moods that, like Walt Whitman, he could claim to contain multitudes. At a time when patriotism ("the last refuge to which a scoundrel clings," as Dylan quoted in "Sweetheart Like You" back in 1983) had become a new religion, Dylan's return to form, or better, his full achievement of a seasoned form, bolstered the singer's standing as an American icon, and gained "the legend" many new fans. Hearing his brand of Americana at that time consoled a great many people deeply conflicted about the course America was following.

Time Out of Mind, with its dark grousing and morose outlook, could be seen as an album of personal dissatisfactions. What Dylan gave voice to in *"Love and Theft"* was indeed a love of theft, of stealing from the great American songbook, creating songs that tipped the hat to some of his heroes and forebears in the world of song. This was Dylan as a reborn force in contemporary music. The "roots music" revival, building on the low-fi and alt-music forms of the nineties, proclaimed the virtues of analog recording in the digital age, and eschewed electronic drums and keyboard-based "orchestrations" in favor of the feel and sound of recordings of the forties and fifties. While those periods are generally acknowledged as highpoints for jazz and blues recordings, rock had for some time been supposed to have come to full maturity in the sixties and seventies. Now those assumptions were up for grabs. *"Love and Theft"* finds Dylan proudly sporting grooves that unite him with jazz and blues as well as the kind of rockabilly that would've been influential to his elders—performers like Johnny Cash, Elvis Presley, Jerry Lee Lewis, and Carl Perkins, the great staples of Sun Records in Memphis. Indeed, most of the geographical reference points on the new album point to Tennessee and points south, both to the east and west. When Daniel Lanois said that Dylan had made "Not Dark Yet," on *Time Out of Mind*, a "Civil War ballad," he pointed to a latent tendency of that album that became fully manifest on *"Love and Theft"*: the South as the heartland of America, a mythical region full of grim realities and down-home charm. In one of the most trying periods in recent history, Dylan's new album was an irresistible shot of vintage Americana.

Dylan, to avoid being a "nostalgia act," had for a long time reinvented his back catalog in live performance, but in the recording studio was often too easily swayed by contemporary sounds or too insistent on a basic rock-gospel-blues approach that had become predictable well before the eighties were out. Work with Lanois had shown the ability to find a consistent sound, but even the much-celebrated *Time Out of Mind* contained songs rather unadventurous in lyrical content. On *"Love and Theft"* every song contains gems, and each song, while pursuing definite themes, contributes lines that further extend the frame of reference of the album. On vinyl, the song sequence is structured as three songs per side for four sides. Each side contains one of the four major songs on the album, but as with most great albums no song is dispensable. The lighter songs provide facets that add to the overall effect. And that effect is of a voice and persona that has taken the full measure of American music to create a sound that is "retro" but also vital.

"Tweedle Dee & Tweedle Dum" starts the album with the kind of loping rock song fairly standard in Dylan's repertoire—it harkens to the initial electric albums in its riff-based tune, recalling songs like "From a Buick 6" or "Obviously Five Believers." Like those songs, "Tweedle" tends to be a song more of mood than meaning, drawing a sketch of the eponymous duo with a whirling mix of throwaway cliché and entertaining detail: "noses to the grindstone," "taking a streetcar named Desire," "the Land of Nod," "a whole lot more than some," "they're a day older and a dollar short / they got a parade permit and a police escort." The characters have a darker side at times as well—"Tweedle Dee is a lowdown, sorry man / Tweedle Dum, he'll stab you where you stand"— but the overall sense is of two ne'er-do-wells on the run, or at least knocking about to little purpose. The song captures something feckless and unpropitious about American life, with our history of criminal pairs and other kinds of wanna-bes striving for a good life that eludes them. Comic pairs like Laurel and Hardy—"Said Tweedle Dum to Tweedle

Dee, 'your presence is obnoxious to me'"—dance on the periphery of the song.

"Mississippi," the major song on the first side, finds the singer in a sort of permanent *locus poenitentiae*, trying to make up for or account for "only one thing that I did wrong." The singer "feels like a stranger," has painted himself into a corner, and his days are numbered. The sense of foreboding remains throughout the song, but there are intimations that some things, even if they went wrong, might still pay off: "But my heart is not weary, it's light and it's free," and "things should start to get interesting right about now." Perhaps the dominant feeling of the song is summed up by "you can always come back, but you can't come back all the way." The "dread realities" that Dylan began to get a handle on in *Time Out of Mind* have now become the source of a deep-seated wisdom. The singer of "Mississippi" can admit to failings in his "powers of expression" and his "thoughts so sublime," and yet the song does not feel disillusioned. "Mississippi" joins songs Dylan is unusually gifted at composing, such as "Don't Think Twice" with its wry "Ain't no use to sit and wonder why, babe, if'n you don't know by now." "Mississippi" returns us to a folk-based clarity that is both unassuming and compelling.

The side closes with "Summer Days" which sounds suitable for jitterbugging, a celebration of Prohibition Era high times that even cribs a famous line from *The Great Gatsby* to cement its debt to the wide-open possibilities of the United States between the great wars. That said, there's also a sense, in this jump-cut tour of summer nights, of Dylan's own youth—"I'm standing on a table, I'm proposing a toast to the King." There's no explicit reason to assume "the King" is Elvis except for the debt to rockabilly that underpins the song. Dylan is having fun with a certain frenetic effort to stay young not uncommon in our culture—"the girls all say, 'you're a worn out star,'" and roll their eyes and tease, and the singer gives a memorable figure for "performance anxiety": "I got my hammer ringing, pretty baby, but the nails ain't goin' down." The song swings with all the bounce of a jalopy rum-running its way across the Great Plains, chasing the dream of the quick score or, more importantly for the aging singer, the elusive "second act" that Fitzgerald said American lives never have.

Side 2 continues a feel for olden days with "Bye and Bye," with its bubbling organ playing as if for slow-dancing couples just after World War II. Despite lean times: "I still got a dream that hasn't been repossessed," the singer tries to assure himself. The melody and treatment buoy the song with a sense of surviving the Depression with one's dreams and love intact. We begin with anodyne lyrics about "singin' loves praises with sugar-coated rhymes," "paintin' the town," "swingin' my partner around," only to end with lines that belong with a fire-and-brimstone preacher—"I'm gonna baptize you in fire, so you'll sin no more"—and a tyrant, "I wanna establish my rule through civil war." The images recall the notion of the "baptism of fire" endured by so many raw recruits in the Civil War, imbuing the song with the powers of fundamentalism and war—key aspects of the American character. "Bye and Bye" is a bit like encountering a poisonous snake under a pretty rose bush. The song feels perfect for mint juleps in a hammock but hints at forms of ruin and trial that could take their toll at any moment.

"Lonesome Day Blues" seems to take up from the darker intimations of the previous song, though now we seem to be very much in a Vietnam-era setting, with a sound akin to "Outlaw Blues" or "Leopard Skin Pillbox Hat." The song steps lively in a 12-bar blues, its singer dropping details such as a brother who "got killed in the war," and a decorated captain who doesn't care "how many of his pals have been killed." The down-and-dirty groove has the appeal of a long drive to clear one's mind, cranking along to no clear destination. "I set the dial on my radio / I wish my mother was still alive." The singer is a bereft and fractured "clean cut kid" left to his own devices, alternating with deft aphorisms about life—"funny how the things you have the hardest time partin' with are the things you need the least"—and love—"you might need my help, sweetheart, you can't make love all by yourself." The song doesn't create a portrait or narrate a situation so much as express a feeling of unease, frustration, and regret. "I want to teach peace to the conquered / I want to tame the proud."

The key song on side 2 is "Floater (Too Much to Ask)," a ruminative waltz that captures a lazy afternoon spent fishing without much ambition. A "floater" could be a drifter or someone who does any odd jobs required, as well as a boat floating with the tide. The lyrics convey wonderfully a drifting mind, mulling over disparate facts—"my grandfather was a duck trapper, he could do it with just dragnets and rope"; "I fish for bullheads, / I catch a lot, sometimes too many"—and advice, "get up near the teacher if you can if you want to learn anything." The singer has much to say, none of it to much purpose. No longer certain if he has any dreams or hopes—"I had 'em once though, I suppose"—he comes down in the final verse to a reflection we suspect is close to home. After telling us that it can be an unpleasant task to kick someone out, he opines, "sometimes somebody wants you to give something up and, tears or not, it's too much to ask." We have the sense that this feckless floater is going to be thrown out for something he can't give up. Could be drinking, could be drugs, could be women, could be . . . floating. The song has the kind of easy, understated grace of songs like "Went to See the Gypsy," "I'll Be Your Baby Tonight," and "Copper Kettle." It's as if Dylan's reclusive country squire has returned, aged and garrulous, to float before us his defiant indifference to the things of this world.

Side 3 opens with one of the album's best tracks: "High Water (for Charley Patton)." Taking its title and a few images from Charley Patton's song "High Water Rising" (about the famous Louisiana flood of 1927), the song transmits a sense of rising fears, not just of literal flood waters typical of the delta of Louisiana and the Gulf Coast of Texas. There are many references in the song to key places and people in the history of the blues—such as Kansas City and Big Joe Turner, Clarksdale, where Robert Johnson made his apocryphal deal with the devil (Johnson is quoted in the lines "I get up in the morning, I believe I'll dust my broom"), and Vicksburg, Mississippi, which, seated high on a hill, was a refuge point during the 1927 flood. The song also recalls a famous song about the flood, "When the Levee Breaks," that was adapted by Led Zeppelin, referenced in "High Water" in "like balloons made out of lead." (Dylan adapts the song on his next album.)

The themes of a flood (always a figure for apocalypse for Dylan) and the history of the blues don't quite exhaust the song's interests. The sense of danger—"it's tough out there," "things are breakin' up out there"—applies to the times concurrent with the song. There's always a next time, as Hurricane Katrina showed only too well in 2006. A strange line about Charles Darwin—"trapped out there on Highway Five / The judge says to the high sheriff, 'I want him dead or alive'"—might indicate Southern fundamentalism, still able to perceive Darwinism as a godless challenge to belief. Dylan has George Lewis, a jazz man of old New Orleans, tell an Englishman, an Italian, and a Jew that "you can't open your mind, boys, to every conceivable point of view." The comment is a check to relativism that sees all points of view in matters of faith or fact as equally valid. With its sprightly banjo, the song reeks of the tensions of the South: floods, blues, set-in-their-ways locals, and fears of the wrath of God. "High Water" is, as they say, an instant classic.

The other two songs on side 3 are much lesser, though not without interest. "Moonlight" finds Dylan practicing the old soft shoe; it's a song one could imagine a crooner popular in the forties handling, like Bing Crosby. The lyrics, like "Bye and Bye," are predominantly mellow, packed with more natural description than ever before in a Dylan song. One of the gems—"The clouds are turnin' crimson / The leaves fall from the limbs 'n' / The branches cast their shadows over stone"—is delivered so sweetly, the playful rhyme sets the tone of the entire song. But there are odd moments, such as the use of the commonplace, "Who does the bell toll for, love, it tolls for you and me"—if wedding bells, this may be benign, but the usual meaning of the bell tolling "for" someone is to announce a death. Elsewhere "my sad heart" and air "thick and heavy / all along the levee" make for a creeping sense of despair. The reiterated call "won't you meet me out in the moonlight alone" comes to feel more and more ghostly and intangible. It's a strik- ing performance and harkens to *Self Portrait*-era Dylan in its ease with a classic soft-jazz melody.

"Honest With Me" has some of the disquiet that one associates with "Just Like Tom Thumb's Blues," a tale of dissociation where "I'm stranded in the city that never sleeps" and "some of these women they just give me the creeps" recall being "lost in the rain in Juarez" and those "hungry women there that really make a mess out of you." A ten- verse mini-epic, each second verse ends with a version of the couplet: "You don't understand it, my feeling for you / You'd be honest with me if only you knew." The subjective position of the song sketches someone we might call an ornery cuss, aggrieved and proud and pissed-off, but not above a deadpan pun: "I'm stark naked but I don't care / I'm goin' off into the woods—I'm huntin' bare." Elsewhere he claims he's "here to start the new imperial empire"—a funny redundancy indicative of this glib speaker, who "won't come here no more if it bothers you." Musically, the song is considerably enlivened by slide guitar, one of its strengths, but Dylan's harmonica is regrettably absent.

The final side of *"Love and Theft"* is its best as all three songs are particularly strong and, as usual with Dylan's best albums, ends with one of his most haunting songs. "Po' Boy," the start of the side, is an absurdist classic. Dylan channels the likes of Groucho Marx, vaudeville jokesters, and the kind of daft humor one associates with the funny papers, even telling a knock-knock joke. The song takes its title from a sandwich common to the South, as well as, in the song's final couplet, identifying the titular figure with the archetypal poor boy, the prodigal son: "washin' them dishes, feedin' them swine." Like every song on *"Love and Theft,"* "Po' Boy" has its share of lines that jump out for the listener through a combination of words and delivery. Here, "Had to go to Florida, dodgin' them Georgia laws" is priceless, as is "They went down the Ohio, the Cumberland, the Tennessee / And all the rest of them rebel rivers" in "Floater." The songs are linked by the sheer brava-do of their fecklessness, with Dylan capturing a sense of humor close to the spirit of an American great like Mark Twain. One suspects that Twain would have been delighted by the character of the singer of "Po' Boy."

"Cry a While" is a more caustic number. Here Dylan's long vaunted command of the "put-down song" resurfaces in a song about trying to settle a score: "I always said you'd be sorry and today could be the day / I might need a good lawyer, it could be your funeral, my trial." In part, one listens to hear how many different rhymes Dylan will find for "a while." And there are also great throwaways that set the rather lusty mood, like "Doc Pasquale makin' the 2 a.m. booty call," and "I'm lon-gin' for that sweet fat that sticks to your ribs." The song is another extended blues, this time with a barrelhouse intonation that struts like a man with a loaded rod in his pocket.

As the concluding song, "Sugar Baby" harkens in spirit to many notable closing songs in Dylan's long career: "It Ain't Me Babe," "It's All Over Now, Baby Blue," and more recent examples like "Every Grain of Sand," "Dark Eyes," and "Shooting Star." The song has a discursive quality, seeming to sum up a long period in a relationship to someone who could be a lover, a longtime friend, or Dylan's audience itself in some ways. "One day, you'll open up your eyes and you'll see where we are." Dylan stretches out the line to get maximum effect; we can only assume that "where we are" is not very good and that if we really grasped how bad we'd be shaking in our boots. The singer, as on most of the album, is not forthcoming about what the actual situation he's alluding to might be: "you've always got to be prepared but you never know for what." An aside on how much "trouble women bring" is met by the comment that "love's not an evil thing." The world of the song is not defeated so much as rueful. "Every moment of existence seems like some dirty trick." Quoted out of context, many lines in the song have the surliness of much of *Time Out of Mind*, but the delivery here is much sweeter, full of the resignation and mellowness of age. "You went years without me, might as well keep goin' now," the refrain says, a sort of "It Ain't Me Babe" farewell that apprises us of how little we've grasped of all Dylan has been telling us over the years. "Sugar Baby," who "ain't got no brains, no how," is another "idiot, babe," and the singer forthrightly tells us so. Yet unlike the attack of the put-down songs or the "you'll rue the day" tone of his Christian era, or even the eyes upon the prize of "Every Grain of Sand," "Sugar Baby" doesn't preach or try to console. It simply, elegantly, sadly shrugs off any obligation to enlighten us.

Dylan, more than ever before in his extensive recording career, has with *"Love and Theft"* given utterance to the actual language and idioms of America in its fierce regionalisms, its storied places and knowing turns of phrase. The album is a virtuoso performance and won the Grammy for Best Contemporary Folk Album, losing Album of the Year to the soundtrack for the Coen Brothers film *O Brother, Where Art Thou?* which, interestingly, features various versions of "Man of Constant Sorrow," a song Dylan performed on his very first album. One might say that the Coens' soundtrack would not be quite what it is without the indelible influence of Bob Dylan on popular music. In any case, both albums attested to the vitality of roots music at the turn to the twenty-first century.

As if to remind old listeners and to apprise new listeners of who they are hearing on *"Love and Theft,"* a special double disc version of the CD contained "I Was Young When I Left Home," a song the twenty-year-old Dylan made as a home recording on a visit back to Minnesota. The song is a gem that should have graced the first album, an indication that, from the start, choices about what to include on Dylan's LPs were hit and miss. Listening to the song in 2001 gives the song, admittedly, more power than it might have had in 1962. We hear the youthful Dylan trying to sound as old and weathered as Dylan at sixty, his age when the song was finally released. Dylan was indeed "young when he left home" and young when he recorded the song, and now, all these years later, has arrived again, in the great late stage of his career.

LOOKING BACK

In a discussion with Mikal Gilmore at *Rolling Stone* published a few months after the release of *"Love and Theft,"* Dylan refused to compare his latest work with his earlier work, mentioning that he feels like he's walking around "in the ruins of Pompeii all the time," accountable to "all the old stereotypes." "Compare this album to the *other* albums that are out there. Compare this album to other artists who make albums," Dylan challenged (425). It's a fair point. The old songs could still be encountered on the original albums, regularly reissued on CD, and in reworkings in live performance. The hiatus from new material in the nineties should have established enough distance between Dylan's youth, middle age, and his current "senior" years.

When we look at the work by those in some way comparable to Dylan in the last two decades, the strongest parallels can be made to Leonard Cohen, Neil Young, Van Morrison, Bruce Springsteen, and Tom Waits. Cohen's *The Future* (1992) earned him much respect among those who were children or not yet born when his recording career began; less prolific than Dylan, even in the nineties, Cohen did not return with a new album until *New Songs* (2001), the same year as *"Love and Theft."* It was a return to form for Dylan's elder, with a warm production and songs like "That Don't Make It Junk," a wry reflection on devotion, and "Here It Is," an unabashed shedding of romantic illusions. Young released a string of great albums in the nineties, including *Harvest Moon* (1992) and *Sleeps with Angels* (1993); early in the new century he released the ambitious song-narrative called *Greendale* (2003), a surprisingly coherent take on three generations of Americans disillusioned with the direction of their country. Van Morrison also made the move from the nineties to 2000 with strong albums: *Back on Top* (1999) and a venture into country and American roots rock on *Pay the Devil* (2000) where he treads upon the terrain of country great—and sometime Dylan collaborator—Willie Nelson. Springsteen, after the lean and mean *The Ghost of Tom Joad* (1995), an album that walks in the footsteps of Woody Guthrie and early Dylan, was silent until the dispiriting election of 2000 and the 9/11 attack inspired *The Rising* (2002), which renewed the vitality of Springsteen's commitment to songwriting. After *Devils and Dust*, another album dominated by acoustic guitars and storytelling in 2005, Springsteen put together a fully realized recording of songs made famous by Pete Seeger with *We Shall Overcome* in 2006. Waits released two masterpieces in the nineties: *Bone Machine* (1992) and *Mule Variations* (1999), both working through versions of Americana at least tangentially related to the territory of *Time Out of Mind*. In 2002, Waits put out two albums simultaneously, both good but neither a move in a new direction. Then, in 2004, *Real Gone*, with a much more processed sound, contained a song in response to the ongoing conflict in Iraq and, with "Hoist That Rag," commented on the tattered condition of America's exceptionalism. Dylan's albums of 1997 and 2001 can be seen as part of a general move toward revisiting Americana shared by his most notable contemporaries.

In the wake of Dylan's latest masterpiece, Columbia continued to release material from his "back pages": 2002 saw the release of live recordings from the Rolling Thunder Revue in 1976, and 2004 saw the famous Halloween show at the Philharmonic in New York in 1964. Both concerts allowed fans of earlier versions of Dylan to touch base again, and both created a fuller impression of the variety of Dylan's live appearances over the years. These releases were followed in 2005 by alternate takes and unreleased versions of songs, some of which appear in *No Direction Home*, a lengthy documentary about Dylan's early career. Edited by veteran New York–based filmmaker Martin Scorsese from compiled materials, including interviews with people who knew Dylan early in his career (like Dave Van Ronk, Suze Rotolo, Allen Ginsberg, and Joan Baez), the documentary does a fair job of getting down unique aspects of Dylan's origins, but too much of the film smacks of the very thing Dylan alluded to as "walking around in the ruins of Pompeii." Reminiscences were combined with footage from a long video interview with Dylan by his manager Jeff Rosen in 2000, as well as clips of concert footage dating from 1961–1966. The soundtrack features some interesting materials—notably early pre-professional recordings and many previously unreleased live tracks—and there is value as oral history in the chatter of Dylan's famous friends. The man him-

self, wily and cagey before the camera, comes across as someone looking on in wonder at his own story.

The effort to tell that story in earnest was demonstrated by the
publication of what may be the first volume of an ongoing autobiography. *Chronicles Vol. 1*, published by Simon & Schuster in 2004, finds
Dylan reflecting on different periods in his career. The main focus
again is on the earliest period. Not only is it fascinating for Dylan's fans
to hear his thoughts and memories about his arrival in New York and his
early enthusiasms, but the length of time between his reminiscences
and the events make his tale both a legend and a personal history of a
bygone time. Dylan includes two chapters that cover the period of *New
Morning* and the recording process for *Oh Mercy* respectively, thus
giving readers a glimpse of the seventies and the late eighties as he
experienced them. We see the degree to which his own name and
reputation could become a burden for Dylan. And yet, as told without
much in the way of score settling, but with a lot of name-dropping, the
main theme remains a commitment to a search for what works. Dylan
the artist seems very much a pragmatist, finding inspiration catch-as-
catch-can. Anyone who has listened intently and sympathetically to his
albums over the decades meets a familiar figure in *Chronicles*, at times
amusing, at times laconic, at times acerbic, at times nostalgic, at times
poignant in his praise of greats now gone. Dylan, the reader realizes,
lives in a world full of ghosts, more so than most people his age, due to
the keen attention he has paid to his elders all along.

Late in the book Dylan speaks of his first encounter with the music
of Robert Johnson and his admiration of how "Johnson's mind could go
in and out of so many places . . . he even throws in Confucius-like
sayings whenever it suits him" (286). Certainly, this description, and the
one Dylan writes about "Pirate Jenny," the Bertolt Brecht/Kurt Weill
composition he heard around the same time in his apprenticeship, describes the kinds of songs Dylan was writing around the time *Chronicles*
appeared. He speaks of Brecht and Weill writing a song that
"transcended the information in it, the character and plot" (276). The
phrase, together with the idea of going in and out of "places" (or voices
or personae), has considerable relevance for Dylan's next album. *Modern Times* offers a version of the blues as a grand old game, a way of
invoking standards, cribbing from classics (such as Ovid and the nineteenth-century American poet Henry Timrod), so that, as Van Ronk

pointed out to Dylan about Johnson's mimicry (in Dylan's words): "this song comes from another song and that one song was an exact replica of a different song" (282). On *Modern Times*, Dylan treats "the tradition" as his happy hunting ground, just as he did when he was learning and stealing from everyone he heard play in the Village.

"I FOLLOWED THE WINDING STREAM"

In the five years since *"Love and Theft,"* the Iraq War turned four years older, the Afghanistan War turned six, and the housing bubble peaked in the very year of *Modern Times'* release, with the precipitate slide in prices creating a domino effect among mortgage-backed securities that eventually gave way to the worst economic crisis of recent history in 2007–2008. The United States was more destabilized than it had been since the contentious election of 2000 and the attacks of 9/11. Osama Bin Laden, the leader behind the latter, was still at large; no "weapons of mass destruction"—the ostensible reason for the invasion of Iraq— had been discovered, though Saddam Hussein, a onetime ally of the United States who became a hated enemy under the first President Bush, had been captured and was executed that year. After a somewhat close reelection in 2004 (but a handy victory by the standards of his first election), President George W. Bush lost both houses of Congress to the Democrats in November 2006. Public opinion was turning against the costly and ineffective wars, but even worse was the growing outrage at the precipitous fall in inflated property value and the gradual realization that the unregulated trading in the "shadow banking system" was bringing major financial institutions to the brink of collapse. The worsening situation would continue well beyond the 2008 election of Barack Obama, the first nonwhite man to be president of the United States.

   Modern Times was released during a time that drew comparisons with the 1930s. The sense of failure or the risk of failure in major U.S. financial institutions was high. The crash of bubbles—in dot-coms, real estate, loan insurers like Freddie Mac and Fannie Mae—the flight of capital and the continued amalgamation of interests (making the robber barons of Teddy Roosevelt's day look like magnanimous captains of democracy) created a situation that reminded people, those who still remembered it, of the Great Depression. And the heroism in World

War II of the people called "the Greatest Generation"—born in the teens and twenties and now facing old age, senility, and death—challenged, as history, the debased state of affairs of the existing U.S. government and military, involved in wars that seemed to do little but sap morale, cost lives and money, and create various kinds of anti-U.S. backlash. The global financial crises would not be eradicated by global warfare in the mid-2000s, unlike the last great economic threat to U.S. freedoms "cured" by World War II.

As with *"Love and Theft,"* Dylan's new album doesn't address any particular issues so much as provide a soundtrack derived from hardscrabble living in the United States that has been a staple of Dylan's world view ever since the early influence of Guthrie's thirties vision. During the volatile late sixties, Dylan revisited, in the songs recorded in Woodstock, his sense of a long-enduring backwoods Americana. The strength of *Modern Times* recalls the unsettled insouciance of the Woodstock recordings. Dylan knows well the times he wants to evoke, and *Modern Times* benefits from his grasp of his forebears.

"Thunder on the Mountain," the leadoff track, continues the tongue-in-cheek tone of some of *"Love and Theft"*: "Gonna raise me an army, some tough sons of bitches / I'll recruit my army from the orphanages." Like John Ashbery, a great American poet born in the late twenties whose output of new poems became amazingly prolific in his later years, Dylan's lyrics become a tissue of different voices, full of swift and even bizarre changes in mood. The aspect of Ashbery's poetry that makes him the celebrated epitome of modern American verse is that the notion of narrative, theme, and consistent speaker disappear in commanding turns of phrase, a kind of echo chamber where "American speech" careens about, led by associations and a range of contexts that keep the reader enthralled but also guessing. As in a dream where the identity of any person or setting is in flux, Ashbery poems move among fluid registers of discourse, conjuring a wealth of idioms for any purpose required. Dylan, while tying his lyrical sallies to basic melodic forms, finds a similar freedom on *"Love and Theft"* and *Modern Times*. Modern poetry like Ashbery's is in many ways a magpie poetry, taking its terms, its images, its phrases, and rhythms from a slippery context never distinctly described or firmly fixed. The better songs on *Modern Times* have a similar richness of implication. The weakest song, "Beyond the

Horizon," feels formulaic, as though Dylan were trying to repeat the success of "Moonlight" on *"Love and Theft."*

A better effort at the mellowness of "Moonlight," "When the Deal Goes Down" adapts a tune made famous by Bing Crosby and imbues the song's devotion to a beloved with both simple statements—"we live and we die, we know not why"—and singular touches—"we all wear the same thorny crown," "I felt transient joys / Though I know they're not what they seem." The song is also one of those singled out as indebted to Henry Timrod for phrases like "frailer than the flowers" and "these precious hours," the presence of such allusions adding to the dated rhetoric of the song, which is one of its charms. "Spirit on the Water," another easygoing song in this vein, recreates the mood of many blues tunes about pining for that perfect lover who is at best elusive. "Put some sugar in my bowl" is a commonplace come-on, but elsewhere there are odd sallies that break the familiar mood of the song: "I can't go to paradise no more / I killed a man back there," and "You ever seen a ghost? No, / But you have heard of them." The genial singer concludes by insisting, "Show me what you got / We could have a whompin' good time."

In some ways an extension of *"Love and Theft"*—with Dylan's use of his touring band as the primary musicians in the studio and self-producing the album with a "live in the studio" feel—*Modern Times* is generally less playful, more brooding than the earlier album, as in three standout tracks, "Workingman's Blues #2," "Nettie Moore," and "Ain't Talkin'," and more romantic, as with the lovely lilt of "Deal" and "Spirit." Elsewhere, the steady blues groove that informs the previous two albums shows goodly conviction on "Rollin' and Tumblin'," which deliberately adapts a long-standing blues song, best known as done by Muddy Waters. Dylan keeps the plaint against a woman who is proving more trouble than she's worth—"Ain't nothin' so depressin' as tryin' to satisfy this woman of mine"—but turns in the end to the possibility of reconciliation: "Let's forgive each other, darling, let's go down to the greenwood glen." Along the way, there are sallies toward the macabre or violent that Dylan seems to get a charge out of these days: "I've been conjuring up these long dead souls from their crumbling tombs."

"Workingman's Blues #2" seems a deliberate recollection of Woody Guthrie as the voice of working men shafted by big business and its practices. Dylan's revamping of the workingman's plight is even willing to borrow, in the post–Soviet era, Marxist terminology: "the buying power of the proletariat's gone down / Money's getting shallow and weak." More than a blues, the song actually sounds like an elegy for the country the singer once knew—"the place I love best is a sweet memory / It's a new path that we trod." Sung with chastened affection, the song revives a feeling for "work" as something manual, lifelong, and pleasurable in its sense of accomplishment: an idea remote from the kinds of jobs available in the service sector of the twenty-first century. If feeding the machines made one feel like a machine in Guthrie's day, the ephemerality of tending the computer increases anxiety, as the notion of a trade or skill and the identity they provide gives way to abstract-sounding management terms, interchangeable and impermanent. In the midst of meditative lines ringing with calls to take up arms against enemies, the singer keeps open the possibility of a relationship that could revive and redeem him. In its datedness, the diction feels stately, with associations with Timrod but also recalls old blues songs and even U.S. poets of Dylan's youth like Robert Frost and Carl Sandburg.

"Nettie Moore" also feels derived from an earlier time, rhyming "Moore" with "My happiness is o'er." The song's title and some of the chorus do indeed come from an earlier "Nettie Moore," from 1857. Dylan's adaptation lets the pre–Civil War lines work to make the entire song seem courtly, framed as a rueful meditation by a lover striving to find relief from mourning the past. But the weight of the past is sounded only in the chorus. The verses are lighter—"I'm the oldest son of a crazy man / I'm in a cowboy band" and "Everything I've ever known to be right has been proven wrong / I'll be driftin' along"—and feel, with the song's insistent snare drum counting-off time, almost like "bullet points" in a list of attributes. But attributes of what? Like many of Dylan's songs of this period, the subject matter is hard to place; the lyrics seem a hodgepodge repository of off-the-cuff asides, descriptions of minor exchanges, observations—"they say whiskey will kill ya, but I don't think it will"—and comments on a current love that matters. We might easily believe we are in the mind of a nearly senile oldster who finds it hard to stick to a topic, but the song's delivery is anything but befuddled. The care with which Dylan shapes the lines of yearning in opposition to the more brusque lines of irritation or bitterness is highly effective. And the chorus is sung with a poignant sense of loss—"there's no one left here to tell."

The album's final song, "Ain't Talkin'," is a true tour de force such as Dylan hasn't assayed in some time. At 8:48, the song is not quite as epic as "Desolation Row" or "Highlands," but can be likened to earlier work like "A Hard Rain's A-Gonna Fall" or "Gates of Eden"—songs that conjure a wealth of detail, contained by a certain reference point—the hard rain, the gates of Eden, here the recurring lines, "Ain't talkin', just walkin'" and "Heart burnin', still yearnin'." The song's tempo creeps along, sounding, indeed, creepy. The feeling is sustained by the lyrics, which seem about to spring something unpleasant on the listener. The song opens with the singer walking "out into the mystic garden" with "cool, crystal fountains," only to be hit from behind. The second verse follows that pattern: a potentially benign setup that turns dark: "I'm tryin' to love my neighbor and do good unto others / But, oh mother, things ain't goin' well." The next verse begins in a state of "weepin'" only to become threatening: "If I catch my opponents ever sleepin' / I'll just slaughter them where they lie." At the midpoint of the song—verse five of nine—the singer speaks of avenging his father's death; thereafter, things start to change, with the singer invoking "a faith long abandoned" and "heavenly aid." We have the sense, perhaps, of a crusader and an avenger, at war, as Dylan has been before, with infidels—the final line before the final chorus: "there's no one here, the gardener is gone" resonates with a sense of the godless universe the singer keeps walkin' through—"through the cities of the plague," at one point. Other gestures in the chorus include a possible allusion to Achilles—"a dead man's shield" and "a toothache in my heel"—and a definite crib from Ovid with "the last outback at the world's end," the song's concluding line. We might easily imagine ourselves back in the Bible-informed world of *John Wesley Harding*'s "Poor Immigrant" or "Lonesome Hobo," doomed to keep walking, traveling through a world in which faith has become bitter. As the conclusion of an album called *Modern Times*, the song recalls the detachment from the times that Dylan has always been able to invoke in his more prophetic mode.

BACKWARDS AND FORWARDS

In 2008, Columbia released—in various packages, including double disc and triple disc versions—outtakes, alternate versions, live versions, and a few uncollected movie soundtrack tunes from 1989 to 2006 called *Tell-Tale Signs*. The collection received more positive comment than most of the earlier *Bootleg* releases with the exception of volumes 1–3, and for good reason. The three alternate versions of a key song like "Mississippi," from the *Time Out of Mind* sessions, show how Dylan explores different deliveries and musical settings. In fact, "Someday Baby," which earned Dylan a Grammy for Best Solo Rock Vocal Performance and a nomination for Best Rock Song in the version that appears on *Modern Times*, is included on *Signs* in a version in some ways superior. The song is based on a song popularized by Muddy Waters and the Allman Brothers called "Trouble No More," and the version on *Modern Times* is in more of a rock vein than the quieter, more insistent version on *Signs*. The point is not so much to second-guess the choices on the official releases, but to show that almost any Dylan song is amenable to a variety of approaches and that each time Dylan sings a song, different effects are achieved.

More important than the discovery of alternate versions is the inclusion of songs otherwise unreleased. A stellar example is "Red River Shore," left off of *Time Out of Mind* in part, one suspects, because the lineup of the album couldn't sustain both it and "Highlands." "Red River Shore" is a moody account of how the one that got away becomes over time an almost mythic presence in the singer's life. The song has a slowly unfolding approach, as though the singer is cautiously broaching a subject that has almost endless depth and significance. The recurring refrain brings us always back to the girl from the Red River shore, most likely the Red River Valley area of Minnesota and North Dakota, a landscape that gives the song some of the poignancy of "Girl from the North Country" but with even more sense of the legendary: "everybody who had seen us there / Said they didn't know who I was talkin' about." The statement that he spent nights in the arms of the girl seems to contradict statements that he "never did get that far" with her. Everything is slippery, based on one look at her that said "she should always be with me." As the song goes on, piling up the sense of having lost something one never had, lines can take on powerful overtones of mourning: "every day is another day away from the girl from the Red River shore." The brevity of this line in expressing the irrevocable march of time is impressive, as though one were to say every step is simply a step further from the womb (or closer to the tomb). In the last verse, the song jumps to a reflection on "a guy who lived a long time ago," a figure of "sorrow and strife," who was able to raise the dead. The implication that perhaps the girl has died, or is in need of a less literal resurrection, is all that binds this verse about Christ to the singer's memory of the girl. The final statement, "sometimes I think no one ever saw me here at all / Except the girl from the Red River shore," evokes a sorrowful plight. If "they" don't "do that kind of thing" (i.e., raise the dead) "any more," then, with death, it is as if one were never here. The terms of the song's contrast are stark: fatalism, or the inevitability of death, against the sense of missing out on one's only possible earthly happiness. "Red River Shore" reminds us again of the "dread realities" that Dylan was willing and able to confront in his songs for *Time Out of Mind*.

Tell-Tale Signs has a consistency that makes it seem almost like an anthology. Even songs written for films fit the general tone. Such a summing-up of his recent years might indicate that, with this compendium from his most fruitful recent period, the cup was now empty. Not so; filmmaker Olivier Dahan got in touch with Dylan and asked that he write a dozen songs or so for a film project he had in mind. Dylan complied with one song, "Life Is Hard," written with Robert Hunter, lyricist for the late Jerry Garcia of The Grateful Dead, and then composed an album's worth of songs with Hunter. That album became *Together Through Life*, a fairly light and offhand album released in April 2009, early in President Obama's first term, but still in the midst of an economic crisis.

Hunter's contribution adds a more casual mood than is found on Dylan's previous three records. While a few songs sound the darker outlook of Dylan's recent material—most notably "Forgetful Heart" with its final baleful couplet: "The door is closed forevermore / If indeed there ever was a door"—the main feeling of the album is scrappy and lusty. Two songs focus on the feminine center of masculine attention that rock and roll—such as Chuck Berry's—often celebrates. "Jolene" and "Shake Shake Mama" are both songs that would not be out of place in a Grateful Dead set. Recalling that Dylan had joined forces with Hunter before, on *Down in the Groove*, and played live with The Dead, *Together* revisits the kind of reaching around for material that marked late eighties Dylan—before the forays with Lanois and with the Was brothers initiated the period covered by *Tell-Tale Signs*—which is a way of saying that nothing on *Together* is as good as the best stuff collected on *Signs*.

"Beyond Here Lies Nothing," the leadoff song, has a strong groove that supports the singer's assurance to a lover that what they have is the be-all and end-all. The lyrics are tossed-off but the song pops thanks to George Recile's drums. "My Wife's Hometown" has the strength of Dylan's wry delivery, as if he's counting off the charms of a termagant, but the song shows its sources too readily. "If You Ever Go to Houston" has the appeal of easygoing Tex Mex and seems a backhanded celebration of the city—soon to became the fourth largest in the United States, per the 2010 census. "I nearly got killed there in the Mexican War," Dylan sings with a straight face. Musically, the album's reliance on David Hidalgo's accordion can begin to cloy in places. The playing is spirited and Hidalgo is a fine musician, but when each song uses the instrument in exactly the same way, the listener begins to crave more variety, something to grate or enliven or seduce—the way Dylan's harmonica playing could once be expected to do.

One of the more notable songs, able to hold its own with the lilting songs of love that have graced each of the last three LPs is "I Feel a Change Coming On," which references Billy Joe Shaver and James Joyce, the master of what he himself called a "plagiarist pen," to describe his procedure of working endless references and allusions into his major works. Use of Joyce's name sets up a clunky line: "Some people they tell me I got the blood of the land in my voice." One would like to assume that some of the hokier lines on the album are attributable to Hunter, who has a way with breezy lyrics, but "Change" sports a few lines that are particularly effective because of Dylan's wistful delivery: "If you want to live easy—baby, pack your clothes with mine," and "Everybody's got all the flowers, I don't have one single rose."

The album ends with "It's All Good"—a look askance at a silly expression popular with the young, but also perhaps a wry comment on the waves of praise that now respond to Dylan's every new release. Like a kind of ragged Candide, the singer keeps insisting all is for the best, even as the feel of the song asserts the contrary. Dylan has not ended an album with a fun song in a long time, the change indicating perhaps the more buoyant mood of some after the much desired departure of President Bush and his "what-me-worry?" leadership. The truly appalling situation in American politics—to say nothing of environmental issues and 9 percent unemployment—may in part have stimulated the use of the mindless rejoinder among the young.

Dylan's voice has shown signs of wear—like balding tires—since his two acoustic LPs in the early nineties. The reedy nasal whine of his early years was long gone by the end of the sixties, and the throatier caterwaul of the seventies gradually became an increasingly expressive instrument into the eighties. But with the later years of that decade, a raspier thickness evolved into the familiar gargling voice of his concert appearances in the 2000s. It's a voice that, like some of the vocalizations arrived at by Tom Waits, can take some getting used to. While Dylan never had what would be described as a pleasant singing voice, he has always been capable of pleasing effects. And he has a talent for phrasing and emphasis that is second to none in rock music. With his resolute turn to older styles of music, Dylan summons up a blues man's bark and growl as the best way to deliver many of his current songs. Perhaps for that reason, the decision to record a selection of Christmas chestnuts has to be one of the more surprising acts of his recording career.

"JACK FROST NIPPING AT YOUR NOSE"

Christmas in the Heart, released in October 2009, has at least four tracks that are great additions to the industry of Christmas tunes, usually sung by velvet-voiced crooners. In general, the album sustains the nostalgic Christmas spirit that Dylan seeks to invoke. The genuineness of the project was underscored by the fact that Dylan arranged to have the proceeds from album sales benefit world hunger organizations, thus spreading more than Christmas cheer. Hearing the album, one suspects that Dylan, like so many of his fellow citizens, grew up hearing Christmas songs year after year and has his own childhood associations with at least some of them. Dylan chose to include both secular songs, celebrating Santa Claus as well as getting together at the holidays (such as "The Christmas Song"), and religious songs about the birth of Christ. The strongest of the latter is "Little Drummer Boy," Dylan's version being among the best in its ability to deliver a true musician's sense of humility and pride in playing for "his king." "Must Be Santa," which was the basis for a rollicking video, is another gem, if only for hearing Dylan "laugh this way, ho ho ho." Other numbers benefit from the somewhat bluesy arrangements that Dylan's band mates have become fully conversant with: "The Christmas Blues" is a strong choice, while "I'll Be Home for Christmas" feels like it is being croaked out by a homeless down-and-outer dreaming of the holidays of yore. A standout is "Have Yourself a Merry Christmas" where Dylan's delivery of "Come next year, we all will be together, if the fates allow, so have yourself a merry little Christmas *now*" exudes both a coziness that can keep the chill at bay and an apprehensive sense that one had best celebrate Christmas while one still can.

The hymns, for all the singer's careful phrasing, fare less well if only because the power or subtlety required by the melodies is a bit beyond Dylan's ragged vocals. His odd phrasing at times has comic effects, as on "Hark the Heeeeerrald Angels Sing." But surely it's worth the price of admission to hear Dylan sing in Latin on "Oh Come All Ye Faithful (Adeste Fideles)." At such moments we might believe we're getting a glimpse of little Bobby Zimmerman as part of a Christmas choir, singing his heart out.

ROLL ON BOB

In an article by Douglas Brinkley in *Rolling Stone* upon the release of *Together Through Life*, Dylan responded to the somewhat impertinent question about his longevity as a performing and recording artist with the comment, "My music wasn't made to take me from one place to another so I can retire early" (2). He makes the keen point that persons who have a talent or skill—he mentions plumbers and artisans, but the point certainly extends to painters, writers, even actors—don't generally "retire" while they are still physically capable of using their abilities. To take the point a bit further, we might think of poets who continued into their seventies and eighties. For every Yeats, who produced some of his strongest and most memorable verse late in life, there is a Wordsworth or a Whitman who continues writing while adding little of lasting significance to his work. Wordsworth in particular, after his brilliant *annis mirabilis*, became something of a hack. Poets of Dylan's lifetime, though elders, like Allen Ginsberg and John Ashbery, make interesting points of comparison as well. Ginsberg maintained the skill of being himself in verse but that self had little new to discover, other than the sad attendants of age; Ashbery has so patently perfected his signature form of verse that reading his poems seems like admiring someone for taking their morning constitutional. Dylan, always an erratic, self-willed talent, could easily become a tired spinner of other people's yarns, even a mangler of other people's melodies, should he fail to maintain an edge by writing new songs. Late in his recording career, Johnny Cash recorded a series of albums with "name" producer Rick Rubin beginning in 1994, referred to as the American Recordings, with releases continuing posthumously as late as 2010. Not every song on these albums works, but they are testaments to Cash's enduring way with a song. With a voice in a narrow baritone and guitar-playing skills that he himself considered rudimentary, Cash was a major interpreter of songs, in part because of his sense of phrasing and his deep regard for lyrics; while it's not unimaginable that Dylan might find albums of songs he would be able to do justice to, his fans always hope for verbal coinage as yet unminted.

Dylan's releases in 2009 marked a bit of each—new work, but not particularly adventuresome, and covers of Christmas chestnuts. The year was early in the first term of Barack Obama, the historic victor of the election of 2008. The initial joy among many of Obama's constituents, young voters particularly, abated as the economic woes of the country continued, and the wars U.S. forces were committed to raged on. Obama quickly showed himself incapable of the kinds of serious changes to Washington political culture that many deemed necessary for any useful progress—particularly on matters of climate change and the difficulties of curtailing corporate power or the infractions of Wall Street. For a brief moment, there seemed a chance for improvement, but the virulent rhetoric of partisan politics only increased, to more rabid and irrelevant extents. If ever the mood of existing institutions was dire, if ever the sense of government, business, and financial interests at loggerheads was critical, if ever the ineffectiveness of the press— gutted by the Internet's depletion of money for newspaper advertising—was a cause for alarm, it was in the early years of the second decade of the twenty-first century. A sense of desperation, but also a strong call for communal action in protest and new solutions, came with the Occupy Wall Street movement that lasted through the fall of 2011 in many U.S. cities. Such spontaneous uprisings of the disgruntled were somewhat countered on the right by the rallies of the Tea Party, a radical voice seeking to control and stymie government so as to render Obama's administration ineffectual. Outside the United States, uprisings in many Arab countries beginning in December 2010 and extending into the spring of 2011 and beyond—earning the nickname "Arab Spring" for the period of the most intensive upheaval—were clearly the inspiration for the anti–Wall Street movement in the States. Though each uprising has its own reasons and consequences, an incentive was the desire to exercise claims against the legitimacy of a given government or particular leaders or, as in the States, against the more general system of economic profits and loss.

In September of 2012, in the centennial of the sinking of the *Titanic* and a few months before the presidential race between Barack Obama and Mitt Romney, the business-style candidate of the Republican Party, Dylan released *Tempest*. Its title song commemorates the famous disaster while also darkly suggesting that going down with the ship might be applicable in a more general sense. Indeed, the album does the job that *Together* didn't do, marking the third in a trio of significant releases since the turn of the century: *"Love and Theft," Modern Times*, and *Tempest*.

Again self-produced with Dylan's touring band, *Tempest* finds Dylan more varied in his lyrical approach than he has been in decades. None of the songs use the standard blues form that entails repetitions of lines. Every song, even those that have refrains, is varied, overflowing with imagery, sayings, quotations, description, aphorisms, and the kinds of memorably worded asides that are the delight of Dylan's fans. The tone of several of the songs is lustily violent, as if Dylan has been watching a lot of Westerns or gangster flicks where problems are generally settled with guns and/or fists. Gone are love songs of the lilting soft-shoe variety that recent albums favored; the closest is "Soon After Midnight," where the sensitivity of the vocal delivery is a marvel in and of itself. As a love song, its lines toy with the notion of fatal attraction: "When I first met you I didn't think you would do / It's soon after midnight / And I don't want nobody but you." Elsewhere are outright threats—"Two-Timing Slim, whoever heard of him / I'll drag his corpse through the mud"—and odd asides "I've got a date with a fairy queen." (Given the fact that Dylan has been cribbing from Ovid and Chaucer of late, the spelling might be "Fairie Queene.")

The first track, "Duquesne Whistle," co-written with Robert Hunter, is the only song with the casual feel of much of *Together*. Thanks in large part to drummer George Recile's slapping rhythm track, the song chugs along like the train it's named for (which ran from 1959 until 1971). Dylan plays with some of the associations his recent image has suggested—"you say I'm a gambler, you say I'm a pimp / But I ain't neither one." The song's up-tempo bounce suggests an "all's right with the world" vibe, though lines like "you're like a time bomb in my heart" and "I hear a sweet voice softly calling / Must be the mother of our Lord" almost take us off the rails.

The hopped-up blues of "Narrow Way" is full of a kind of murderous vigor; nothing much develops of interest in the lyrics, but the singer is able to fling off quatrain after quatrain, always returning to the idea of a "long road, a long and narrow way," that might unite separated lovers: "If I can't work up to you, you'll surely have to work down to me someday." We might say the gauntlet has been thrown—can "you" go as low as the singer does? Many statements in the song can be perceived as taunts, dares, or boasts, so that the singer's attitude toward "you" is generally aggressive and dissatisfied—"We looted and we plundered on distant shores / Why is my share not equal to yours?" The persona of the song might easily be the "gambler or pimp" that the singer of "Duquesne Whistle" denies being.

Side 2 opens with a talk-sung song that is the most understated on the album, delivered as a direct address to a woman the singer is trying to charm by speaking frankly. As such it's a surprisingly seductive performance, with Dylan's voice at its most cagey. "Maybe it's the same for you as it is for me," the singer suggests, looking back on a time when "for one brief day I was the man for you." The "Long and Wasted Years" of the title seems to refer to a marriage that is over but for the odd kinship that endures: "I just came to you because you're a friend of mine."

"Pay in Blood" sounds upbeat, defiant, even triumphant. Again the persona of the song is one who thrives on challenge, violence, threats, even insult: "I've been through hell, what good did it do? / You bastard, I'm supposed to respect you?" "I came to bury, not to praise" leaps out as a line that might apply to the album in general, as the body count does get rather high.

"Scarlet Town" with its plunking banjo accompaniment and sense of somber unease strikes a note similar to "Ain't Talkin'"—even to the point of the lyrical violin that slithers in and out of the arrangement. Each line of the song seems to be a brick set in place, constructing an edifice between the singer and the place he sings of. As a portrait of a place, the song shows us a mythic space where "I was born," where "you fight your father's foes," where "cryin' won't do no good." The tales of the American West are full of such rotten towns, places where those who stay do so out of a sense of tragic fatality. "If love is a sin then beauty is a crime"—and all things, and all races—"the black and the white, the yellow and the brown"—can be "beautiful in their time." What is the crime of "Scarlet Town"? The song suggests a kind of penitential space more than a hell, a limbo that swallows the soul.

The leadoff song of the third side is "Early Roman Kings," a Muddy Waters–inspired stomper along the lines of "Mannish Boy." Here Dylan seems both to satirize and to celebrate somewhat the macho ethos of the "gangsta" mentality. It's one of his most rousing recent blues tunes and the most flat-out fun song on the album. One of the entertainments, as is often the case in such songs, is to see how many different rhymes Dylan makes with "kings." One particularly apropos example is: "I ain't dead yet / My bell still rings / I keep my fingers crossed / Like the early roman kings." And a verse that seems to sum up the mood of the entire song: "Ding dong daddy / You're coming up short / Gonna put you on trial / In a Sicilian court." This is the kind of muscular little rocker that it seems Dylan can play forever.

The last three songs on the album are stories, and one of those, "Tin Angel," a largely dialogue-driven narrative, tells a tale with a deliberateness Dylan has not employed since the story-telling seventies with songs like "Isis," "Lily, Rosemary and the Jack of Hearts," and "Black Diamond Bay." The other two—"Tempest" and "Roll On John"—are more impressionistic narratives. Though the fates of the *Titanic* and of John Lennon, the respective subject matter of each song, are well-known, the songs don't aim to tell the actual stories. Rather, the significance of those stories, their immense pathos, is used to provide a known frame of reference to Dylan's at times quizzical choice of detail and allusion.

"Tin Angel" takes its melody from an old traditional song that has been worked into a variety of forms and takes its situation from a different one. Both songs are Child Ballads, early folk songs collected by Francis James Child. Dylan's tune is reminiscent of "Black Jack Davey" (which Dylan covered on *Good as I Been to You*), in which a highborn husband finds his wife has run off with a gypsy or pack of gypsies. He pursues them, finds her, and is rebuked by her. He then takes vengeance. Dylan's lyrics on "Tin Angel" are closer to "Matty Groves," which spells out the duel between the young lover and the husband, which the husband wins. When his wife rebukes him, he kills her and, in some versions, himself as well. Dylan's adaptation freely departs from this basic premise. While seeming to keep the horses and swords of the original era of the song, he also has electric wires and guns. The lover kills the husband, only to be rebuked by the wife, who then draws a knife and kills him: "All husbands are good men, as all wives know, / Then she pierced him to the heart and his blood did flow." After taking revenge for her husband, she kills herself, much like the woman who kills herself after killing her lover in the song "Henry Lee" (indeed, Dylan gives the name Henry Lee to the lover): "'You died for me, now I'll die for you,' / She put the blade to her heart and she ran it through." ("Henry Lee" has a variant known as "Love Henry," which Dylan recorded on *World Gone Wrong*.)

Dylan's version of this tale is made more sordid by the language he employs. The husband calls his wife "a greedy-lipped wench" and her lover "a gutless ape with a worthless mind." There are also odd details, such as the description of the husband coming to spy on the lovers that is gratuitous and clumsy: "He lowered himself down on a golden chain / His nerves were quaking in every vein." Set against the kind of economy and force of the old Child ballad, Dylan's version seems at times rather unwieldy, but at the same time his delivery of the song gives it a lustiness—both the lust of sex and bloodlust—well-served at times by the awkward grace of the lyrics. Meeting in death, the trio may be said to stand for an unholy trinity. There is a kind of absolute justice at work and the singer seems to take grim glee in playing each role and in taking leave with an omniscient view of funeral torches blazing "through the towns and the villages all night and all day."

That sense of being both in and above the story, so important a device of storytelling, is significant in "Tempest," which puts us aboard the sinking *Titanic* while also reminding us, in the chorus breaks, that a sleeping "watchman" is dreaming the *Titanic* is sinking. That dream element is further contained by a female storyteller who opens the song, and under a pale moon shining "on a Western town" tells "the sad, sad story of the great ship that went down." Thus, the story we are getting could be seen as the tale the woman tells, filtered through the dream of the watchman; or the woman's story could contain the watchman as a narrative element. The difference is whether or not one chooses to hear the actual words of the song as a rendering of what the woman tells. Placing this speaker in the song, but narrating her placement, is enough to render all the details somewhat askew. We don't know at what period the woman tells the story, but it seems that she has seen the film *Titanic*, directed by James Cameron and starring Leo DiCaprio as Jack Dawson. The song features a character called Leo who, like Dawson, draws. Yet in no way can "Tempest" be construed as telling the story of Cameron's film. Rather, the details in the song are a freely adapted version of what happened aboard the ship. Some elements—the exact date, and the presence of "the rich man Mr. Astor"—are historically accurate, others aren't.

Dylan (who freely adapted a newspaper story about pandemonium aboard a ship way back in his "Talkin' Bear Mountain Picnic Massacre Blues") lets his imagination go where it likes, giving us, in one of the most effective but entirely sentimental moments, "Jim Dandy," who gives his place on a lifeboat to a little crippled child; and "Davey the brothel keeper," a character reminiscent of the dealer who breaks the bank in the gambling room aboard the sinking island casino in Dylan's "Black Diamond Bay," releases his girls and "sees the changing of his world." The sense of the momentous, apocalyptic event is amplified by the teller's choice of imagery: "All the lords and ladies / Heading for their eternal home"; "the roll was called up yonder"; "the veil was torn asunder"; "he waited for / time and space to intervene"; "they drowned upon the staircase / Of brass and polished gold." Elsewhere, the captain reads "the Book of Revelations," we hear that "brother rose up against brother," and a bishop addresses God: "the poor are yours to feed." Amid the teeming details of the epic song's forty-five verses, the teller keeps a focus on the great reckoning that is being performed—not a disaster, but a judgment: "there is no understanding / on the judgment of God's hand"; "all things had run their course." In one of the most telling verses—"There were many, many others / Nameless here forevermore / They never sailed the ocean / Or left their homes before"—

the notion of anonymity in death blankets those too historically insignificant to merit names: the poor indeed, whose name is legion.

The seesawing ballad tune, a slow Irish jig, makes all the carnage oddly buoyant. All are ultimately swept beneath the sea—even though there were 710 survivors of the actual disaster. Dylan's teller is indifferent to that; we have instead a cautionary tale of sorts, a "look upon my works ye mighty" moment à la Shelley's "Ozymandias." The hubris of humanity is a theme that extends beyond the great ship itself to the world we live in now, with "natural" disasters read more and more in terms of mankind's effect on the ecosystem and the very fabric of the planet as a sustainable "being." The *Titanic*—in its allegedly "unsinkable" superiority—can also be a figure for institutions "too big to fail," as was said of investment firms, like Lehman Brothers, and loan agencies, like Fannie Mae, that fell upon insolvency but for government bail-outs around 2008.

In evoking one of the most famous maritime events in history, subject for one of the highest-grossing blockbuster films of all time, Dylan's "Tempest" participates in folk legend so common to the American media and to the way in which people increasingly live their lives, informed by vague analogy. The reference to Shakespeare is also interesting. Often regarded as Shakespeare's last play *The Tempest* begins with a ship foundering and sinking in a storm stirred up by Prospero, a magician on a nearby island. In "Tempest," the teller notes "The wizard's curse played on." It was not a storm or tempest that sank the *Titanic* but rather a glancing collision with an iceberg, a detail that "Tempest" never mentions, though "icy waters" are referred to once. Dylan's disaster includes a "whirlwind / Sky splitting all around," which has nothing to do with the sinking of the *Titanic* but everything to do with the opening of Shakespeare's play. Dylan has concocted an interesting pastiche of disaster to refer to many kinds of peril and to the kinds of actions that occur when people "meet their maker," as the saying goes. "And it's a big, it's a big, it's a big, it's a big ship's a-gonna sink," we might say.

The final song on the album is one of Dylan's most stirring to date. An elegy for John Lennon, who was killed by a psychotic fan at gunpoint one December night in 1980, the song feels, coming thirty-two years after the event and late in Dylan's career, like an elegy for an entire generation. There are many fallen comrades, in other words, and

Lennon's death, because he was such a figurehead for his contemporaries, speaks for a more extensive sense of loss, indeed, for an era gone for good.

Dylan keeps much of the song close to Lennon, with phrases borrowed from the latter's songs and scattered details from his life. Use of a line like "I heard the news today, oh boy" has immediate recognition from "A Day in the Life," but also recalls that song's use of headlines to describe a certain state of mind. The "news" of Lennon's death arrived very much as the kind of event Lennon's song, from 1967, refers to. Dylan uses a reference to "that deep dark cave" as a witty allusion to "the Cavern" where Lennon and the future Beatles worked as "The Quarrymen" but also, with "they tied your hands and clamped your mouth," recalls Plato's allegory of the cave, which posits that the objects we strive to obtain in this world are but shadows of more substantial things not of this world. At the song's end, Dylan works in a reference to "Tyger, Tyger," one of the best-known poems of visionary poet William Blake, which describes a figure for demonic agency, coupling it with Lennon's complete surrender from activity into endless sleep: "Tiger, tiger, burning bright / I pray the Lord my soul to keep / In the forest of the night / Cover him over and let him sleep." The first and third lines are from Blake, while the second line is from a child's prayer, and the final line arrives as a benediction on Lennon, a prayer for his eternal rest, but also places him, somewhat mystically, in "the forest of the night."

The lyrics are quite understated in their evocation of Lennon's ultimate meaning—Dylan's eulogy "Lenny Bruce" is more emphatic about the purpose and effect of Bruce's work—but the deep attachment to Lennon, as a person, as an artist, and as a memory and spirit come out very strongly. The song's melody and Dylan's delivery fuse to evoke tenderness and sadness and admiration. The way Dylan uses phrasing to put the words of short lines into the long melodic line makes for hesitations and stresses that show consummate care with the song, a fitting tribute to one of the most immediately recognizable voices of his generation. If one focuses only on Lennon, however, one will miss some of the power of the song. Much in the lyrics does not refer directly or even indirectly to Lennon or The Beatles, but rather measures the time already gone for a singer who might indeed be willing to contemplate, as one does when at graveside, a consummation devoutly to be wished.

Bob Dylan is truly one of the great writers of his generation. As the American Academy of Arts and Letters noted in their induction of Dylan in May 2013, Dylan transcends the notions that apply to practitioners of a single art. As songwriter, singer, performer, and poet Dylan combines his talents to create a singular presence in the world of the popular arts. With the last three songs on *Tempest*, Dylan might be said to position himself as a descendant of folk ballads of lust and violence, a poet of major events in American history—as Whitman was, with "When Lilacs Last in the Dooryard Bloom'd," about the death of Lincoln—and a poet of elegy for the lights of his own generation, thus treading on ground common to poets throughout history. And yet Dylan's is not primarily a literary art or achievement. To read the words of "Tempest" against something like "The Wreck of the *Hesperus*" would be silly, to some extent. Dylan does not compose words for the page. His unique art is in his delivery of his words, set to the music he achieves in a studio or live before an audience. As a master of popular song forms, Dylan has done more for the extension of songwriting into areas once considered the province of literature and poetry, but he has also done more for the vitality of the blues and folk traditions and for the legacy of his generation's adaptation of rock and roll, than any other living American musical artist. His is an achievement that is unparalleled in many ways in its sheer magnitude and in its diversity, originality and adaptation of earlier work, riskiness, unevenness, trail-blazing indifference to more comfortable and popular genres and approaches, and devotion to live performance. The latter capacity alone would merit calling Dylan an American troubadour—recalling the early traveling musicians of the Middle Ages—but the phrase also captures something of Dylan's mysterious grasp of long-standing musical traditions that continue to inspire him and to infuse his compositions with the sense that they were not written by one man—the former Robert Zimmerman, formerly of Duluth, Minnesota—but rather by a collective spirit abroad in our country, an ethos of individualism, collaboration, comedy, drama, desire, dream, memory, history, God, man, woman, of races and places, wars and peace and loves and loss, of words, melody, music, rhythm, that inform the song and voice we know as "Bob Dylan."

EPILOGUE

"Now the Rest Is History"

It was the pre-Socratic philosopher Heraclitus who said that no man ever steps into the same river twice because it's not the same river and he's not the same man. The truth of time and change contained in this reflection is one that consideration of a long career such as Bob Dylan's brings to the fore. When we talk about "Dylan," we are never talking about the same man, but rather a succession of personae. And whatever point we first dip into the river of his works colors the experience we will have. Where are we in our own lives? What is happening in the times we are living through? How receptive are we to periods of time now gone?

For a long time, there was a tendency to claim Dylan's early career as definitive and mostly everything since the sixties as derivative or ephemeral. My sense is that, as a succession of albums released at certain times in Dylan's life and at certain points in history, Dylan's work is more homogeneous than it might seem, both at its best and its worst. The uniqueness of the early work in part derives from the fact that no one like Bob Dylan already existed when those albums appeared. Subsequently, later "Dylans" exist in a world where the early work predates them. And where one stops the account determines whether we end on a high point or a low point. When Dylan was largely dismissed as a has-been in the eighties, that standing had in part to do with the times themselves as well as his own output. One effect of a great comeback, such as Dylan has enjoyed since 1997, is earlier periods get reevaluated, too. Currently that is happening with Dylan's work from around 1970, and our reevaluation is aided by a new release in August 2013 of yet another *Bootleg* Series containing more material from the sessions that produced *Self Portrait* and *New Morning* and were the basis for the album *Dylan*. While the period of *Self Portrait* has been notable previously as the point at which Dylan "lost his way" and departed from the style of rock promoted by *Rolling Stone* magazine and the like, the music Dylan has produced on the well-received recent albums "*Love and Theft*" and *Modern Times* naturally send one back to the transition from the sixties to the seventies, the period when Dylan began to stretch beyond folk and blues. Called *Another Self Portrait*, the new release bolsters our current sense of Dylan as someone committed to American songwriting in all its forms, discovering a more relaxed sense of his vocation in song.

Assessing Dylan's work also reflects our own changing critical assumptions and is a result of the tools we choose to measure with. In 1964, when Dylan said, "I got nothin', Ma, to live up to," he at once dismissed his own past as a measurement of his present. Few of his critics seem to have grasped the strength of his assertion. Often, a critic's only purpose seems to be making sure each new Dylan is aware of what it is he's not living up to—whether it's *Freewheelin'*, *Blonde on Blonde*, *Blood on the Tracks*, *Slow Train Coming*, or "Blind Willie McTell." In the Introduction, I took the view that being true to the spirit of "Bob Dylan," whatever that might be conceived to be at any given moment, is the purpose of Dylan's work. We might presume to say what we see as being "authentic Dylan," but if we don't consider the entire picture, we risk creating an unnecessary restriction. If we truly value the creativity and skill and unpredictable inspirations of an artist, we have to value even those side trips down avenues less than fruitful and accept when something is simply "good enough for now."

The most common criticism of Dylan is "phoniness," asserting that he is mimicking a music he has no genuine claim to, or that he is trying to be a certain version of Bob Dylan he no longer has access to. It's a purist's position, ultimately, but I tend to be mystified as to the source of its conviction. No one looking on at Dylan's work could have predicted where it has gone, nor what he has become. If, somewhere along the line, one identifies strongly with a particular album or string of albums, that fact should stand for what it's worth. Those albums don't disappear because of the existence of something much different and perhaps less successful later.

The diachronic argument accepts that an artist changes over time and that such change doesn't alter what has been achieved. When Dylan went electric, for some it meant he invalidated his folk persona, and when he went country, that invalidated his rock persona; or alternatively, when he reached his forties and had to make records in the 1980s, those records were invalidated by his sixties personae. None of those positions make much sense to me, as they rest on a chosen point in Dylan's career from which to judge the rest of his career. And no one, neither Dylan nor his audience, can rest at one point in time indefinitely. When Dylan found Jesus, for example, he put aside his secular songs, but only for a time.

In rock journalism the more common viewpoint is synchronic: taking "the times" in their most contemporary sense as the factor that determines whether or not an album is timely and successful and whether it is cutting-edge or retro. Such judgments are worthwhile only to the extent that we always appreciate a knowing commentary on what is happening now—at the time in which we are alive and reading—but in any historical account such as this book, "now" is not a precise point in time because of the retrospective nature of the endeavor. All along, we are looking back on something that occurred and trying to assess it from a vantage point about which I make no definite claims, regarding its value as measured against other periods. In terms of Dylan's career, the majority of this book was written between the release of *Tempest* and the release of *Another Self Portrait*. There is no conclusion because Bob Dylan has yet to conclude.

My purpose here has been to look at what seems worthwhile in each new Dylan he has offered us, to see how it reflects upon its moment. My sense of timeliness is perhaps different from that of the journalist's, but it is a difference of degree rather than kind. My study addresses the albums chronologically, as existing in time, attempting in part to understand the times as filtered through the songs Dylan writes and releases. That said, led by my own tastes, I can pick out my favorite songs and albums by Dylan, unrestricted by period or sequence. Such a view is the "eternal present" of the listener, who is able to make choices on the basis of what speaks at the moment. There is always some entertainment value and some use value—as a means of reflection on the possibilities of song—in every Dylan album. Dylan, like any artist, is better at some things than at other things, but Dylan, unlike many artists, is often "willing to risk it all" and do things that aren't likely to be popular—which we may think of as a way of proving his love is not in vain. Most accounts by those who have worked with Dylan stress that he hates to do the same thing twice, even if it were wonderfully successful, and that he likes to be unpredictable, even if that quality costs him coherence or precision or professionalism—or any other quality we might consider desirable. We might also say that Dylan's desire is to create something we haven't heard before, whether we wanted to hear it or not, and that desire keeps him from sitting still and resting on his laurels.

It is my hope that this book sends readers to the records to become listeners, willing to hear for themselves what moves them and what doesn't. Albums of popular music such as Dylan makes are not, generally speaking, works of art in the sense that fine-arts criticism uses the term, and in general that's because the popular arts tend to be done quickly, ad hoc, and often simply for contractual reasons. Many of Dylan's albums are flawed as "art." But as a collection of songs and performances, every Dylan album—whether official release or bootleg or official bootleg—offers glimpses of this protean poet of voice, mood, and musical approach at work. And I must admit that I never fail to be fascinated by some aspect of his work. Dylan has lived a life in song and the memorable performances in his corpus are numerous, and quite often even when listening to them over and over, it seems that one never hears the same song twice.

FURTHER READING

Baker, Dean. *The United States Since 1980*. Cambridge: Cambridge University Press, 2007.

Bangs, Lester. "Bob Dylan's Dalliance with Mafia Chic." *Creem*. April 1976. Thompson 210–22. Bangs' takedown of "Joey."

Baughman, James L. *The Republic of Mass Culture: Journalism, Filmmaking, and Broadcasting in America since 1941*. 2nd Ed. Baltimore: Johns Hopkins University Press, 1997.

Brinkley, Douglas. "Bob Dylan's Late-Era, Old-Style American Individualism." *Rolling Stone*. May, 14, 2009: http://www.rollingstone.com/music/news/bob-dylans-america-20090514 1-8; retrieved 7/5/13.

Cherlin, Michael and Sumanth Gopinath. "'Somewhere Down in the United States': The Art of Bob Dylan's Ventriloquism." Colleen J. Sheehy and Thomas Swiss, eds. *Highway 61 Revisited: Bob Dylan's Road from Minnesota to the World*. Minneapolis: University of Minnesota Press, 2009. An ambitious and attentive attempt to catalogue the variety of voices and poses that Dylan utilizes on his second album.

Cohen, John and Happy Traum. Interview. *Sing Out!* October/November 1968. Cott 113–36.

A Concert for Bangladesh. Dir. Saul Swimmer. 1972. DVD Rhino Records, 2005. Dylan's performance at this concert is one of his best on film.

Cott, Jonathan, ed. *Bob Dylan. The Essential Interviews*. New York: Wenner Books, 2006. This collection of some of the best interviews Dylan has given is indeed essential.

———. Interview. *Rolling Stone*. January, 26, 1978. Cott 171–97.

———. Interview. *Rolling Stone*. November, 16, 1978. Cott 251–70.

———. "Introduction." Cott ix–xv.

Creswell, Toby. "Gates of Eden Revisited." *Rolling Stone* (Australia). 16 January, 1986. *Younger* 235–45.

Crowe, Cameron. Liner notes. *Biograph*. Columbia Records, 1985, 2–35. Crowe manages to compress the essentials of the Dylan story into a small space, and Dylan goes on some fun rants about the music business; the comments on individual songs are also interesting.

Denning, Michael. "Bob Dylan and Rolling Thunder." Dettmar 28–41.

Dettmar, Kevin J. H., ed. *The Cambridge Companion to Bob Dylan*. Cambridge: Cambridge University Press, 2009.

Don't Look Back. Dir. D. A. Pennebaker. DVD 1965 Tour Deluxe Ed. New Video Group, 2007. The film that does more to create an image of Dylan than any other—but be careful. It's best to read between the lines.

Dickstein, Morris. *Gates of Eden. American Culture in the Sixties*. 1977. With a New Introduction. Cambridge, MA: Harvard University Press, 1997.

Didion, Joan. *Slouching Towards Bethlehem. Essays*. 1968. Farrar, Straus and Giroux, 1990.

———. *The White Album. Essays*. 1979. Farrar, Straus and Giroux, 1990.

Dylan, Bob. *Chronicles, Volume 1*. New York: Simon and Schuster, 2004. Dylan has his say in print about different phases of his career. The prose is straightforward with occasional flourishes. His gloss on events isn't always completely accurate, but it's his story and he tells it his way.

———. "Advice for Geraldine on Her Miscellaneous Birthday." *Writings*: 118–19.

———. "11 Outlined Epitaphs." Liner notes. *The Times, They Are A-Changin'*. Columbia, 1964. *Writings*: 100–110.

———. "Joan Baez in Concert, Part 2." *Writings*: 75–82.

———. "Last Thoughts on Woody Guthrie." *Writings*: 52–56.

———. Liner notes. *Bringing It All Back Home*. Columbia, 1965. *Writings*: 157–58.

———. Liner Notes. *Highway 61 Revisited*. Columbia, 1965. *Writings*: 181–82.

———. Liner Notes. *Planet Waves*. Asylum, 1974.

———. Liner Notes. *World Gone Wrong*. Columbia, 1993.

———. "My Life in a Stolen Moment." *Writings*: 49–51.

———. "Some Other Kinds of Songs." Liner notes. *Another Side of Bob Dylan*. Columbia, 1964. *Writings*: 139–50.

———. *Tarantula*. 1966. 1971. New York: Scribner, 2004. This original prose work shows what happens when Dylan works without a band; it's a kaleidoscope of one-liners and odd locutions and presents the stream of consciousness of an unusual mind with a distinctive way with words.

———. "Three Kings." Liner Notes. *John Wesley Harding*. Columbia, 1967. *Writings*: 255–56.

———. *Writings and Drawings by Bob Dylan*. A Borzoi Book. New York: Knopf, 1973.

Ehrenreich, Barbara. *Hearts of Men. American Dreams and the Flight from Commitment*. 1983. Garden City: Anchor Books, 1984.

Ephron, Nora and Susan Edmiston. Interview. "Positively Tie Dream," August 1965; *Cavalier*, Feb. 1966. Cott 47–54.

Frith, Simon, ed. *The Cambridge Companion to Pop and Rock*. Cambridge University Press, 2001.

———. *Sound Effects. Youth, Leisure, and the Politics of Rock'n'Roll*. New York: Pantheon, 1981. This interesting account of the music industry from the birth of rock to punk touches on the ideology of making records and is a good introduction to the different aspects of rock as business and culture.

Gill, Andy and Kevin Odegard. *A Simple Twist of Fate: Bob Dylan and the Making of* Blood on the Tracks. Cambridge, MA: Da Capo Press, 2004.

Gilmore, Mikal. Interview. *Rolling Stone*. 17 July, 1986. Cott 333–46.

———. Interview. *Rolling Stone*. 22 December, 2001. Cott 411–28.

———. Interview. *Rolling Stone*. 27 September, 2012: 44–51, 80–81.

Gitlin, Todd. *The Sixties. Years of Hope, Days of Rage*. New York: Bantam Books, 1987.

Gould, Jonathan. *Can't Buy Me Love: The Beatles, Britain, and America*. New York: Three Rivers Press, 2007.

Gray, Michael. *Bob Dylan Encyclopedia*. London: Continuum, 2006.

Hajdu, David. *Positively 4th Street: The Lives and Times of Joan Baez, Bob Dylan, Mimi Baez Fariña, and Richard Fariña*. New York: Farrar, Straus, and Giroux, 2001.

Hebdige, Dick. *Subculture: The Meaning of Style*. 1979. London: Routledge, 2001.

Heiman, Bruce. Radio Interview. KMEX (Tucson, Arizona). 7 December, 1979. Cott 271–74.

Hentoff, Nat. "The Crackin', Shakin', Breakin,' Sounds" *The New Yorker*. 24 October, 1964. Cott 13–28.

———. Liner notes. *The Freewheelin' Bob Dylan*. Columbia Records, 1963.

Heylin, Clinton. *Bob Dylan: Behind the Shades*. 20th Anniversary Ed. London: Faber and Faber, 2011. Heylin is an unflagging Dylanologist, full of opinions and apt to take potshots at whoever displeases him. One wishes at times he had an editor, or a word limit.

———. *Bob Dylan: A Life in Stolen Moments: Day by Day 1941–1995*. New York: Schirmer Books, 1996.

————. *Bob Dylan: The Recording Sessions, 1960–1994*. New York: St. Martin's Griffin, 1995. The main argument of this book is that every Dylan album would be better, if only Dylan had consulted Heylin first. Some might agree, but the author tends to overplay the view that almost every discarded track and alternate take is a revelation that the released versions can't compete with. That's only true some of the time. But the sessionographies are well worth having.

Hilburn, Robert. Interview. *Los Angeles Times*. 23 November 1980. Cott 279–84.

The Last Waltz. Dir. Martin Scorsese. 1978. DVD MGM, 2002. One of the best rock and roll movies ever, even if everyone is already far along in their careers and might seem middle of the road. The film actually gives you hope that great rock acts can age gracefully.

Loder, Kurt. Interview. *Rolling Stone*. 21 June 1984. Cott 285–307.

McGregor, Craig, ed. *Bob Dylan. A Retrospective*. New York: William Morrow & Co., Inc., 1972.

Marcus, Greil. *Bob Dylan. Writings 1968–2010*. New York: Public Affairs, 2010. The stultifying effect of reading these occasional pieces in book form comes from the fact that Marcus is relentless in his journalese and knee-jerk reactions, and so each new album falls into the inevitable space created by the simple fact that, no matter what happens, Bob Dylan will never record another *Blonde on Blonde*. It's just not possible.

————. *The Old, Weird America: The World of Bob Dylan's Basement Tapes*. A special edition with a new introduction and updated discography. New York: Picador, 2011.

Marqusee, Mike. *Wicked Messenger: Bob Dylan and the 1960s*. New York: Seven Stories, 2005.

Marwick, Arthur. *The Sixties*. Oxford: Oxford University Press, 1998.

Masked and Anonymous. Dir. Larry Charles. 2003. DVD Columbia Tristar, 2004. Much maligned by people who want films to be tidy and never amateurish. For anyone who finds Dylan's lingo irresistible and his screen presence fascinating. Otherwise, why bother?

Nashville. Dir. Robert Altman. 1975. DVD Paramount, 2000.

Negus, Keith. *Bob Dylan*. Bloomington: Indiana University Press, 2008. This is a short, deft book that says useful things about Dylan's music *as* music.

No Direction Home. Dir. Martin Scorsese. DVD. Paramount Home Video, 2005. There's some great concert footage. But the performances that speak for themselves, and excite the eyes, ears, and mind, are interrupted again and again for a bunch of old apologists for Village lore sitting around reminiscing. Every now and then there's Dylan looking into the camera and trying to make sense of how great he was.

O'Dair, Barbara. "Bob Dylan and Gender Politics." Dettmar 80–86.

The Other Side of the Mirror: Bob Dylan Live at Newport Folk Festival 1963–1965. Sony, 2007. Worth a look to see how quickly Dylan and his world changed in three short years. Speaks volumes, especially if you weren't around in the sixties.

Pareles, Jon. Interview. *New York Times*. 28 September, 1997. Cott 391–96.

Pat Garrett & Billy the Kid. Dir. Sam Peckinpah. 1973. DVD 2 Disc Special Ed. Warner Home Video, 2006.

Poirier, Richard. "Learning from The Beatles," *The Performing Self: Compositions and Decompositions in the Language of Contemporary Life*. Forward by Edward W. Said. New Brunswick: Rutgers University Press, 1992: 112–40. An essay on *Sgt. Pepper* by a top literary critic; makes a lot of music criticism seem silly.

Renaldo and Clara. Dir. Bob Dylan. Lombard Street Films, 1978. Hard to find and hard to sit through, but if you want to talk Dylan in the seventies, you have to see it at least once. I'm pretty sure I saw it three times, in a theater.

Ricks, Christopher. *Dylan's Vision of Sin*. London: Penguin, 2003. Ricks writes while word-drunk—so like any alcoholic drink, it's best taken in moderation. And the book follows a thematic approach, which means that all of Dylan's writing occupies the same time and is always inspired. "And as to the forms that may be taken by knowledge, one of the best is knowing when one has had enough." That knowledge came to me quite quickly when reading this book.

Riley, Tim. *Hard Rain: A Dylan Commentary*. New York: Da Capo Press, 1999.

———. *Tell Me Why: A Beatles Commentary*. New York: Knopf, 1988.

Rosenbaum, Ron. "Born-again Bob: Four Theories," *New York Magazine*. 24 September, 1979. Thompson 233–37. Astute.

———. Interview. *Playboy*, March 1978. Cott 199–236.

Scaduto, Anthony. *Bob Dylan*. 1971. London: Helter Skelter Publishing, 2001. The first Dylan bio is still a landmark because it was written fairly close to the years of Dylan's first three "periods." Some of its facts have been disputed or disproved, but Scaduto is as scrupulous and unsensational as one could be at the time.

Schreiber, Ronnie. "Dylan's Grammy Acceptance Speech Explicated," *Dylan and the Jews* website: http://www.radiohazak.com/Dylgramm.html.

Shelton, Robert. *No Direction Home. The Life and Music of Bob Dylan*. 1986. Revised and updated edition edited by Elizabeth Thomson and Patrick Humphries. Milwaukee: Backbeat Books, 2011. Shelton, who "broke" Dylan with his *New York Times* article, was close enough to his subject to spend time with Dylan and the book benefits from his personal take on the man, though that vantage provides distortion as well.

Silber, Irwin. "An Open Letter to Bob Dylan," *Sing Out!* November 1964. McGregor 66–68.

Slaughter, J. "Marijuana prohibition in the United States: History and Analysis of a Failed Policy." *Columbia Journal of Law and Social Problems* 21(1) 1988: 417–75.

Sloman, Larry "Ratso." *On the Road with Bob Dylan*. London: Helter Skelter, 2005.

Sounes, Howard. *Down the Highway. The Life of Bob Dylan*. New York: Grove Press, 2001, 2011. This biography goes after the newsworthy aspects of Dylan's life and career—its most famous nugget is the fact that Dylan married and divorced Carolyn Dennis. Unlike Heylin, Sounes has little opinion about how any facts about Dylan influence his music and that's actually refreshing.

Spencer, Neil. Interview. "The Diamond Voice Within," *New Musical Express*. August 15, 1981. *Younger*, 171–85.

Spitz, Bob. *Bob Dylan: A Biography*. New York: McGraw-Hill, 1989.

Taylor, Derek. *It Was Twenty Years Ago Today: An Anniversary Celebration of 1967*. A Fireside Book. New York: Simon and Schuster, 1987.

Thompson, Hunter S. *Fear and Loathing in Las Vegas*. 1971. New York: Modern Library, 1998.

———. *Fear and Loathing: On the Campaign Trail '72*. New York: Popular Library, 1973.

Thomson, Elizabeth and David Gutman. *The Dylan Companion*. 1990. Da Capo Press, 2001. There are many interesting pieces of occasional Dylan journalism collected here.

Troy, Gil. *Morning in America. How Ronald Reagan Invented the 1980s*. Princeton: Princeton University Press, 2005.

Troy, Gil and Vincent J. Cannato, eds. *Living in the Eighties*. Oxford: Oxford University Press, 2009.

Van Ronk, Dave. *The Mayor of McDougal Street: A Memoir*. Cambridge, MA: Da Capo Press, 2005.

Wenner, Jann S. Interview. *Rolling Stone*. 29 November 1969. Cott 139–60.

Wilentz, Sean. *The Age of Reagan, A History: 1974–2008*. New York: Harper Perennial, 2009.

———. *Bob Dylan in America*. New York: Doubleday, 2011. Dylan as seen by a historian. The best chapters put some aspect of Dylan's career or a given song, like "Blind Willie McTell," or album, like *Blonde on Blonde*, into a relevant context, and Wilentz's summaries of different aspects of Dylan's career cover a lot of detail quickly.

Williams, Paul. *Bob Dylan Performing Artist. 1960–1973: The Early Years*. London: Omnibus, 1990.

———. *Bob Dylan Performing Artist: The Middle Years 1974–1986*. London: Omnibus, 1992.

———. *Bob Dylan Performing Artist: Volume 3: Mind Out of Time 1986 and Beyond*. London: Omnibus, 2004.

Willis, Ellen. "Dylan," *Cheetah*, 1967. McGregor 218–39.

Wolfe, Tom. *The Electric Kool-Aid Acid Test*. 1968. New York: Bantam, 1972.

Woodstock. Three Days of Peace and Music. Dir. Michael Wadleigh. DVD 2 Disc 40th Anniversary Director's Cut. Warner Home Video, 2009.

Yaffe, David. *Bob Dylan. Like a Complete Unknown.* New Haven: Yale University Press, 2011. Yaffe takes the stream-of-consciousness approach to Dylan, which is maybe what Dylan at his best inspires, and at least it's a thin book.

Young, Israel G. "Frets and Fails," *Sing Out!* November 1965. McGregor 93–94.

Younger Than That Now. The Collected Interviews with Bob Dylan. New York: Thunder's Mouth Press, 2004.

FURTHER LISTENING

*This annotated discography contains every official Bob Dylan release,
followed by selected live albums and compilations.*

Another Side of Bob Dylan (August 8, 1964), 4th album, Columbia Records. This album
showcases Dylan's move toward more personal and introspective songs, as well as returning to the jokiness so notable on his second album. Recorded in one long session, the
album captures Dylan at a key moment of transition.

The Basement Tapes (June 26, 1975), 16th album, Columbia Records. Technically a compilation album, combining tracks recorded at home in Woodstock with the musicians later
known as The Band and tracks The Band recorded later, the album is the only official
release of the unusual songs Dylan wrote in seclusion in 1967.

Blonde on Blonde (May 16, 1966), 7th album, Columbia Records. Arguably the best album
Dylan ever made, it was recorded in Nashville with brilliant session men, creating a
unique sound to match Dylan's extended treatment of the vagaries of romantic love.

Blood on the Tracks (1975), 15th album, Columbia Records. Dylan's return to form in the
mid-seventies with an album that furthers *Blonde on Blonde*'s concerns with women, love,
and romantic dysfunction, generally interpreted in the light of the Dylans' marital problems at the time.

Bob Dylan (March 19, 1962), debut album, Columbia Records. Notable for showing where
Dylan began, but not definitive, as some of the song choices are questionable. Features
two early original compositions, "Song for Woody" and "Talkin' New York Blues," and
standout performances of standards like "In My Time of Dyin'" and "House of the Rising
Sun."

Bringing It All Back Home (March 22, 1965), 5th album, Columbia Records. The first album
with electric instruments and a rock and roll / boogie/blues approach on most of the songs
on the first side; side 2 features four challenging songs that demonstrate both the poetic
pretensions of Dylan's material as well as the incisive and memorable phraseology of this
period in his songwriting.

Christmas in the Heart (October 13, 2009), 34th album, Columbia Records. Something of an
oddity, but likeable enough. An album of holiday standards, the secular Christmas songs
fare better than the religious hymns.

Desire (January 16, 1976), 17th album, Columbia Records. An uneven album with a distinctive sound thanks to the use of violin and back-up vocals from Emmylou Harris and Ronee
Blakely; songs co-written with Jacques Levy have a cinematic quality that continues the
vein of "Lily, Rosemary and the Jack of Hearts" from *Blood on the Tracks*.

Down in the Groove (May 31, 1988), 25th album, Columbia Records. A low point in Dylan's career, a collection of odds and ends, none of which strongly urge release. I'll only endorse "90 Miles an Hour Down a Dead-end Street" and "Death Is Not the End."

Dylan (November 16, 1973), 13th album, Columbia Records. Unlucky album 13 isn't an official Dylan release, as it was compiled by Columbia from outtakes for *Self Portrait* and *New Morning* and was released only because Dylan signed with Asylum. Some of the album is better than what appears on *Self Portrait* and, with the 2013 release of more work from those sessions as *The Bootleg Series Vol. 10*, deserves to be included.

Empire Burlesque (June 8, 1985), 23rd album, Columbia Records. An uneven record that should have been much better. For the most part, the songs feel vital enough, but the processed sound imposed on the whole by Arthur Baker makes this the most dated Dylan album, boasting a "club mix" sound that might give it historical interest.

The Freewheelin' Bob Dylan (May 27, 1963), 2nd album, Columbia Records. The one that really started it all; Dylan displays his songwriting skill and demonstrates his unique grasp of how to capture the mood of each of his original songs in this varied assortment, including classics like "Blowin' in the Wind," "A Hard Rain's A-Gonna Fall," and "Don't Think Twice, It's Alright."

Good as I Been to You (October 1992), 28th album, Columbia Records. Shortly after turning fifty, Dylan elected to record a collection of standards. None of the songs seem like definitive versions, but the album has a casual charm that feels like we're sitting around at home with Dylan as he plays some favorites.

Highway 61 Revisited (August 30, 1965), 6th album, Columbia Records. One of the definitive albums of Dylan's career, the first album on which he showed what he could do with rock and electric blues, as well as boasting signature songs, memorable lyrics, and some of his most commanding vocals—"exercises in tonal breath control."

Infidels (November 1, 1983), 22nd album, Columbia Records. Gets my vote for best Dylan album of the eighties, though some might prefer *Oh Mercy*. The musicians are excellent and the lineup of songs is a good mix of the kind of things Dylan does well, sounding off about the state of the world, the state of romantic affairs, and his own psyche. And it's a relief to have no songs dedicated to Christ.

John Wesley Harding (December 27, 1967), 8th album, Columbia Records. As time goes on, this album just seems to get better. Something of an anomaly, the album is concise, cryptic, mellow, and edgy all at the same time. It's also far removed from Dylan's forays into rock, returning to folk via country-tinged blues and ballads. His last great album of the sixties.

Knocked Out Loaded (August 8, 1986), 24th album, Columbia Records. Essentially this is an album of middle-of-the-road filler to accompany the release of "Brownsville Girl," an epic of narrative sleight of hand, myth making, and mourning of the Old Hollywood Western, co-written with Sam Shepard. The song is not to be missed.

"Love and Theft" (September 11, 2001), 31st album, Columbia Records. Welcome enough when it was released, on the very day the World Trade Towers fell, this warm and witty album of vintage Americana improves with age. Dylan shows himself again to be a man of many moods and this one's good enough to retire on, had he been so inclined.

Modern Times (2006), 32nd album, Columbia Records. The "follow-up" (after five years) to *"Love and Theft"*, this album seems to suit the mood of its moment surprisingly well. Coming after a Dylan film, *Masked and Anonymous*, an autobiographical book, and a retrospective documentary, the album shows Dylan to be convincingly ensconced in Americana. The first time an album by an artist of sixty-five years hit number 1 upon release.

Nashville Skyline (April 9, 1969), 9th album, Columbia Records. Famous for Dylan's use of his crooner voice, the album contains more filler than one would like, but it's an easy album to listen to because Dylan is willing to court Easy Listening arrangements. The duet with Johnny Cash is more a curiosity than a success.

New Morning (October 19, 1970), 11th album, Columbia Records. Best-known as the album that saved the day after the debacle of *Self Portrait*, this album features short, likeable songs and good musicianship. The lyrics never get too adventurous and some are a little cloying, but in general it's a listenable document from a very odd year for anyone who remembers the sixties.

Oh Mercy (September 22, 1989), 26th album, Columbia Records. Dylan's first pairing with producer Daniel Lanois produces his best sounding album of the eighties, a pleasure to listen to. The songs run toward the darkly foreboding and that suits the era well, to say nothing of a guy's late forties.

Pat Garrett & Billy the Kid (July 13, 1973), 12th album, Columbia Records. Dylan's only soundtrack album to date, the music suits well the vision Sam Peckinpah put on celluloid of a played-out Old West and a rift between friends when one goes straight and one stays an outlaw. "Knockin' on Heaven's Door" says it all.

Planet Waves (January 17, 1974), 14th album, Columbia Records. Dylan reunites with The Band and delivers a mostly upbeat album of funky rockabilly-style songs with, here and there, soul-searching statements like "Dirge" and "Wedding Song." The album lets us know that Dylan is ready to start writing songs again, as in the follow-up, *Blood on the Tracks*.

Saved (June 20, 1980), 20th album, Columbia Records. You don't have to love Jesus to like this album of original gospel tunes, but it helps. This, the second album of Dylan's apostle period, finds him with a hot band and vigorous tunes, but not much lyrical magic. "In the Garden" is the keeper, and "Saving Grace" boasts a vocal like nothing else.

Self Portrait (June 8, 1970), 10th album, Columbia Records. The second Dylan album to display a dearth of original material, this record is infamous for its gaffes—like "The Boxer" and an embarrassing live version of "Like a Rolling Stone"—though it can also be appreciated for its oddity and for the types of songs Dylan is willing to assay. If you've never been too partial to rockin' Dylan or Dylan the scribe of the sixties, you might find something to your liking here.

Shot of Love (August 12, 1981), 21st album, Columbia Records. At the time, it was easy to be disappointed by this album, though its stature has grown. It more creatively meets the Bible-thumping themes of the previous two releases and gave new hopes of a songwriter who doesn't have to crib from Christ. There's a lack of sharpness to some of the songs. The CD includes "The Groom's Still Waiting at the Altar."

Slow Train Coming (August 20, 1979), 19th album, Columbia Records. Dylan won a Grammy for telling the world to "Serve Somebody" in a funky little offhand gem. The first side of this album cuts like a knife, while the second side is so much flab—until "When He Returns" rolls the stone away.

Street-Legal (June 15, 1978), 18th album, Columbia Records. If this had been recorded with a slightly fastidious producer, it would be the second great album of Dylan's thirties. As it is, it's a much underrated offering. The problems are not with the material or the performances, but with Dylan using his own recording facilities and doing his music a great disservice.

Tempest (September 11, 2012), 35th album, Columbia Records. The scope of this album is rather daunting, coming from a guy in his seventies still able to crank out verse after verse, many offering the kind of pithy gems we've come to expect. Listening to Dylan at this point requires the love of a voice that's seen too much use, and a fondness for how the same verse, even the same line, can contain clichés, stolen lines, and original turns of phrase. "Tempest," the song about the *Titanic*, may be overlong, but it sure as hell beats sitting through Cameron's film.

Time Out of Mind (September 30, 1997), 30th album, Columbia Records. This is the album that put new Dylan material back on playlists with one of the great comebacks of any career. The songs are subdued, the production—from Daniel Lanois again—is highly conceptual, and the record grabbed Album of the Year at the Grammys. Not every song is the gem you might like it to be, but it all has its place.

The Times, They Are A-Changin' (January 13, 1964), 3rd album, Columbia Records. When people talk about Dylan "the protest singer," this is the album they're thinking about, mostly. Twenty-two when he recorded this record, Dylan sings anthems, topical songs, thwarted love songs, songs of hardship and songs of personal introspection, which is what he did on his second album, except here the offerings are rather more humorless.

Together Through Life (April 28, 2009), 33rd album, Columbia Records. Dylan cooked up an album's worth of songs with his friend Robert Hunter and gave it mostly a spritely sound with David Hidalgo's accordion. Two or three gems are sprinkled among the proceedings, and nothing is bad, so let's say "It's All Good."

Under the Red Sky (September 11, 1990), 27th album, Columbia Records. Following *Oh Mercy* is what makes this album seem less than it is. If compared to Dylan's LPs of the mid-eighties, this album shines, but . . . There's nothing here that would make a believer out of you if you weren't already inclined. "Handy Dandy" does it for me.

World Gone Wrong (October 26, 1993), 29th album, Columbia Records. Dylan's second stab at an all-acoustic solo LP recorded at home serves up more interesting material than *Good as I Been*, and that's because Dylan sounds like he's fed up with everything. This is crotchety folk blues delivered by someone not asking any quarter and not in a mood to give it.

SUPPLEMENTAL LISTENING

Bob Dylan at Budokan (April 23, 1979), double album, Columbia Records. These shows from early on, in Japan, are certainly not the best performances from the 1978 world tour, but there's an appealing insouciance to Dylan's vocals here and the band truly rings changes on songs way too familiar in their originals—it's pretty much laid-back as only the seventies can be.

Bob Dylan's Greatest Hits Vol. 2 (November 17, 1971), double album, Columbia Records. This eclectic collection revisits top tracks from all Dylan's albums to that point, except the first and third, and supplements them with a few non–album tracks, a lovely live rendition of "Tomorrow Is Such a Long Time," and amiable revisits of three Woodstock tunes.

The Bootleg Series Vol. 1–3, Rare and Unreleased, 1961–1991 (March 26, 1991), 3 discs, Columbia Records. There is much here that supplements the official releases, and the sound improves on most of the unofficial bootleg versions.

The Bootleg Series Vol. 4, In Concert 1966 (October 13, 1998), 2 discs, Columbia Records. When I first heard the unofficial bootleg of this concert in 1978, it was a revelation. "So this is how that period of Dylan sounds live!" Forget all the buzz about audience heckling and such nonsense, the electric album delivers a version of Dylan that can be found nowhere else. The acoustic album is one of those records for when you've been up all night and it's starting to get light.

The Bootleg Series Vol. 5, Live 1975 (November 26, 2002), 2 discs, Columbia Records. I generally find it hard to get caught up in this official release of Dylan live with The Rolling Thunder Revue because there are so many great unofficial releases from these shows and the sequence on these two discs doesn't give an account of an RTR show. Still, it was a good period for Dylan live. The duets with Baez feel more contentious and thus more interesting than the duo in the Sixties.

The Bootleg Series Vol. 6, Live 1964 (March 30, 2004), 2 discs, Columbia Records. Since this show is often referred to in the accounts of Dylan's early career, it's great to have, even if mainly as a document. It is an extraordinary concert, in terms of its material and Dylan's ease with his many different moods, and it showcases Joan Baez and Dylan at the height of their mutual admiration.

The Bootleg Series Vol. 8, Tell-Tale Signs: Rare and Unreleased, 1989–2006 (October 6, 2008; deluxe version, October 7, 2008), 2 discs or 3, Columbia Records. A collection from late period Dylan. The alternate versions are all of interest, and some are standouts, then there are great unreleased tracks like "Red River Shore" and songs from film soundtracks, like "'Cross the Green Mountain." The consistency on this hodgepodge collection is impressive.

The Bootleg Series Vol. 10, Another Self Portrait, 1969–1971 (August 27, 2013), 3 disks or 4 discs, Columbia Records. These selections from the sessions for *Nashville Skyline, Self*

Portrait, and *New Morning* bring to light some interesting mixes—horns on "New Morning"!—some familiar tracks undubbed and thus more "Woodstocky," like "Copper Kettle," and some tracks that are just fun to have: covers like "Thirsty Boots," "Railroad Bill," and "Annie's Going to Sing Her Song" and demos like "When I Paint My Masterpiece"— "sure wish I hadn't a-sold my old Victrola." A very congenial collection from Bob's mellow days. The extra CD contains the Isle of Wight concert for those inclined to revisit and revise.

Hard Rain (September 10, 1976), Columbia Records. Most accounts of Rolling Thunder, phase 2, remark how it lost the sense of purposive camaraderie that inspired the initial tour. The evidence is here in what is to me one of Dylan's most satisfying records of this period. Every song is rawer than its studio recording and the ramshackle sound here is of the essence.

Traveling Wilburys Vol. 1 (October 18, 1988), Warner Brothers Records. When Dylan joined with George Harrison, Jeff Lynne, Tom Petty, and Roy Orbison to lay down a B-side for a Harrison single, the song, "Handle with Care," was too much fun and too good to leave at that. The album is short on substance but is more fun than just about anything that dates from the late eighties.

INDEX

ABOUT THE AUTHOR

Donald Brown has taught writing and literature at Yale and published essays on Thomas Pynchon, James Joyce, and others. He is an editor and critic for the *New Haven Review*, and has a degree in art history and comparative literature from the University of Delaware and a Ph.D. in comparative literature from Princeton University, as a Mellon fellow. Since 2006, he has maintained *blogocentrism*, a blog on music, movies, books, and writing. A native of Delaware, he has lived in New Haven, Connecticut, since 1999 where he supports local theater. He has attended over twenty Dylan concerts, beginning in 1978 and most recently in 2013, and prefers vinyl records to other music technologies. And he still makes mix tapes.

CPSIA information can be obtained at www.ICGtesting.com
Printed in the USA
BVOW04*0243150114

341881BV00004B/15/P